THE NEW YORK CITY POLICE DEPARTMENT

The Impact of Its Policies and Practices

THE NEW YORK CITY POLICE DEPARTMENT
The Impact of Its Policies and Practices

JOHN A. ETERNO
Molloy College
Rockville Centre, New York, USA

CRC Press
Taylor & Francis Group
Boca Raton London New York

CRC Press is an imprint of the
Taylor & Francis Group, an **informa** business

CRC Press
Taylor & Francis Group
6000 Broken Sound Parkway NW, Suite 300
Boca Raton, FL 33487-2742

Printed on acid-free paper
Version Date: 20140807

International Standard Book Number-13: 978-1-4665-7584-4 (Paperback)

Library of Congress Cataloging-in-Publication Data

The New York City Police Department : the impact of its policies and practices / John A. Eterno, editor.
    pages cm
    Summary: "Studying the flagship New York City Police Department is critical to understanding policing and democratic society. An examination of the department by experts who have been watching it for years, this book reviews qualitative research on how the community views the NYPD, police culture, resistance to change, and the drop in the homicide rate in recent years. It explores hiring, firing and retention, discusses crime-fighting strategies, and reviews legal concerns and the response to public demonstrations such as the Occupy Wall Street movement. The final chapter demonstrates how the lessons relate to other departments throughout the world"-- Provided by publisher.
    Includes bibliographical references and index.
    ISBN 978-1-4665-7584-4 (paperback)
    1. New York (N.Y.). Police Department. 2. Police--New York (State)--New York. 3. Police administration--New York (State)--New York. 4. Crime--New York (State)--New York. I. Eterno, John, 1959-

HV8148.N5N497 2014
363.209747--dc23
    2014028242

Visit the Taylor & Francis Web site at
http://www.taylorandfrancis.com

and the CRC Press Web site at
http://www.crcpress.com

Contents

Acknowledgments

My wife, JoAnn, and daughters, Julia and Lauren, are the treasures of my life. Their love and understanding allow me to accomplish so much.

The contributors to this book are more than authors; they are the men and women who are willing to speak out—for better or worse. They are brave, accomplished scholars who have my everlasting respect.

About the Editor

John A. Eterno earned his PhD from the State University of New York at Albany. He is a professor, associate dean, and director of graduate studies in criminal justice at Molloy College in Rockville Centre, New York, and is also a retired New York Police Department captain. He has penned numerous books, book chapters, articles, and editorials on various topics, including democratic policing, human trafficking, data-driven policy, police management, policing within the law, investigations, combating terrorism in democracies, global policing, and many others.

Contributors

Christine S. Barrow is an assistant professor of criminal justice at Molloy College in Rockville Centre, New York. She earned a PhD in criminal justice from Rutgers University in 2012. Dr. Barrow has spent several years performing qualitative research on how involvement in community organizations contributes to pro-social behavior among urban youth.

Robert Gangi served as executive director of the Correctional Association of New York for more than 29 years and founded the Police Reform Organizing Project (PROP) in the spring of 2011. He has been an activist, community organizer, and public policy advocate in New York City for nearly 50 years. Also, he is a recognized expert on criminal justice and law enforcement issues with a particular focus on police and prison concerns.

Delores Jones-Brown, JD, PhD, is a professor in the Department of Law, Police Science, and Criminal Justice Administration in John Jay College at the City University of New York. Her book, *Race, Crime, and Punishment,* won a New York Public Library award in 2001. Dr. Jones-Brown has also written multiple articles, book chapters, and legal commentaries. Her research interests include race, crime and justice, juvenile justice, police–community relations, and the legal socialization of adolescent males.

Andrew Karmen earned his PhD in sociology from Columbia University in 1977. Since 1978, he has been a professor at John Jay College of Criminal Justice, where he was a codirector of the Masters Program in Criminal Justice for nearly 20 years. He is the author of *New York Murder Mystery: The True Story of the Crime Crash of the 1990s* (NYU Press, 2006) and *Crime Victims: An Introduction to Victimology, 8th Edition* (Cengage, 2013).

Harry G. Levine is professor of sociology at Queens College and the Graduate Center, City University of New York. His research focuses on drugs, alcohol, and food in a historical context. His writings have received seven distinguished scholarship awards for his work on addiction, alcohol prohibition and regulation, international drug policy, crack cocaine, the war on drugs, and racial bias in marijuana possession arrests. In 2013 he was awarded a Senior Scholar Distinguished Achievement Award from the Society for the Study of Social Problems.

Joseph E. Pascarella, PhD, MPH, is a research associate at Rutgers University and a retired police captain from the New York Police Department. His research interests include measuring policing performance, police organization, management, and strategic planning. He has published several articles relevant to policing personnel performance, planning, and management, including an analysis of police salaries in 2000, police disability pensions in 2004, and Operation Ceasefire in Newark, New Jersey, in 2010.

Loren Siegel is an attorney and co-director of the Marijuana Arrest Research Project. From 1981 to 2001 Siegel was a senior staff member of the American Civil Liberties Union and served as the organization's principal spokesperson on criminal justice and drug policy issues. She is the author of chapters in several books, including *Crack in America* (Eds. Levine & Reinarman, University of California Press, 1997) and *Gangs and Society* (Eds. Kontos, Brotherton, & Barrios, Columbia University Press, 2003).

Eli B. Silverman, PhD, is professor emeritus in the John Jay College of Criminal Justice and Graduate Center at the City University of New York. He served with the U.S. Department of Justice and National Academy of Public Administration, Washington, DC, and as an exchange professor at the Police Staff College in England. He has consulted and trained police agencies in the U.S., U.K., Canada, Mexico, Europe, Asia, and Australia. Areas of interest include police performance management, community policing, policy analysis, stop and frisk, and CompStat. His recent works include *The Crime Numbers Game: Management by Manipulation* (coauthored with John Eterno) and *NYPD Battles Crime: Innovations in Policing*.

Christopher Sullivan earned his law degree in 1985 from St. John's University Law School in Queens, New York, and his master's in criminal justice from Long Island University, Greenvale, New York in 1980. He is currently chairperson of the Criminal Justice Department of Molloy College in Rockville Centre, New York, where he teaches both graduate and undergraduate courses. Sullivan has written on international legal issues relating to law enforcement and employment law in policing. Prior to joining the faculty at Molloy, he spent 28 years with the New York City Police Department, where he attained the rank of lieutenant special assignment and served as legal advisor to the chief of personnel.

Kerry Ulmer earned her master's in criminal justice from Molloy College in 2014. While at Molloy College she worked as a graduate assistant, conducting both criminal justice and legal research.

Alex S. Vitale is associate professor of sociology at Brooklyn College, where he teaches criminology, sociology of law, and social movements. His research focuses on the politics of policing and the policing of politics. He is senior policy advisor to the Police Reform Organizing Project and serves on the New York State Advisory Committee of the United States Commission on Civil Rights.

Introduction

1

JOHN A. ETERNO

Contents

Evidence-based policing is a term used for developing and improving policy based on scientific study: what works. It is forward thinking. It is not a rubber stamp for existing programs. A study based on sound scientific methods is conducted and then policy is developed, tested, or reformed based on the results. This requires an open-minded, transparent department willing to allow data to be given to an outside, independent research team. Good examples of this include: Taylor et al.'s study of sex crime victims in Victoria, Australia (see Taylor et al., 2012) or Engel's various works with the police of Cincinnati, Ohio, United States (see, e.g., Thompson, 2009 or Engel & Whalen, 2010).

Conversely, the New York City Police Department engages in what has been described as *policy-based evidence making*. It is a pejorative term meaning they work back from a policy that has been in place for years and try to find evidence for it. One strategy is to invite those likely to be friendly to them from outside (e.g., RAND Corporation, 2007; Smith & Purtell, 2006) who work closely with the department, sometimes in a give-and-take manner, in a likeminded pursuit, ultimately to justify at least some of the necessary evidence to defend the status quo. Indeed, such researchers can be hired by friends of the police department or even the police department itself (no independent funding sources such as federal or private grants or other government sources are used), making independent findings unlikely (e.g., see NYCBAR, 2009, exposing numerous concerns with the RAND report and *Floyd v. City of New York* case excerpts on the Center for Constitutional Rights (2014) website specifically showing how the police department changed key wording of the RAND report based on conversations with NYPD's upper echelon).

Another similar policy-based evidence-making tactic is to set up commissions or panels supposedly to check into their policies. For example, when sex crime victims' groups went to the commissioner complaining of problems with officers not taking reports, the commissioner set up a panel of friendly advisors. Ultimately, the only changes that are made from such panels are window dressing. In this way, then, the status quo is again maintained.

Another example of this is crime report manipulation in which the department asks some former federal prosecutors known to the commissioner to
make a report on a finely tuned subject, not on all the questionable practices
but on auditing only. The committee is, in reality, nearly useless and impotent; such committees fend off criticism, gaining time for the department.
Invariably such panels make some recommendations and the department
makes superficial changes, again maintaining the status quo.

Trumpeting supposed success (without calling attention to any weaknesses) year in and year out is yet another policy-based evidence-making
tactic to maintain the status quo. That the NYPD claims their policies are
solely responsible for the crime decline regardless of evidence to the contrary
is a good example. Although the crime decline is most certainly real, to claim
sole credit is another matter completely. In fact, crime has declined approximately 40% throughout the United States during this same period. To defend
the NYPD's assertions, the usual friendly scholars are given access to reports
and data that no others can obtain. The predictable result is a defense of the
department's policies and claims—maintaining the status quo—regardless
of contradictory evidence that may come from the outside.

Linking a policy to saving lives or bringing down crime is another policy-
based evidence-making strategy. The overuse and abuse of stop and frisk is
an example of this. The reason supporting the policy of stopping hundreds
of thousands of people, they claim, is to prevent guns from getting into the
hands of criminals. Unfortunately, when examining their own reports, the
number of guns taken off the street through forcible stops is so minimal it
is clear that this explanation is weak, at best. The NYPD will then engage
in other policy-based evidence-making strategies until they eventually
gain some traction with the public. They try to find something, anything,
to defend the policy, even if the policy is unconstitutional (see Center for
Constitutional Rights, 2014, and *Floyd v. City of New York,* 2013a).

In this book an elite group of scholars who have examined the NYPD's
policies and practices are brought together. These scholars have varied viewpoints and concerns. Ultimately, however, the common denominator among
us is that we are adding our data and interpretations to what should be a free
and open discussion about the NYPD. As of this writing, William Bratton
has only recently become the police commissioner. As his tenure progresses
we hope that significant changes will be made. The bulk of these writings
were penned prior to his appointment.

The chapters can be categorized into the good, the bad, and the downright
ugly. The most favorable view of NYPD is presented by Pascarella. He rightly
points out the NYPD's grasp of technology and its use in crime-fighting. In

addition, the innovation of CompStat clearly belongs to the NYPD which, at least initially, brought some good, more efficient management changes to the NYPD. However, as time went on some of these successes have become problematic and even malignant. Karmen exposes some of the negative aspects especially not focusing on victims. Eterno and Silverman see key problems with a management system gone awry with a myopic focus on the numbers of index crimes even to the point of looking the other way with respect to crime report manipulation by officers. Although Vitale sees some positive aspects to the NYPD's handling of crowds, his overall theme is also negative: that the NYPD fails to respect basic rights in its policing of protests. Barrow and Jones-Brown get into the neighborhoods of the city and certainly do not find a favorable view or treatment in communities of color. Levine and Siegel unveil an unbridled policy of NYPD marijuana arrests that is also racist. Gangi provides his personal experiences in creating a grassroots movement in an attempt to change the police. In this book, then, we openly present varied viewpoints: the good, the bad, and the ugly.

Ultimately, however, the NYPD has not allowed impartial external examination. Recently, the blowback from the city council includes a new inspector general. This is what happens when a department is obsessed with protecting its public image and allows no meaningful outside scrutiny over many years. The NYPD has defended the status quo using policy-based evidence-making techniques such as inviting friendly scholars, claiming success due entirely to their efforts regardless of evidence to the contrary, and appealing to saving lives or fighting crime/terrorism or impotent commissions. There is no transparency and, therefore, precious little evidence-based policing is taking place.

At times, then, this book with independent analyses will make the NYPD and other political powers uncomfortable, especially when we challenge the public image and the status quo. In a democratic society it is our duty to speak out: good, bad, or ugly. We will not be silent. That is how it should be. It is in the crucible of democracy where ideas are truly tested, if ideas are allowed a forum. At a conference where my colleague Eli Silverman and I spoke about problems with NYPD crime numbers, the organizers tried to silence us; we continued to speak then and we continue now. At a conference where I presented the overwhelming case for crime report manipulation, a low-ranking FBI special agent came to me quietly. He took me aside, away from any curious onlookers. His whispers were barely audible, "Your words are falling on deaf ears." It is our hope that these "deaf ears" will one day hear, listen, and act on the evidence presented herein.

These are our thoughts ....

References

Center for Constitutional Rights. (2014). *Floyd v. City of New York* updates and excerpts. Retrieved from http://ccrjustice.org/floyd-trial-updates

Engel, R.S., & Whalen J.L. (2010). Police-academic partnerships: Ending the *Dialogue of the Deaf,* the Cincinnati experience. *Police Practice and Research,* 11, 105–116.

Floyd v. City of New York order on liability (2013a). http://ccrjustice.org/files/Floyd-Liability-Opinion-8-12-13.pdf

Floyd v. City of New York order on remedy (2013b). http://ccrjustice.org/files/Floyd-Remedy-Opinion-8-12-13.pdf

NYCBAR. *Statement of the New York City Bar Association concerning the NYPD's stop-and-frisk practices.* (2009). Retrieved from http://www.nycbar.org/pdf/report/NYLit_2508504_1.pdf

RAND Corporation. (2007). Analysis of racial disparities in the NYPD's stop, question and frisk practices. Retrieved from http://www.nyc.gov/html/nypd/downloads/pdf/public_information/TR534_FINALCompiled.pdf

Smith, D.C. & Purtell, R. (2006, August). Managing crime counts: An assessment of the quality control of NYPD crime data (occasional paper), New York: New York University School of Law.

Thompson, A. (2009, September 16). *Cincinnati police partner with academics.* Retrieved from http://www.npr.org/templates/story/story.php?storyId=112847746

Taylor, S.C., Muldoon, S., Norma, C., & Bradley, D. (2012). Policing just outcomes: Improving the police response to adults reporting sexual assault. Social Justice Research Centre, Edith Cowan University, Western Australia. Retrieved from http://www.ecu.edu.au/_data/assets/pdf_file/0004/483016/Policing-Just-Outcomes-in-Sexual-Assault-Final-Report.pdf

Unreasonable Suspicion
Youth and Policing in New York City

2

CHRISTINE S. BARROW
DELORES JONES-BROWN

Contents

> The right of the people to be secure in their persons, houses, papers and affects, shall not be violated. ...
>
> **Fourth Amendment to the United States Constitution, 1791**

2.1 Introduction

According to the records of the New York City police department, between 2008 and 2009, 1,121,470 New Yorkers were stopped. Of these stops, 37% (or 416,350) were targeted at youth between the ages of 14 and 21 (Stoudt, Fine, & Fox, 2011). Community anecdotes confirm that an untold number of such stops occur without ever being recorded in official statistics. Community members tell the story of unmarked cars that "roll-up" in neighborhoods designated as "high crime;" often, plainclothes officers emerge from such vehicles, and young Black or Latino men "assume the position" against walls and on hoods of cars and are "patted down" en masse or are ordered to empty their pockets or backpacks. If nothing illegal is found, which departmental statistics confirm is often the case, the young men are allowed to continue along their way. The officers return to their cars. No forms are filled out.

Apologies or explanations may or may not be offered by the police. On occasion the incidents are captured on cell phones or video recorders. For a generation of youth, these stops have become commonplace, ordinary, a fact of life. So much so that one source confirms that during 2011 the number of recorded stops for African-American youths between the ages of 14 and 24 exceeded the actual number of such youths in the city: 168,126 stops compared to 158,406 Black youth in the age range (NYCLU, 2012). These statistics confirm that many of the city's youths experience being stopped by the police not once or twice but multiple times. In a recent report by the VERA Institute of Justice, 44% of youthful respondents reported having been stopped nine or more times (Fratello, Rengifo, & Trone, 2013). Other departmental statistics confirm that only rarely do such stops result in an arrest of any kind.

2.2   Reasonable Suspicion: Definitions and Overview

NYPD officers conduct these so-called "reasonable suspicion" stops under the auspices of a 1964 New York State law with authority confirmed by the 1968 United States Supreme Court decision in *Terry v. Ohio* and its companion cases of *Sibron v. New York* and *Peters v. New York*. The statute authorized the use of "stop and frisk" as a means of detecting crime based on reasonable suspicion rather than "probable cause," the legal standard called for by the Fourth Amendment. Under the U.S. Supreme Court's 8 to 1 decision in *Terry v. Ohio,* a police officer may briefly detain a civilian if, based on a set of facts that the officer observes and can articulate, there is reason to believe that the individual has engaged or is about to engage in criminal activity. During the detention, the officer may ask questions in order to heighten or dispel her suspicion. If there are additional facts to suggest that the individual may be armed and dangerous, the officer may conduct a pat-down of his outer clothing for the purpose of discovering any weapons that the civilian possesses. The officer must also be able to articulate why she felt the civilian was armed and dangerous.

The majority ruling in the *Terry* case makes clear that such stops are not justified based on mere hunches about the criminality of the person stopped, and the language in the Fourth Amendment suggests that the facts leading to suspicion must be personal. Groupwide suspicion, for example, suspecting all young Black or Latino males who live in "high crime areas" of being about to engage in crime, is not constitutionally permissible.

In determining whether suspicion is "reasonable," the U.S. Supreme Court has developed a "totality of the circumstances" test that requires an examination of all of the facts known to the officer prior to making the stop. This test gives the officer wide latitude in deciding whether criminal behavior has taken or is about to take place but it still requires that suspicion be specifically focused on the observed behavior of the individual who is stopped.

2.3   Policing Youth in Urban Communities

Research on policing in urban communities documents a wide range of harms to minority residents including slow police response time, police harassment, disrespectful treatment, verbal abuse, and excessive use of force (Anderson, 1999; Browning et al., 1994; Brunson & Miller, 2006; Brunson, 2007; Jones-Brown, 2000; Mastroski, Reisig, & McCluskey, 2002; Weitzer & Tuch, 1999). Studies have also found that residents living in disadvantaged areas were less likely to see the police as helpful and expressed less satisfaction with the police (Silver & Miller, 2004; Sun et al., 2004).

A major concern about policing in urban communities is the impact on neighborhood youth. In regard to police stops, youth in New York City are disproportionally targeted as compared to other age groups. Stoudt et al. (2011) examined the NYPD Stop, Question, and Frisk dataset for the years 2008 and 2009. This examination concluded that stop and frisk is a policy heavily focused on the younger citizens in New York City (Stoudt et al., 2011). Fratello et al. (2013) found that the same was true for 2012.

Recent studies have identified the negative effects on youth of being stopped or arrested. Findings from an investigation conducted by Wiley and Esbensen (2013) revealed that being stopped or arrested not only increases future delinquency but also amplifies deviant attitudes. The study found that police contact affects pro-crime attitudes by decreasing anticipated guilt and increasing agreement with neutralization statements, which may suggest that these youths are beginning to take on increasingly deviant identities (Wiley & Esbensen, 2013). The results of this study suggest that although police officials believe that the aggressive use of stop and frisk deters youths from committing crime, the opposite may be true. That is, by labeling certain youths as criminal and deviant through disproportionate stop activity, such youths may come to identify with those labels and act accordingly. The study also suggests that because youths feel that they cannot turn to police for help, they may engage in self-protective violence. Hence, rather than having a deterrent effect, frequently being stopped by the police may add to delinquent behavior and negative attitudes.

A recent study of police attitudes toward minority communities revealed that police conceptions of minority communities are heavily influenced by the perceived quality of their encounters with the public and whether the officers feel respected by community residents (Sanchez & Rosenbaum, 2011). Officers interviewed in this study felt that most of the negative sentiment originated from African-American young people. Police had particularly harsh feelings about youth in minority neighborhoods, describing them with a wide range of negative attributes. No particular subset of youth was immune from this criticism. In a nutshell, officers felt that youth and young adults have no respect for them and, therefore, the feelings and behaviors can be reciprocated (Sanchez & Rosenbaum, 2011). Given the high level of police contact for youth in certain NYC neighborhoods, especially in the absence of criminal activity on their part, it is important to attempt to understand how such contact occurs and its impact on the youth who endure it.

2.4   Research Methodology

Data for this investigation came from a broader study of youth involvement in neighborhood organizations. Qualitative interviews were conducted with young men and women at a Brownsville Brooklyn Recreation Center (BRC). The BRC has been serving the Brownsville community since 1964. This facility has been responsible for helping the community by running an array of programs and services out of the facility. These programs range from meal and food banks to programs for senior citizens, homework help for adolescents, and computer and sports programs for younger members (Richardson, 2010). Brownsville is among the top 10 stop precincts for the years 2003–2012 (Jones-Brown, Stoudt, Johnston, & Moran, 2013).

A total of 35 participants was selected for this study. Data collection took place in two stages: a snowball sample of 15 respondents was selected during July of 2009 and a random sample of 20 respondents was selected during December 2010 for this analysis. Prior to setting up interviews with youth and staff members, a letter was sent to the chief of the New York City Department of Parks and Recreation describing the purposes of the study. Permission was granted to conduct the investigation in June of 2009. Prior to each interview, the researcher explained the full purpose of the study and administered full consent procedures. An age-appropriate consent form was given to youths to sign. The respondents were assured confidentiality and were informed about the potential risks of the study.

The interview began with asking for basic demographic information, including place of residence, family structure, racial and ethnic background, and school attended. Lastly, respondents were asked to report about their engagement in deviant and illegal behavior. To do this, the researcher obtained the list of "personal questions" from the Internationalization of Legal Values Inventory instrument (Finckenauer, Louin-Tapp, & Yakovlev, 1991). This instrument provides an extensive list of questions about delinquent offenses. If the respondent answered "yes" to the offense, the researcher inquired about the nature of the incident, if the respondent had been arrested, and if he/she had served time in a juvenile facility.

One of the goals of the investigation was to examine how respondents perceive different forms of controls in their lives. In this particular instance the focus was on respondents' perceptions and experiences with the police in their communities. "Do you have respect for the police?" followed by a probe, "Can you talk a little bit about any experiences or encounters you have had?" Also, "Do you have respect for the law?" followed by a probe, "Can you tell me a little more about that?"

The interview ended with respondents discussing their perceptions and experiences with the police in their communities. They were asked whether they respected the police and the laws, and most important whether they felt the police were effective in keeping the neighborhood safe. Both waves of respondents were asked identical questions addressing these issues of policing. Data analysis for this investigation was achieved using grounded theory methods where the researcher systematically generated theory from the data (Glaser & Strauss, 1967).

2.5 Research Findings

As previously discussed, a total of 35 qualitative interviews were conducted with the recreation center participants. A total of 24 male and 11 female respondents were interviewed. Participants ranged in age from 14 to 21 with a mean age of 18. Respondents' ethnic backgrounds varied. Many of them identified themselves as being of Caribbean origin from countries including Guyana, Haiti, Jamaica, Trinidad, and St. Lucia. Others identified themselves as African American, Latino, Cherokee Indian, or Polish in origin, as well as African nations, Nigeria and Kenya.

Respondents provided descriptive information about their family structures. In the female-headed households, respondents reported that there was limited contact with their fathers. The extended family was very common among this sample. Many resided with mother, siblings, aunts, and grandparents, as well as nieces and nephews in one household. There were a number of reported reasons for these different living arrangements. Lastly, the majority of respondents were currently in high school, and a small number had recently completed high school.

Involvement in the recreation center varied for these respondents. For some, this was an institution where they attended school daily. There was a group of alternative high school students who spent their days at the facility continuing their education and obtaining work experience in a work-study program at the BRC. Each of these young men had transferred from other alternative high schools in Brooklyn. They were either in their third or fourth year of high school. For others, the recreation center was a place of employment where they gained skills and work experience.

During the summer hours when school was not in session, young men and women worked as BRC summer camp counselors for the younger children. At the center, youth are provided with opportunities for career instruction and social development. Interns attended school during the afternoon and early evening hours at a high school in a community adjacent to Brownsville. The internship provided financial compensation for working 10–15 hours per week. Lastly, for the remaining respondents this institution was a place of leisure and recreation.

Youth perceptions of the police were formed through direct and indirect contact with these officers. Many respondents had had their own personal interactions with police, whereas others based their opinions on friends' or relatives' experiences. Lastly, many formed their opinions based on what they had witnessed in the news media or in public. For many, these experiences shaped their views about trust and belief in the police.

2.5.1 Youth and Unreasonable Suspicion

Multiple stops that do not result in a finding of criminality are easily seen as unreasonable. The fact that such stops are focused in some communities and not others gives rise to serious social and legal questions. Analysis of police data reveals that stops are highest in 10 of 76 precincts. As noted previously, Brownsville is one of those ten. The justifications offered for such stops may be laudable, for example, that crime is higher in those areas and therefore the community is in greatest need of police services. But, the fact that there is very little crime detected during such a high number of stops suggests that a recalibration of the volume of stops and a rethinking of reasons for them may be in order. New York City CompStat reports indicate that overall Brownsville has experienced a decline in violent and property crimes in the last two decades.

Police department data confirm that the majority of all stops are based on information about the setting in which a person appears. In 2012 the majority of stops were reported as having occurred in a "high crime area." Other reasons for stops were related to the "time of day, day of week, [or] season corresponding to reports of criminal activity" or "proximity to [a] crime location." Taken together, the use of these factors suggests that a pedestrian may have very little personal control over being seen as a criminal suspect (Jones-Brown et al., 2013).

Most respondents in the current study reported that they had experienced direct contact with the police in their communities. The following sections discuss reactions to these occurrences. In sum, these young men and women were stopped, searched, and questioned often. For certain young men, these were the only instances where they had some form of interaction with the police. In many cases, these experiences left them feeling belittled and frustrated, because the officers were demeaning. When asked, "Do you have respect for the police?" many young men and women stated having little respect for the police due to negative encounters. Responses to these questions also revealed how frequently these participants had interactions with the police. For example, Thomas, a 17-year-old intern, shares how often police officers stop him. He stated: "Three times a week. Yes, it's a shame; it's sad. 'Cause they think I sell drugs, the way I look, the way I dress. Where I live is a drug area."

When asked the same question Albert, an 18-year-old alternative high school student, shared his contempt for the police. He had been repeatedly a target of their stop and search approach. "I don't like cops; they always harassing me for no reason. Plenty of times they harass me. They see you with anybody and they think you up to something. They ask for ID, I give it to them, and then they leave me alone."

Gregory, an 18-year-old intern, also shared that he had experienced repeated stop and searches by the police. In one instance, the police appeared to be monitoring his behavior while waiting for him to react to their presence. He was questioned about possessing illegal items, although his response was "No" to having these items, the police officers carried out the search. He stated:

Every three months I get stopped. They search me. Like one time I'll be close to my house, coming from the store. I had my earphones in my ear and they driving slow next to me, and all of a sudden he told me to stop and just searched me. I don't know if they were waiting for me to look at them. I didn't pay them no attention. When I looked, they asked if I had anything. I said, "No." And then they searched me.

John, an 18-year-old basketball player, shared that he was stopped coming from his aunt's barbecue. He was told he fit the description of a suspect when he believed he didn't. He explained:

Most of the time the regular people that look regular be doing things and we could be standing on the corner and somebody could have just got robbed and they'll be right up the block and they'll come mess with us sitting in the park but they won't mess with the people. Before they always do surveillance in the area and they'll see us in the park talking in the joking and they'll give us a ticket for loitering.

I can understand the after 8 pm thing, there's like the rules, and they'll ask for IDs and flash the flashlight in our face and we're just sitting there, and they'll just come mess with us and then somebody will get robbed right around the corner from us and won't even know nothing.

James, an 18-year-old alternative high school student, shared his interaction with a transit police officer. He felt this officer should have approached him in a more respectful manner about listening to his music in the subway. Had the police officer addressed him courteously, he would have been more willing to cooperate, even though he felt what he was doing was not illegal. His narrative suggests that the police officer was consistently monitoring his behavior. He explained:

> I was in the subway. I had my headphones on and bopping to my music and bouncing the basketball. The cop said, "Stop bouncing the basketball." I saw my friend; she wants to be like a boy, so she takes the ball and starts bouncing it. So now the cops come up the stairs and say, "You want to be a wise guy." My friend walked away. The cops said, "If you bounce that ball again I'm giving y'all all a ticket." Then he said, "You can't listen to music on the platform." He asked me for ID. He just wrote my name down. All he has to do is talk to me man to man to turn the music off. These guys, just because they got that badge, they think they can do whatever they want.

Both James' and Gregory's experiences suggest that the police were trying to intimidate them while they were in their communities. Neither of these individuals reported engaging in any illegal activity during these incidents. However, in both cases their actions were scrutinized by local law enforcement. Neither of these occurrences resulted in an arrest. These narratives suggest that police pay close attention to young individuals even when they are not involved in criminal behavior. Conclusions drawn from these narratives are consistent with previous literature on policing in urban communities where young males, particularly minority males, feel harassed and disrespected by the police (Brunson & Miller, 2006; Jones-Brown, 2000; Mastroski et al., 2002).

There were respondents in the sample who admitted to having respect for the police even though they were subjected to frequent stop and searches. This was expressed among the young women in the sample who were not immune to police contact. There were also additional concerns about how the police went about enforcing the laws: primarily about the areas and individuals they targeted.

Stacey respects the police; however, she feels because she lives in public housing the police are more aggressive with their enforcement tactics than in other parts of the community. She explained: "Yes, much respect for the police. But just because you live in the projects, they just treat people different. They stopped me in the projects, because I had an Arizona [iced tea] and they smelled it and thought it was beer. I threw it away, because their nose touched it."

Andrea, a 14-year-old summer youth worker, shared her recent experience about spending time with her friends in the neighborhood. Police went as far as having her friends searched against the gates.

The police, well I feel like yeah they here to protect you but sometimes they just pick with you. Like my teacher said to me today, "Why do you think the police stop you on the street today, because y'all don't know y'all rights. And they know y'all don't know your rights, so they like pick with us." Plenty of times, it could be five of us just talking and having fun without doing nothing bad, but they stop us and want to search us, have us on the gate, on the floor, all of that.

This was like last month. Sometimes they just do the boys if there's just male cops; they'll just leave us at the side, and I know that they can't check me because they are male so sometimes they'll come with a female in the car, and if they don't have the car they'll come in the paddy wagon. And they'll have males and females in there so they'll just check all of us. And they just start for nothing.

Ian, a 17-year-old intern, had also experienced multiple stops by the police, however, he reported that he used these interactions to his advantage. He did not report feeling any tension or animosity after the incidents took place. He shared that once he completes high school he would begin to pursue a career in law enforcement. Perhaps he wants to be placed in the authoritative role that the police exhibit in his community. He explained: "My future is going to be a SWAT officer, so I have respect of law enforcement. I've talked to like three of them, because they would stop me and search me. I would ask them about how to become a police officer. They told me things I didn't know about. And they would tell me what paperwork to do."

Jean, a high school intern, also had experience with being stopped and searched by the police. He stated that he had been stopped and questioned in the New York City subway stations in his community. However, he did not appear to classify these events as an infringement of his rights. Although Jean did not report that he was engaged in any wrongdoing while being stopped and searched, he did not identify his encounters with the police as a negative experience nor did he report demonstrating any hostility toward the police during questioning. He saw the encounter as an illustration of police performing their duties. His narrative suggests that he respects authority figures regardless of their actions.

This perception appears to be consistent with findings from a study conducted by Nihart and colleagues (2005) in which they found that student attitudes toward the police were significantly and positively correlated with their feelings toward their parents and their teachers. He stated, "The police stop me once in a while. Like in the train station. I have the utmost respect for the police. Because if you are going to respect one adult, you have to respect all. I haven't had any bad experiences with them. If they ask me a question, I cooperate."

Narratives from both Ian and Jean suggest that being stopped and searched by the police is commonplace in their communities. Therefore neither appears to view these experiences as an infringement of their rights, even though no illegal behavior was reported during the incidents. Neither individual reported feeling any tension or animosity after the incidents took place.

The belief that attracting police attention is the norm is also expressed in current research studies as well. In the study conducted by Stoudt et al. (2011), one young person in their sample explained police stops as just part of living in New York City. Yet, according to the NYPD, nearly all of the young people stopped were not arrested, given a summons, or found to be in possession of a weapon or other contraband. In other words, nearly all of these young people were innocent (Stoudt et al., 2011).

There is one final example from the narratives illustrating unfair police enforcement in the community. In the section on positive police disposition, Cindy, a summer youth intern, spoke of how the visible police presence in her community made her feel safe. She reported no personal interaction with the police, but she was not immune to witnessing law enforcement administer undeserved punishment to those around her. She spoke briefly about a friend who was stopped and searched by police with no identified explanation. "Police enforce the law, but I've seen them stop people for no reason. We were just walking with a friend from school, and just stopped my friend for no reason. We were coming down the steps from the train by my school by the Brooklyn Museum."

Procedural justice can explain respondent reactions to police experiences. Procedural justice perspectives argue that the legitimacy of police is linked to public judgments about the fairness of the processes through which the police make decisions and exercise authority (Sunshine & Tyler, 2003). Respondents made it apparent that they would like a police presence to remain in the community; however, it is the manner in which police enforce the law that concerns them. Police develop and maintain legitimacy through their effectiveness in fighting crime (Sunshine & Tyler, 2003). It is evident to the respondents in this sample that increasing police presence after a severe incident takes place and targeting youth not engaged in illegal behavior is not an effective crime-fighting strategy.

Prior negative contact with the police is significantly associated with young people's judgments of lower police legitimacy. Similar studies have shown that young people's attitudes toward police legitimacy are positively linked to police use of procedural justice. In a recent study conducted by Hinds (2007), young people who rated their recent contact with police as negative viewed police as having lower legitimacy compared to young people who said they did not have a recent negative experience with police. This study's findings show that police can enhance their legitimacy by using fair procedures when dealing with youth.

Similar results were shown in a study of adolescent attitudes toward the police in a Canadian city. Adolescents who reported no prior police mistreatment or harassment experience expressed more favorable attitudes toward the police (Chow, 2011).

2.5.2 Appearance Profiling

In addition to targeting certain areas of the community, respondents reported, the police targeted certain individuals based on their attire. Ian shared an experience about how his clothing attracted police attention. He is not at liberty to wear clothing of his choice without harassment from the police. Ian resides in an area where gang activity is prevalent and it is possible that he has accepted being stopped and searched as a tactic to fight gang activity. He explained: "Police are the ones that protect you, so I have respect for them. Sometimes when you wear a color in a specific neighborhood, like I live in a Blood neighborhood … and if I wear red, they would stop and search me because of the color."

A number of other respondents made references to sagging pants attracting police attention. When asked, "What is your opinion of the police in your neighborhood?" John, an 18-year-old alternative high school student, explains how he avoids wearing this particular style of clothing. He explained: "I stay out they way, 'cause if you don't, they always try to lock you up for something, 'cause basically when you are Black or young Black male they tend to pick on you sometimes, depending on how you carry yourself, how you look. I could walk around with my pants sagging and they will swear to God that I am a drug dealer or they will swear to God that I will fit the description and they will always pick on you."

Stacey also talked about how she avoids associating with certain individuals because their clothing is likely to draw police attention. Her statement suggested that police harassment could be reduced if some individuals were not conspicuous. She shared: "I don't hang out with a lot of people that attract the cops. Like the cops start with anybody like the guys. They start with people that have their pants down low; they see them with a blue or red flag and I don't hang around those people."

Sean also concurred and avoided wearing certain attire because the police targeted youths dressed in a certain manner. He shared: "All this pants low, all this nonsense, when you bring this upon yourself, the police suspect. I don't bring that 'vibe' to me. When I walk down the street, I don't draw attention to myself with the pants sagging."

Narratives from Ian, Stacey, and Sean all indicate that they've witnessed police focusing on certain individuals because of their apparel. Although each of these young men and women expressed having respect for the police, they were all aware of the circumstances that increase one's chances of being stopped and searched by the police. Therefore, young men and women have developed strategies to reduce police attention. In this case, it is refraining from certain attire the police associate with criminal behavior. They also avoid contact with individuals who wear this attire. This mentality is also evident in other studies on policing. In an investigation on policing in urban communities, Brunson & Miller (2006) learned some young men attempted to reduce their chances of coming under suspicion by avoiding certain areas and certain people altogether.

2.6 Improving Relationships Between Youth and Police

Because the current study points to distrustful relationships between police and youth particularly in minority communities, it is important to explore possible solutions to improve these relationships. A number of programs that allow youth and police informal interactions have been shown to improve relations. For example, Teen Empowerment programs facilitated in the city of Boston were shown to build meaningful relationships between youth and police. Here police officers and youths were given the opportunity to take part in small group interactions where they were allowed to hear each other's concerns. The goal was to help both parties work together effectively to build community. It helped both youth and police to look beyond the stereotypes they have of one another and begin to replace them with an understanding of the common interest (Fusoni, 2005).

In an evaluation of outreach programs with police in schools, school-children established real relationships with police officers during weekly program sessions. These interactions led to changes in attitudes toward police and their role in the community. Children's feelings of safety and protection are enhanced as they become able to identify and internalize the positive, pro-social attributes that the officers embody. Post participation, significantly fewer students believed negative statements about police officers such as "police beat up on people for no reason" or "police try to act like big shots." Not only were perceptions of youth shaped during these interactions, but police officers who work in the children's community became familiar with the conditions children face on a daily basis (U.S. Department of Justice, 2003).

Similar changes in police attitudes toward youth were expressed in research conducted by Rabois and Haaga (2002). Participants were recruited by the local PAL to participate in a basketball program. Results indicate that officers reported positive attitudes toward minority youth team members and demonstrated a positive attitude change regarding minority youths as an overall out-group.

In an evaluation of community police youth development programs, Anderson, Sabatelli, and Trachtenberg (2007) studied how youth assisted police departments while broadening their understanding of law enforcement. Police worked with youths in a variety of roles, including educating youth on the use of the Internet, chaperoning field trips to local museums, and learning sports-related skill training in such areas as golf and sailing. Many of the programs offered community service and volunteer opportunities that included food and toy drives, community clean-up projects, and other types of community service.

Lastly, a training evaluation of the "Effective Police Interaction with Youth" program was shown to increase patrol officer awareness of disproportionate minority contact and increase patrol officer knowledge of youth behavior and strategies for interacting effectively with youth. Program participation resulted in police officers' reporting feeling increased comfort in starting conversations with youths they did not know. They also reported feeling confidence in having the skills necessary for interacting with youths, and commitment to the idea that patrol officers can have a positive impact on youths without taking time away from their other enforcement activities. At follow-up, patrol officers still reported more knowledge of adolescent development, police–youth interactions, and disproportionate minority contact than they did before they received the training (Center for Applied Research in Human Development, 2008).

2.7 Discussion

Youth in urban communities such as Brownsville continue to be disproportionately targeted by aggressive policing tactics. The Brownsville Recreation Center has worked with various agencies to address the needs of youth residing in urban communities. The research suggests that informal interactions between youth and police help build trust and understanding. Because so many BRC participants expressed unfavorable police interactions, perhaps facilitating some leisure activities for youth and police at the center would help change perceptions for both police and participants. Positive contacts could be cultivated through community policing programs (e.g., school liaison officers), whereas negative contacts could be reduced by avoiding overly aggressive enforcement and by treating young people with respect, dignity, and fairness (Chow, 2011). Poor police–citizen relationships may lead to noncompliance with the law generally, and in specific encounters with police, and the nonreporting of offenses and suspicious events and people (Tyler, 1990). Young men and woman would be more likely to cooperate with the police to help deal with the actual criminals in their communities.

At the same time, if police officers learn more meaningful tactics to approach urban youth, this could reduce the groupwide suspicion that appears to exist in these communities. Respondents in the sample who were congregating in public spaces with their friends would not have experienced the harsh inappropriate treatment from police, especially because the narratives from the young men and women in the sample suggest that the multiple stops they had experienced did not lead to a finding of criminality.

Although dissatisfied with enforcement tactics, respondents believed the police had the ability to serve as a form of social control in their communities. They recognized the need for a police presence but voiced their need for punishment and enforcement to be administered fairly. Many young men and women in the sample were not opposed to police presence but complained instead about unfair law enforcement. Therefore, officers should carefully assess the conditions under which they stop and question youth to reduce the negative effect that contact may have on attitudes toward the police and other government entities and the possible development of a deviant identity (Wiley & Esbensen, 2013).

A small number of respondents were included in this analysis, however, these findings provide support for the continued analysis of how youth and police relationships can be improved in urban communities. In this current study, youth who had face-to-face interaction with the police reported it to be a negative experience. Interviewing youth participants at other Brownsville organizations might help determine if there are any consistencies with policing contact in Brownsville. Future research may also include an increase in female respondents. This would make it possible to perform a gender comparison of police contact experiences.

References

Anderson, E. (1999). *Code of the Street: Decency, Violence and the Moral of the Inner City*. New York: W.W. Norton.

Anderson, S.A., Sabatelli, R.M., & Trachtenberg, J. (2007). Community police and youth programs as a context for positive youth development. *Police Quarterly*, 10, 23–40.

Babbie, E. (2007). *The Practice of Social Research*. Belmont, CA: Thomson Wadsworth.

Bailey, C. (2007). *A Guide to Qualitative Field Research*. Thousand Oaks, CA: Pine Forge Press.

Browning, S.L., Cullen, F.T., Cao, L., Kopache, R., & Stevenson. T. (1994). Race and getting hassled by the police: A research note. *Police Studies*, 17, 1–11.

Brunson, R.K. (2007). Police don't like black people: African American young men's accumulated police experiences. *Criminology and Public Policy*, 6, 1, 71–102.

Brunson, R.K., & Miller, J. (2006). Young black men and urban policing in the United States. *British Journal of Criminology*, 46, 613, 1–28.

Carr, P.J., Napolitano, L., & Keating. J. (2007). We never call the cops and here is why: A qualitative examination about legal cynicism in three neighborhoods. *Criminology*, 45, 2, 445–480.

Center for Applied Research in Human Development. University of Connecticut. (2008). Effective Police Interactions with Youth: Training Evaluation. Storrs, CT.

Chow, H.P. (2011). Adolescent attitudes towards police in a western Canadian city. *Policing: An International Journal of Police Strategies & Management*, 34, 4, 638–653.

Eterno, J., & Silverman, E. (2012). *The Crime Numbers Game: Management by Manipulation*. Boca Raton, FL: CRC Press.

Finckenauer, J.O., Louin-Tapp, J., & Yakovlev, A.M. (1991). *American and Soviet Youth: Comparative Study of Legal Socialization*. Edison, NJ: Transaction.

Fine, M., Freudenberg, N., Payne, Y., Perkins, T., Smith, K., & Wanzer, K. (2003). Anything can happen with police around: Urban youth evaluated strategies of surveillance in public places. *Journal of Social Issues*, 59, 1, 141–158.

Fratello, J., Rengifo, A., & Trone, J. (2013). *Coming of Age with Stop and Frisk: Experiences, Self-Perceptions, and Public Safety Implications*. New York, NY: Vera Institute of Justice, Center on Youth Justice.

Fusoni, M. 2005. Teen empowerment: Youth, police, and neighbors in partnership. *New Directions for Youth Development*, 106, 61–71.

Glaser, B., & Strauss, A.L. (1967). *The Discovery of Grounded Theory*. Hawthorne, NY: Aldine Publishing Company.

Hinds, L. (2007). Building police-youth relationships: The importance of procedural justice. *Youth Justice*, 7, 3, 195–209.

Jones-Brown, D. (2000). Debunking the myth of Officer Friendly: How African American males experience community policing. *Journal of Contemporary Criminal Justice*, 16, 2, 209–229.

Jones-Brown, D., Stoudt, B., Johnston, B., & Moran, K. (2013). *Stop, Question and Frisk Policing Practices in New York City: A Primer* (revised). Center on Race, Crime and Justice, John Jay College of Criminal Justice, City University of New York.

Lurigo, A.J., Greenleaf, R.G., & Flexon, J.L. (2009). The effects of race on relationships with the police: A survey of African American and Latino youths in Chicago. *Western Criminology Review*, 10, 1, 29–41.

Mastroski, S.D., Reisig, M.D., & McCluskey. J.D. (2002). Police toward the public: An encounter-based analysis. *Criminology*, 40, 515–551.

New York Civil Liberties Union. 2012. Stop-and-Frisk Activity in 2011: NYCLU Briefing. New York, NY.

Nihart, T., Lersch, K.M., Sellers, C.S., & Mieczkowski, T. (2005). Kids, cops, parents, and teachers: Exploring juvenile attitudes toward authority figures. *Western Criminology Review*, 6, 1, 79–88.

Phillips, S.W., & J.J. Sobol. (2011). Police decision making: An examination of conflicting theories. *Policing: An International Journal of Police Strategies & Management*, 35, 3, 551–565.

Rabois, D., & Haaga, D.A.F. (2002). Facilitating police-minority youth attitude change: The effects of cooperation within a competitive context and exposure to typical exemplars. *Journal of Community Psychology* 30, 2, 189–195.

Richardson, C. (2010, April 2). Former NBA man Gregory Jackson needs help getting aid from Brownsville Recreation Center to Haiti. *New York Daily News*, 1–2. New York, NY.

Rusinko, W., Knowlton T., Johnson, W., & Hornung, C.A. (1978). The importance of police contact in the formulation of youths' attitudes toward police. *Journal of Criminal Justice, 6*, 53–67.

Sanchez, V.C.G., & Rosenbaum, D.P. (2011). Racialized policing: Officers' voices on policing Latino and African American neighborhoods. *Journal of Ethnicity in Criminal Justice, 9*, 152–178.

Skogan, W. (2006). Asymmetry in the impact of encounters with police. *Policing & Society, 16*, 99–126.

Stoudt, B.G., Fine, M., & Fox, M. (2011). Growing up policed in the age of aggressive policing policies. *New York Law School Law Review, 56*, 1331.

Sun, I.Y., Triplett, R.A., & Gainey, R.R. (2004). Social disorganization, legitimacy of local institutions, and neighborhood crime: An exploratory study of perceptions of the public and local government. *Journal of Crime and Justice, 27, 1*, 33–60.

Sunshine, J., & Tyler, T.R. (2003). The role of procedural justice and legitimacy in shaping public support for policing. *Law and Society Review, 37, 3*, 513–547.

Tyler, T.R. (1990). *Why People Obey the Law*. New Haven, CT: Yale University Press.

Tyler, T.R. (2006). *Why People Obey the Law*. Princeton, NJ: Princeton University Press.

U.S. Department of Justice. (2003). Community outreach through police in schools. Washington, DC: Office for Victims of Crime.

Weitzer, R., & Tuch, S.A. (1999). Race, class, and perceptions of discrimination by the police. *Crime and Delinquency, 45, 4*, 494–507.

Wiley, S.A. & Esbensen, F. 2013. The effect of police contact: Does official intervention result in deviance amplification? *Crime and Delinquency, 59, 7*, 1–25.

An Examination of the Constitutional Issues Related to New York City Police Department Policing Tactics and Policies

CHRISTOPHER SULLIVAN
KERRY ULMER

Contents

3.1 Introduction

One of the most controversial areas of modern police activity concerns aggressive police tactics for order maintenance and criminal investigative purposes. Since the 1990s aggressive policing styles have become the norm in many large urban areas, including cities such as Philadelphia, Boston, Chicago, and New York City. These aggressive policing strategies have recently come under fire from a concerned public and have been subjected to critical scrutiny by criminal justice scholars. A classic example of aggressive policing strategy is the widespread use of the stop, question, and frisk tactic in high crime areas of New York City. Modern police tactics have evolved over the last few decades from a reactive approach to a proactive approach, and stop and frisk, considered a proactive tactic, is one of the ways in which police attempt to prevent crime and reduce violence. However, application of aggressive policing tactics comes at a price. Proactive policing in the form of stop and frisk stakes claim to short-term gains in terms of crime reduction but arguably has also had the effect of promoting police community tension, increasing police officer disillusionment, and ultimately reducing police legitimacy. The danger lies in the delicate balance between short-term gain and long-term negative consequence.

This chapter examines the evolution of aggressive proactive policing policies, the legality or constitutionality of these policies, and their legal validity or illegitimacy, as well as the impact of proactive policing on crime and the community, and the possible long-range consequences of these tactics. The potential consequences of both continuation and reversal of such policies as well as discussion of more effective police management models to replace existing models is presented and examined.

3.2 New York City: Social, Ecological, Political, and Historical Environment

In order to understand the adoption of aggressive policing tactics it is important to understand the environment in which these policies developed. The experiences and attitudes of the people of New York City, its elected officials, and its police leaders are the products of their experiences and understanding of the issues. New York City is the largest urban area in the United States, with a population of over eight million people. New York is a port city whose natural boundaries include the Atlantic Ocean, the Hudson River, and the Long Island Sound. There are features unique to New York City that make it an unusual place to live and work. The city encompasses five different counties, which unlike any other city in the United States, are policed by one police agency, the NYPD. New York is not a city in the traditional sense of the term, but it is rather its own separate entity, self-governing and self-policing. In addition to its unusual structure, New York is a culturally diverse area, surrounded by and including people of all different ethnic backgrounds, races, religious beliefs, economic standings, and political backgrounds. All of these distinctive characteristics make New York City a very different kind of place to police. As a matter of course city officials and police department administrators are pressured to develop creative policies that are unique and specifically geared to NYC crime prevention needs in order to police the city effectively. This burden falls most visibly on the mayor and the police commissioner. Since the 1970s, police commissioners appointed in New York City have been expected to be innovators as well as leaders. The police commissioner is expected to produce concrete results in terms of crime reduction statistics while maintaining good community relations and responsiveness to the various political groups that are active in the city.

Prior to the mid-1970s in New York City, the police department could be characterized as a reactive force. Answering calls for service and attempting to maintain omnipresence were the primary tactics employed by the department. Police performance was measured by arrest rates, and an absence of scandal.

In the 1960s major cities throughout the country experienced devastating race riots. Televised instances of police overreaction and media examination of police tactics, in combination with an apparent increase in crime rate, led to national concern over crime and the ability of the criminal justice system to manage the crime problem. In response, President Lyndon Johnson commissioned the President's Commission on Law Enforcement and the Administration of Justice, also known as the President's Crime Commission. In 1967, the commission issued its final report, *The Challenge of Crime in a Free Society*. The report was highly critical of police nationally and cited poor training, low educational levels, police brutality, and a lack of police contact with communities served. In 1964, New York City witnessed the mayhem of the Harlem race riots. Throughout the 1970s communities endured uncontrolled violence and arson in the Bronx much of which was regularly broadcast on television. Responding to political and public pressure the NYPD was forced to engage in large-scale hiring of police personnel. In the early 1970s a major police scandal was uncovered involving systematic and ongoing organized police corruption, particularly in the area of vice, in minority neighborhoods. The scandal resulted in the Knapp Commission, which investigated these allegations and confirmed the existence of a culture of corruption within the NYC Police Department.

The 1960s also saw increased legal challenges to police procedural tactics. Willingness emerged on the part of the U.S. Supreme Court to hear cases challenging the constitutionality of police practices. This period has come to be known as the Warren Era after Chief Justice Earl Warren or the Due Process Revolution. Legal challenge to accepted police tactics complicated police procedures significantly. Officers were now expected to know and understand a complex body of law upon which even the Justices of the Supreme Court disagreed. The combination of the Due Process Revolution and the findings of the President's Crime Commission changed policing dramatically.

By the mid-1970s a significant amount of funding was being poured into policing through the Law Enforcement Administration Program (LEAP), a federal program intended to elevate the level of professionalism of American police agencies. As a result of federal funding, the 1970s saw significant increases in police training, a focus on higher education for police personnel, and the emergence of criminal justice as an academic discipline. Academics developed theories such as problem-oriented policing (Goldstein, 1979), "broken windows" (Wilson & Keling, 1982), and community-oriented policing. These theoretical paradigms promised to make police more effective at reducing crime and disorder. The concept of police effectiveness evolved as professional policing emerged. The use of police to resolve or at least address underlying individual and community problems, a concept foreign to traditional policing, became the desired outcome. This was an ambitious goal and the more complex the area policed, the more complex and onerous the goal became.

In 1975, New York City fell into a fiscal crisis and in June of that year the department laid off approximately 3,000 police officers. By 1980 uniform personnel levels fell from 30,000 to under 20,000 and innovative policing took a back seat to simply handling calls for service. The priority in the early 1980s was on hiring practices. In the 1980s and early 1990s a number of drug-related scandals rocked the department. These scandals corresponded with the crack cocaine epidemic and crack wars of that era. In 1992, Judge Milton Mollen was appointed to head a New York City commission to investigate allegations of police corruption and anticorruption procedures. The commission found that the corruption of the eighties and early nineties was different from the corruption uncovered by the Knapp Commission in that it was based on disorganized opportunistic acts of greed and brutality.

The late 1980s and early 1990s also saw an intense effort to transform the department into a community policing agency. These efforts, however, were overshadowed by increasing crime and deteriorating street conditions. New York City had its share of traditional crimes and was also plagued by the problems associated with increased homelessness, rampant subway graffiti, and aggressive panhandling. In 1994, newly elected Mayor Rudy Giuliani appointed William Bratton as police commissioner. Commissioner Bratton, who had been successful in addressing crime conditions in the New York City transit system through the application of policies based on the broken-windows theoretical framework, immediately implemented a number of initiatives designed to target crime-related problems in the city (Rosmarin, 2012). Bratton's initiatives marked an end to the reactive form of policing that dominated NYC policing and introduced a proactive model based on specific strategies, monitoring problems through statistical analysis and accountability.

Although scholars disagree on the exact reason for the decline, implementation of more aggressive policing tactics corresponded to a dramatic decrease in the crime rate. According to the Uniform Crime Report, in 1985, the violent crime rate in NYC was 1,881.3, meaning that for every 100,000 people in the city, just over 1,881 violent crimes occurred. Since then, the violent crime rate has dropped exponentially every year, with last year's crime rate at just 639.3 (FBI, 2012). Aggressive policing continued through Mayor Giuliani's term of office as well as through Mayor Bloomberg's 12 years in office. New York City's war on crime took the form of performance-driven management which led to proactive aggressive policing methods. Proponents of the city's tactics routinely touted crime reduction statistics as a by-product of proactive methods.

Crime rate is a complex construct and is difficult to measure. Crime rate will increase or decrease based on a number of demographic, economic, and other social and policy-driven factors. For example, the violent crime rate spiked in the early 1990s due to the crack cocaine epidemic and turf wars between distributors. The notion that the police can actually have an impact on the crime rate is a relatively new concept and may be a by-product of the police professionalization movement which emerged after the publication of President Johnson's Crime Commission report, *Challenge of Crime in a Free Society.* Although it appears that the drop in the crime rate which occurred in the mid-1990s is attributable to police tactics this issue is still unresolved and is the subject of continued debate.

Adoption of aggressive policing tactics, therefore, was probably the result of multiple factors. A spike in the crime rate, visible signs of street disorder, and an overall focus on crime control starting in the early 1970s coupled with the belief that the police can make a difference made it clear that the police were a good investment for change. Aggressive policing, especially if supported by a theoretical basis such as broken windows, were easily implemented, easily measured, and simple to maintain and expand.

In addition to aggressive policing, the department adopted an equally aggressive management model known as "CompStat" which is discussed elsewhere in this text. CompStat essentially elevated performance measures such as arrest and summons rates to iconic importance. Implementation of CompStat drove the department into a frenzied effort to reduce crime report statistics lower and lower. This included a drive to increase recorded police contacts, such as stop and frisks. Stop-and-frisk encounters are recorded on a departmental form[1] and are an easy measure of police officer activity. Intangible measures of police performance such as citizen satisfaction were not measured directly so they were less important. The CompStat era ignores the fact that the crime rate is a complex issue and is related to other greater issues such as poverty and demographics (Meares, 2013). Also, long-range consequences of a single tactic are not considered.

One of the issues related to the public's understanding of aggressive police tactics is the question of whether the carrying out of such tactics (good or bad) is the product of policy or individual police officer initiative or a combination of the two. This is a critical issue. If the policy is sound and citizen dissatisfaction stems from inappropriate or illegal officer practices then change or remediation can be achieved by improved selection procedures, training, and discipline. If the policy is flawed, either on its face or in the manner in which it is executed, then policy change should achieve the desired result. Complicated policy questions persist. Is the policy specific enough, is it comprehensive, is it being carried out intelligently by middle management, and so on?

According to Meares (2013), "There are two dominant ways to evaluate police. The first is whether their conduct comports with the law. The second approach assesses whether they are effective crime fighters." In *Floyd v. New York City* (2013) the Federal District Court for the Southern District of New York dealt with the question of whether New York sacrificed legality for effectiveness.

3.3   Basic Legal Principles and the NYPD: Origins of Supreme Court's Supervision of Local Law Enforcement

"The Constitution is what the Supreme Court says it is" (Chief Justice Charles Evans Hughes). The relationship between the U.S. Constitution and the U.S. Supreme Court and local law enforcement is a complex one, which is important to understand. As originally envisioned by the framers, the Constitution left the states (e.g., New York) politically and legally intact and created the federal government to address specific mutual needs such as defense and interstate trade. The Tenth Amendment specifically states that "The powers not delegated to the United States by the Constitution, nor prohibited by it to the States, are reserved to the States respectively, or to the people" (USC amend. X). Under this framework, federalism, the "general police power," that is, the power of the government to assure the health and safety and welfare of the public remained a power and responsibility of the state government and not the federal government. Enactment of criminal laws and procedures to enforce these laws were to be state matters. The Bill of Rights, originally thought to be unnecessary because of the limited nature of the federal government, was ratified in 1791 to protect against abuse by the federal government, not the states. This principle was affirmatively asserted in *Barron v. Baltimore* (1833). This concept remains largely intact with the legislative and executive branches having limited involvement in the state administration of justice; however, the judicial branch is highly involved in state criminal procedure today.

Had it not been for the ratification of the Fourteenth Amendment in 1868, state and local criminal procedural rules and doctrines would be purely a matter of state law and would probably be significantly different from state to state as is the case in other areas of the law such as criminal law. Although uniformity among the states is generally seen as a good thing, it does reduce an individual state's ability to respond to unique state needs.

The Fourteenth Amendment was one of three reconstruction amendments intended to assure that Southern states which fought in the Civil War did not simply ignore their defeat and continue the institution of slavery in one form or another. The due process clause of the Fourteenth Amendment states, "[N]o state shall deprive any person of life liberty or property without due process of law" (USC amend. XIV). The significant words are "no state" because in ratifying the amendment every current and future state (and all political subdivisions within the state) agreed to honor due process rights of persons within their borders or be subject to rulings of federal courts and potentially the force of the federal government to enforce this obligation.

At the time there was uncertainty as to whether the amendment meant that the Bill of Rights, which assures specific due process rights such as the protection against self-incrimination (as opposed to a general concept of due process), were applicable to the states. Put simply, if the Fourteenth Amendment requires the states to honor the due process rights of persons within their states and the Bill of Rights is essentially due process rights, logically, the Bill of Rights should apply to the states. The issue is not simple and led to what is referred to as the "incorporation debate" with some justices of the Supreme Court advocating total incorporation and others advocating a more cautious selective incorporation strategy. Today, therefore, police procedures, such as arrest, stop, frisk, search, and the like, must conform to the U.S. Constitution and Supreme Court decisions interpreting the U.S. Constitution. Police procedures must also conform to state constitutions and state court decisions interpreting them, when state constitutions provide greater protections than the federal Constitution based on independent state grounds. (See discussion of *Terry* and *DeBour* below.)

Throughout the early 1900s, more and more cases were heard by the Supreme Court dealing with defendants arguing that their Fourteenth Amendment due process rights were violated by state law enforcement officers and that the applicable law was the law decided by the Supreme Court interpretation of the Bill of Rights cases. This led to the incorporation of the Bill of Rights protections to the states selectively and only where the right at issue was "fundamental" in what came to be known as the "fundamental rights selective incorporation approach." The first of these cases, *Gitlow v. New York* (1925) focused on the First Amendment right to free speech and the court held that freedom of speech does apply to New York and there-fore to all of the states. Following the *Gitlow* decision, the rights outlined in the Bill of Rights were systematically applied to the states in cases such as *Near v. Minnesota* (1931), which incorporated freedom of the press; *Palko v. Connecticut*, (1937) applying the Fifth Amendment right forbidding charging a criminal defendant with the same crimes following a lawful trial (1937); and a series of criminal procedure cases including *Gideon v. Wainwright* (372 U.S. 335, 1963), *Miranda v. Arizona* (384 U.S. 436, 1966), and *Benton v. Maryland* (395 U.S. 784, 1969) and *Wolf v. Colorado* (338 U.S. 25, 1949), incorporating the Fourth Amendment at the state level. The Court's deci-sions in these cases incorporated the rights contained in the Bill of Rights to the states one by one and today virtually all rights contained in the Bill of Rights have been selectively incorporated "jot for jot" and "bag and baggage" to the states. This means that existing and future case law must be followed as well. The case law that existed and continues to be developed is federal case law and is handed down by the Supreme Court. Another Constitutional pro-vision, the Supremacy Clause, establishes that when a conflict exists, federal law supersedes state law. However, as noted above, state law providing greater protections may coexist with federal constitutional law.

By the end of the 1960s most of the rights outlined in the Bill of Rights were applied to the states through the Fundamental Rights Selective Incorporation Approach. The Incorporation doctrine both added a layer of doctrines and substituted U.S. Constitutional principles for existing state doctrines and principles onto those that were already in practice in New York, thus creat-ing a multilevel system of laws by which the police department is governed. Consequently, policies and policing methods must be constitutional accord-ing to not only the state constitution, but also the U.S. Constitution.

3.4 Street Encounters: Fourth Amendment Probable Cause, Reasonable Suspicion, and Stop, Question, and Frisk

The American concept of liberty includes the belief that ordinary inno-cent persons should be free from police interference absent a valid reason. As Judge Schiendin notes in *Floyd v. NYC* (2012), "The security of one's pri-vacy against arbitrary intrusion by the police—which is at the core of the Fourth Amendment—is basic to a free society" (quoting *Wolf v. Colorado*, 1949). Aside from social contacts such as an officer asking for the time of day or approaching a citizen to discuss the weather, police contacts include rea-sons such as asking for information about an incident or condition such as a car accident or the location of a reported broken traffic light. They also include approaching a citizen because the officer suspects the individual is involved in criminal or unlawful activity and seizing or arresting a person because he or she has committed a crime. These encounters occur on a continuum, or at levels, and they all involve some degree of interference with freedom.

The Fourth Amendment to the U.S. Constitution, which was incorporated to the states in 1949 in *Wolf v. Colorado*, assures that "the right of the people to be secure in their persons, house, papers and effects against unreasonable searches and seizures shall not be violated and no warrant shall issue but upon probable cause." The Supreme Court has interpreted these clauses to mean that "all warrantless searches are per se unreasonable absent several well delineated exceptions to the warrant requirement" (*Katz v. U.S.*, 1967). Because a warrant must be based on probable cause, all searches and seizures must be based on probable cause "absent several well delineated exceptions to the warrant requirement" (*Katz v. U.S.*, 1967).

In 1968 the Supreme Court was confronted with a case in which a police detective seized three individuals during a street encounter, without probable cause. The circumstances, however, indicated that the seizure was reasonable. According to the Court, the facts in *Terry* represented a "whole rubric of police activity" which is usually based on little information in a fast-moving series of events (*Terry v. Ohio*, 1968). In *Terry*, the Court ruled that a brief investigatory detention based on a standard which is lower than probable cause was such a well-delineated exception to both the warrant requirement and the probable cause requirement. Essentially, in *Terry* the Supreme Court held that not all police intrusions must be based on probable cause and the Court accepted a reasonableness analysis.

Significantly, the New York legislature had already dealt with the issue of police investigatory detentions in 1962 when it debated and ultimately passed New York CPL 140.50 known as the stop-and-frisk law. The legislature's efforts were a response to the incorporation of the exclusionary rule to the states in *Mapp v. Ohio* in 1961 and a belief that *Mapp* would unravel the criminal justice system in New York, because this ruling required that states exclude evidence secured in violation of the Constitution from use in a criminal trial (Segal, 2012).

Before the stop-and-frisk statute was passed in New York, officers were told to stop individuals based on their "... judgement, training, knowledge and ability as a law enforcement officer" (Segal, 2012). The New York State legislature, concerned that the ruling would turn "New York's law enforcement apparatus to ash," set to "put out the flames" by pre-emptively passing legislation that would "authorize officers to stop and question individuals suspected of past, present or potential criminal conduct and, when officers reasonably suspect danger, conduct a limited search for weapons." The law, which rendered the fruits of such actions admissible in state criminal proceedings was the product of a New York State law enforcement effort to argue that police professionalization resulting from the reform era of policing requires that the "law respect the judgment of thoroughly professionalized police officers when those officers stopped suspicious persons on the street, a practice which was clearly a standard police tactic. The argument succeeded in securing the passage of the New York Stop and Frisk Law and later influenced the Supreme Court when it heard *Terry v. Ohio* in 1968" (Segal, 2012).

3.4.1   *Terry v. Ohio* (1968)

The *Terry* decision is at the heart of the legality of aggressive police tactics and the use of stop-and-frisk to control crime. Chief Justice Earl Warren, the author of the Court's opinion in *Terry*, "understood well the incendiary interplay between police behavior, race and *stop and frisk*. In the opinion he referred specifically to wholesale harassment by certain elements of the police community of which minority groups, particularly Negroes, frequently complain" (Zeidman, 2012/2013).

The facts in *Terry* are of necessity long and often cited and repeated. This is because every nuance is important. Detective McFadden was assigned to pickpocket patrol in downtown Cleveland, Ohio. He was 62 years old and had 30 years of police experience. Detective McFadden observed the defendant and three other men acting suspiciously. McFadden was able to explain in articulate detail, which is now referred to as with *articulable facts,* what specifically he observed that made him suspicious. This was important because it permitted the court to examine his observations and evaluate reasoning to determine if they were reasonable. These facts included the suspects walking back and forth in front of a row of stores, pausing to stare into the same window, repeating the same ritual about a dozen times, and stopping at the corner and conversing. The suspects were then joined by a third man (Katz) whom McFadden had seen in a car talking to one of the pair (Chilton). These observations, in combination with McFadden's police experience led McFadden to believe that the three were "casing" the store for a robbery. At that point, McFadden approached the three and identified himself as a policeman and asked their names. The men "mumbled something" whereupon McFadden spun Terry around, patted down his outside clothing and felt a pistol in his overcoat pocket. Another gun was found when McFadden patted down Chilton's overcoat pocket. McFadden then arrested the men for possession of concealed weapons.

Terry was convicted and appealed. On appeal *Terry* argued that (1) McFadden did not have probable cause to believe that he was going to commit a crime, (2) McFadden seized him when he stopped him and spun him around and that the Constitution forbids seizures absent probable cause, and (3) McFadden searched him when he "patted him down" and that the Fourth Amendment forbids a law enforcement officer to search absent probable cause. Finally, *Terry* argues that *Mapp v. Ohio* requires that the evidence (the gun) be excluded from being introduced at trial as evidence of Terry's guilt.

The state's argument was simple. The state argued that the Fourth Amendment simply did not apply. McFadden did not seize Terry because he did not arrest him and the intrusion was so minimal that it did not trigger a Fourth Amendment protection. McFadden did not search him because a "pat down" was not a search, again arguing that the intrusion was minimal. The police only needed probable cause actually or formally to arrest and actually search, not stop and frisk. Essentially, the state admitted that McFadden did not have probable cause, but argued that he did not need it to take the action he did.

Chief Justice Warren's opinion rejected both arguments. First Warren rejected the state's argument that the Fourth Amendment was not applicable, holding that a stop such as the one McFadden employed was a Fourth Amendment seizure but that it was not a full seizure and the frisk was a Fourth Amendment search but not a full search. The Fourth Amendment was therefore applicable; however, because the stop was not a full seizure and the frisk was not a full search, the reasonableness clause not the warrant clause governed. Or to put it another way, because probable cause is attached to the warrant clause, it is reasonableness that is constitutionally required for such an intrusion.

Justice Douglas' dissent, however, warned that to give police complete discretion to determine whether there is the correct level of suspicion in a given situation could lead down a slippery slope. He specifically stated, "To give the police greater power than a magistrate is to take a long step down the totalitarian path. Perhaps such a step is desirable to cope with modern forms of lawlessness. But if it is taken, it should be the deliberate choice of the people ..." (*Terry v. Ohio*, 1968). Here, Douglas did not completely condemn the decision handed down by the majority in this case, but he cautioned that it could create larger issues if the police abused the power granted under the decision. He called for a vote from public opinion; because the police derive their authority from the government and the government is of the people, the people should decide to give police that power. Douglas further suggested that there be an amendment to the Constitution outlining the regulation of these types of stops that should be ratified by a public vote.

Essentially the *Terry* court modeled its decision after NY CPL 140.50, although it buried its approval in criticism of the law (Segal, 2012). The *Terry* decision gave constitutional approval to a police tactic that was historically practiced but probably was not consistent or congruent with the culture and expectations of many. This decision, therefore, has been both criticized because not only did it create an exception to the probable cause requirement, it created the exception in the highly sensitive area of police encounters and applauded because it provided the police with the ability to prevent crime. In light of the chief justice's concerns and the reservations expressed in Justice Douglas' dissent, however, it is unlikely that the Supreme Court meant to condone 685,000 stop and frisks a year in a city with a population of just over eight million, when it decided *Terry* in 1968. Is such a sweeping application of stop and frisk a means of crime prevention or a tactic of social control? If it is a form of social control, should the police be the institution to decide and implement such a tactic?

3.4.2 *People v. DeBour*

New York's stop-and-frisk law was further defined in 1976 when the New York State Court of Appeals (the highest appellate court in New York State) decided *People v. DeBour*. Although *Floyd v. New York City* was primarily decided on *Terry* analysis, *DeBour* is important because it both restricts and expands a police officer's authority to approach citizens. According to *DeBour*, police street encounters occur at four levels in New York (*Debour* is limited to New York). In this case uniformed officers stopped DeBour because the officers suspected that he might be involved in a narcotics violation. Officers observed him walking alone in a high crime area after midnight. According to the officer, DeBour crossed the street, possibly to avoid contact with the officers. Based on this observation the officers approached and asked DeBour for identification, which he said he did not have. The officers then asked him what he was doing, to which he responded that he had just parked his car and was going to a friend's house. It was then that the officers noted a strange bulge under his coat and the officers asked him to open his coat. They found a loaded gun and subsequently arrested DeBour for carrying a concealed weapon (*Debour v. N.Y.*, 1976).

DeBour appealed his case on the grounds that the police did not have the right to approach him and that when the two officers confronted him and "caused him to stand still he was *seized* within the meaning of the Fourth Amendment."

On appeal, the Appellate Division (the intermediate appeal court in New York) held that the initial contact between DeBour and the officers was constitutional and the encounter that followed was lawful. Essentially the court saw the encounter as an approach, not a stop. Specifically, it was an approach coupled with questions based on an objective credible reason.

Upon appeal to the New York State Court of Appeals, the highest appeal court in New York, the conviction was affirmed and (in a companion case) the court outlined the four levels of intrusion and predicate indicators needed for each of four increasingly intrusive encounters. According to the court, at Level I the police may approach a person if they possess an objective credible reason for the approach. In addition they may ask questions, and the questions asked of DeBour (identification, explanation of what a person is doing) were permitted. At Level II the police needed a founded suspicion of criminal activity. At Level II a founded suspicion of criminal activity permitted the police to ask more intrusive questions related to such suspected criminal activity. At Level II, however, the police are not permitted to stop the individual and the individual is free to go and refuse to answer the officer's questions. Questioning of this nature is exercised pursuant to the common law right of inquiry and is sometimes referred to as "mere suspicion questioning." At Level III the officer needs reasonable suspicion and may forcibly stop the individual for a reasonable period of time for the purpose of conduction of a brief investigation, the purpose of which is limited to confirming or dispelling the officer's concerns. Level III is the equivalent of a *Terry* stop. At Level IV the police officer must have probable cause and with probable cause may constitutionally arrest a person without violating the Fourth Amendment (*People v. DeBour*, 1976).

Subsequent case law established that at Level I encounters an officer may ask nonthreatening questions regarding a person's name, address, and destination, and can query about something unusual they are carrying. Although police can approach a person because they have an objective credible reason to suspect criminal activity, they cannot ask for permission to search. Level I encounters should be brief and nonthreatening and there should be an absence of harassment or intimidation (*People v. Hollman* 79 N.Y. 2d. 181, 1992). Please see Table 3.1.

Table 3.1 Comparison of Levels of Intrusion

DeBour Level of Intrusion	Predicate	Terry or NY CPL 140 Equivalent	Police Can	Police Cannot
I	Objective credible reason Criminal or non-criminal		Approach Ask non-threatening questions	Approach on a whim Ask threatening questions
II	Founded suspicion	Mere suspicion	Engage in common law right of inquiry	Stop or use force Suspect is free to leave
III	Reasonable suspicion	Reasonable suspicion	Forcibly stop Frisk if there is separate reasonable suspicion that suspect is armed	Hand cuff suspect Transport suspect
IV	Probable cause	Probable cause	Arrest	

3.4.3 *Floyd v. NY* and the Reasonable Suspicion Standard

In a pretrial proceeding Judge Scheindlin summarized the law from several precedents and articulated the reasonable suspicion standard needed for the police to conduct a forcible stop or stop and frisk:

> [T]he police can stop and briefly detain a person for investigative purposes if the officer has a reasonable suspicion supported by articulable facts that criminal activity may be afoot, even if the officer lacks probable cause.
>
> This form of investigative detention has become known as a *Terry* stop.
>
> While "reasonable suspicion" is a less demanding standard than probable cause and requires a showing considerably less than preponderance of the evidence, the Fourth Amendment requires at least a minimal level of objective justification for making the stop.
>
> The officer [making a *Terry* stop] ... must be able to articulate something more than an inchoate and unparticularized suspicion or hunch.
>
> Reasonable suspicion is an objective standard; hence, the subjective intentions or motives of the officer making the stop are irrelevant. *Floyd v. New York City* 813 F. Supp. 2d. 457 (2012)

Of the four levels of intrusion permitted by *DeBour*, it is the first that opens the door to police criminal investigation motivated encounters. It both limits and permits the police to approach (not stop or even ask threatening questions) anyone, provided the approach is based on an objective credible reason, which as one can see in *DeBour* can be a very low level of suspicion. Although being present in a high crime area alone is clearly not a sufficient objective credible reason, very little additional information is needed to permit a Level I encounter and the asking of "nonthreatening" questions. *DeBour* does forbid "whimsical" or baseless approaches; however, it permits approaches based on a very low level of suspicion which is difficult to review after the fact. Although it may objectively appear reasonable, the subject of the approach may react in a manner that escalates the encounter due to a subjective appreciation of the situation. This in combination with the impracticality of monitoring conduct at such a low level invites extensive approaches of individuals in high crime areas whatever their behavior (whether they cross the street or not).

As noted above, *DeBour* restricts police authority to approach an individual at Level I or approach and exercise the common law right of inquiry in a criminal investigation context at Level II. This is more restrictive than *Terry* or CPL 140.00 but it does provide law enforcement with a constitutional justification for an approach and it is easy to see how crime control policies and efforts could maximize this authority. Assuming that CPL 140.50, *Terry*, and *Debour* are all intended to restrict the police in order to assure that the

American concept of liberty, which includes the belief that ordinary innocent persons should be free from police interference absent a valid reason, is
adhered to by the police, what mechanisms are in place to prevent the police
from violating statutory and constitutional requirements?

3.4.4 Exclusionary Rule: Its Limitations and Alternatives

The primary remedy available for an individual who is the subject of a police
encounter, which is a violation of CPL 140.00, *Terry*, or *DeBour*, is the exclusionary rule. Unfortunately, this remedy has not proven effective in controlling police behavior (agency, individual officer, or both). Because most
subjects of stop and frisk are not arrested, the exclusionary rule is irrelevant. In those cases where unconstitutional seizures are made and evidence
secured, it is the role of the courts to apply the exclusionary rule aggressively
in order to control and instruct the police. Zeidman (2013), however, notes
that there have been virtually no suppressions hearings during this period,
and he argues that the criminal courts have failed to control the police even
when arrests are made.

Other possible remedies such as criminal actions against the officer,
state civil suits, departmental discipline, and Civil Complaint Review Board
sanctions have all proven to be relatively ineffective for a variety of reasons.
Those reasons include difficulty in determining the difference between the
permissible levels of intrusion under *Terry* and *DeBour*, the fact that officers
generally act under a qualified immunity from prosecution, and the possible
reality that subjects of improper stops often lack the means necessary to pursue the matter and civil suits.

Even the Civilian Complaint Review Board, which one would expect to
be the primary enforcer of standards of police behavior, has proven to be ineffective. Kabakova (2012) argues that NYPD stop and frisks are "unreviewable"
and the lack of success of the Civilian Complaint Review Board is due to a
lack of cooperation on the part of the NYPD itself.

In addition to the individual remedies above, an individual or a class of
individuals may be able to challenge such practices under 42 U.S.C. 1983,
which provides that every "person" who, under color of any statute, ordinance, regulation, custom, or usage of any State subjects, or "causes to be
subjected," any person to the deprivation of any federally protected rights,
privileges, or immunities shall be civilly liable to the injured party. Although
civil liability may and frequently does include damages to an individual
victim (where damages are shown) § 1983 also provides an opportunity for
injunctive relief. § 1983 therefore provides the mechanism to bring a civil suit
against a person acting under color of law. The next question relates to the
right or rights violated.

3.5   Fourteenth Amendment and Equal Protection

In addition to the due process clause the Fourteenth Amendment contains two other clauses intended to assure the permanent end of slavery (overt or covert). They are the privileges and immunities and the equal protection clauses.

In 1873, the Supreme Court decided three cases that have come to be known as the Slaughterhouse cases in which it narrowly interpreted the Fourteenth Amendment privileges and immunities clause to protect only U.S. citizenship rights, not state citizenship rights, essentially making the privileges and immunities clause irrelevant in most legal actions. The equal protection clause, however, remains a somewhat viable constitutional remedy. The equal protection clause provides that "no state shall deny to any person within its jurisdiction the equal protection of the laws" (U.S. Const. Amend XIV). It was specifically intended to prevent racial discrimination, although the Supreme Court has extended its reach to other classifications referred to as suspect classifications. Today suspect classifications include national origin, religion, and alienage as well as race. Gender is considered a quasi-suspect class.

The concept of a classification is very broad. Every governmental action classifies persons to some extent. Laws requiring a license to drive classify persons between persons with driver's licenses and those without driver's licenses. Enforcement policies targeting minority neighborhoods, therefore, would potentially be a race-based classification under the Fourteenth Amendment.

The central purpose of the equal protection clause is the prevention of official (government) conduct discriminating on the basis of race (or other suspect classifications). In *Washington v. Davis* (1976), a case involving police selection testing in Washington, DC, the Supreme Court ruled that the official discrimination must be intentional noting that intentional discrimination may be established without demonstrating intent in the traditional sense. "Frequently the most probative evidence of intent will be objective evidence of what actually happened rather than evidence describing the subjective state of mind of the actor" (*Washington v. Davis*, 1976). Later cases clarified the concept in which a plaintiff could establish that a state governmental entity could act intentionally. However, many misinterpret the concept of intentional discrimination believing that evidence of significant statistical differences alone are sufficient to establish discrimination. This belief is based on employment discrimination cases based on federal civil rights statutes, not the equal protection clause and the line of cases interpreting the statute. Equal protection cases require a greater proof of intent, which is generally difficult to establish because governmental actions are based on decisions made by legislatures, committees, and other groups of individuals and are frequently based in part on legitimate objectives such as crime control.

But what if policy makers know (or should/must know) that their policy has created an actual systemic violation of the Constitution (both the Fourth Amendment and the Fourteenth Amendments as discussed above), but they are consumed with the positive effect, the reduction of crime, or more specifically reported crime? (Remember, you can eliminate crime if you put everyone in jail.) Is this intentional discrimination under the equal protection clause? The answer apparently is yes if it is extreme, ongoing, and implemented with no regard or concern for the adherence to the requirements of the Fourth Amendment. Extreme indifference can be deliberate (conscious), which is deliberate indifference or the equivalent of intentional.

The Second Circuit Court of Appeals, which is the Federal Intermediate Court covering New York City, has outlined several ways for a plaintiff to plead intentional discrimination. "First a plaintiff could point to a law or policy that expressly classifies persons on the basis of race. Second a plaintiff could identify a facially neutral law or policy that has been applied in an intentionally discriminatory manner third a plaintiff could also allege that a facially neutral statute or policy has an adverse effect and that it was motivated by discriminatory animus" (*Floyd v. New York City*, 2013, citing relevant Second Circuit cases).

According to Starkey (2012), "the Intent Doctrine which requires the claimant to trace purported equal protection deprivation back to a discriminatory motive (and because establishing such motive is so difficult) the Supreme Court has nearly nullified the clause." Starkey, however, "presents a moderate fix for equal protection jurisprudence: Plaintiff Burdened Deliberate Indifference (PBDI)." Starkey's analysis of deliberate indifference illuminates the elements of this basis for assigning intent.

> Under PBDI the plaintiff carries the burden of proving that (1) the plaintiff alerted the state [NYPD] to the existence of a law, policy, or manner of conducting business which constrains races unequally; (2) the plaintiff provided the government body with an alternative ... likely to greatly diminish or solve the complained of racial disparities; and (3) the government failed to act. After these three prongs are proven, (4) the government carries the burden of proving that its failure to act furthered a compelling governmental interest, equal protection has been denied (Starkey, 2012)....

Ultimately, evidence in *Floyd v. New York* led Judge Scheindlin to conclude that

> NYPD's senior officials have violated § 1983 through their deliberate indifference to unconstitutional stops, frisks, and searches. They have received actual and constructive notice since at least 1999 of widespread Fourth Amendment violations – Despite this notice they deliberately maintained and even escalated policies and practices that predictably resulted in even more widespread – violations. (*Floyd v. New York*, 2013)

If a law or other government action or policy is based on race, the court will look very closely to determine if the law, action, or policy violates the Fourteenth Amendment. When an allegation of a race-based classification is made, the court will apply a strict scrutiny analysis. For a race-based policy to survive strict scrutiny the need for the policy must be compelling or extremely important and the means must be necessary, meaning there must be no other way to address the need. It is usually extremely difficult for a policy to survive strict scrutiny analysis.

Therefore, if police stop-and-frisk tactics are an official policy and that policy intentionally, as defined above, targets minority neighborhoods, this is potentially a race-based classification, and if challenged under the Fourteenth Amendment, it will be subjected to a strict scrutiny analysis.

3.5.1 *Floyd v. New York* (2013)

Before discussing the decision it is important to note that although the city originally appealed the decision in late January 2014, Mayor DiBlasio announced that the city would not pursue the appeal and would accept the remedies imposed by Judge Scheindlin. In a sense this is unfortunate because the decision will not receive the benefit of an appeal, which would test the holdings and principles of the case and expand its precedential effect beyond the Southern District. The decision not to appeal increases the importance of understanding what the case involves and what it means for policing as an institution.

Judge Scheindlin begins her opinion in *Floyd v. New York* by noting "This case is about the tension between liberty and public safety in the use of the proactive policing tool called 'stop and frisk'" (*Floyd v. New York*, 2013). During the eight-year period from 2004 to 2012 the department recorded 4.4 million recorded stops. These stops resulted in frisks 52% of the time; however, guns were recovered in only 1.5% of these frisks, and 80% of the stops occurred in minority neighborhoods (*Floyd v. New York*, 2013). Although these tactics resulted in few weapons arrests, they did generate a significant number of quality of life arrests or summonses such as trespass in city housing developments (Fagan, Davies, & Carlis, 2012) and misdemeanor marijuana arrests (Rosmarin, 2012). Both trespass arrests and marijuana arrests have received close examination that reveals questionable policy implications.

In this action there were two central legal issues involved in evaluating the legality of the NYPD stop-and-frisk policy. The first was whether stops are being performed in a constitutional manner and consistent with the requirements of *Terry v. Ohio* (1967). Second, was whether the policies violate the equal protection clause because of the disproportionate number of Blacks and Hispanics subjected to stop and frisk. These issues were addressed in May 2013 in an evidentiary trial in the Southern District of New York and an August

2013 decision by Judge Scheindlin, in which she held that these policies did violate the Fourth and Fourteenth Amendments to the U.S. Constitution.

In order to determine if stop and frisk was being conducted constitutionally the court examined various factors including statistical analysis, testimonial evidence, and a close examination of the 19 police encounters considered. The statistical analysis was based on data contained by the department and evaluated by the plaintiff's expert, Dr. Jeffery Fagan. The analysis revealed that simply based on the information recorded by the officer many were unjustified.

The testimony revealed that although some of the training was appropriate, the police department aggressively pressured commanders and officers to make more and more stops but essentially never took any measures to ensure that those stops were being conducted in a constitutional manner, in spite of the fact that the police department was on notice that there were problems. For each of the 19 individuals, Judge Scheindlin heard testimony and answered questions of fact (where there was a dispute as to the facts of the incident) and questions of law. Ultimately, Judge Scheindlin held that the stop-and-frisk policy violated the Fourth Amendment.

Judge Scheindlin also found that the department's policies violated the equal protection clause. As noted above, in order to succeed in an equal protection case, the plaintiff must establish intentional discrimination. That is, did the NYPD intentionally target minority neighborhoods for aggressive police stop-and-frisk tactics. Again, proving intentional discrimination requires that the plaintiff trace back to a discriminatory motive on the part of the city and that the existence of other motives such as crime control do not eliminate the possibility of success. Additionally, if proven, deliberate indifference may establish intentional discrimination. At trial extensive evidence was introduced establishing that the city was aware of the impact of its stop-and-frisk policies and that in spite of this the policies continued. The city, however, argued that this was appropriate because it is in these areas that the crime rate is the highest. In order to answer this question the court again examined both statistical information and testimonial evidence. The court's finding, that the city's policies did target minority neighborhoods was ultimately based on the statistical information and analysis provided by the plaintiff's expert witness, Dr. Fagan. Specifically, Judge Scheindlin found credible Dr. Fagan's analysis which indicated that "NYPD carries out more stops in areas with more Black and Hispanic residents even when other relevant variables are held constant," and that "the best predictor for rate of stops in a geographic unit is the racial composition of that unit" (and) "not the crime rate" as the city had argued (*Floyd v. NYS*, 2013, p. 59) and testimonial evidence revealing pressure on precinct commanders to increase stops, supporting survey data revealing the existence of such pressure, and tape recordings made by police officers demonstrating that the pressure was communicated directly to police officers on patrol.

Ultimately, Judge Scheindlin found that the city was liable for violation of the plaintiffs' Fourth Amendment rights through the widespread practice and deliberate indifference to Fourth Amendment violations, of which the city had been made aware. Judge Scheindlin also found that the city violated Fourteenth Amendment rights by a policy of indirect racial profiling through the application of a facially neutral policy.

3.5.2   New York after *Floyd v. New York*

On August 22, 2013, less than two weeks after the *Floyd* decision, the New York City Council overrode a mayoral veto and passed the Community Safety Act. One of the two main parts of the act provides for the appointment of an inspector general to oversee certain aspects of the operation of the NYPD, and the second part will permit an expanded class of New Yorkers to bring discrimination claims against the city if they feel they have been unfairly targeted by the police.

The combination of the Community Safety Act and the *Floyd* decision make the likelihood that nothing will change extremely remote. So, there will be fewer stops, fewer summonses, and fewer trespass and marijuana misdemeanor arrests. But will the crime rate remain low or will the crime rate soar? Will guns return to the streets of inner-city New York? If this does happen, the academic question will be, was it a consequence of a change in policy or the natural cycle in the crime rate? The practical question will be what to do about it. New York will have to evaluate its alternatives and decide whether to return to aggressive policing or do something better or more effective.

Floyd calls for the police department to address the crime problem intelligently. Aggressive policing without concern for its consequences has proven to be problematic. Problem- and community-oriented policing strategies or new models based on an evaluation and assessment of the NYC experience are needed. This, however, is no simple task. No true model exists that has the implementability of aggressive policing which can apparently be turned on and off at the press of a button.

3.6   Alternatives to Police Administration and Policy Making

Police management styles continue to be based on a military centralized command structure. Benefits of the military structure are the ability to respond quickly to problems such as terrorism, natural disasters, and changes in crime patterns (such as the murder rate during the crack cocaine epidemic). It can be argued that the NYPD is highly successful at rapid response and resolutions to police problems and emergencies. The police department was essentially remade after 9/11 under the leadership of Commissioner Kelly.

Responding to Hurricane Sandy, 9/11, blackouts, and other emergencies, however, is not the same as the constructive long-term management of social issues or successful solutions to complex problems. Resolution of complex problems is the new business of policing that problem-oriented policing, community policing, broken windows, and other theoretical models advocate. CompStat was fashioned from a corporate model and focuses on measurable results and police officer activity (e.g., stops and summonses). Rather than manufacturing cars or widgets, however, police departments produce summonses, arrests, and stop and frisks. The problem is that people do not buy summonses, arrests, or stops as they do cars, so there is no way to determine if the product is addressing what the community wants and needs. There is no way to tell if the product is a lemon or a limousine. The main issue in policing today should be how to move to a new model of police administration that embraces citizen satisfaction as well as crime control. Currently there are two ways to evaluate the performance of an individual police department or agency. In the first a legal measure looks to see if the department fulfills its mission in a lawful manner, honoring the Constitution and assuring due process. The second measures effectiveness in crime control. Meares (2013) suggests that a better measure of police agency performance would be "rightful policing" where the agency seeks to accomplish both goals, legal policing and effective policing. Several initiatives could help move the NYPD toward such a new model.

The element of the corporate model, which is missing in the CompStat model, is the presence of a board of directors. The function of a board of directors is to develop corporate policy, based on multiple factors, which is carried out by the company chief executive. Members of the board are selected for their expertise and have defined legal and fiduciary responsibilities. In its place the NYPD and the police institution generally rely on the political system to measure satisfaction. If the police executive is not doing a good job, the mayor should replace him or face defeat in the next election. This is a slow process and the recent NYC mayoral campaign may indicate that the damage is done before change can occur. Another problem with the political model is overcorrection. It would be unfortunate if the NYPD (or the city) were to overreact and return to a wholly reactive model. If a politician runs on a reform agenda, future decisions must conform to that agenda or face criticism. In addition, the political process is not always responsive to the needs of minority segments of the population. In the case of policing the damage can be significant.

If, however, policy were directed by a board of commissioners, policies might be forged in a more representative manner. As with a board of directors, a board of commissioners should include some members with expertise in policing as well as representatives from the community and other affected groups. The greatest benefit would be community participation in policy making and problem solving. In a sense it would be a CompStat for the police commissioner.

Opponents might argue that the creation of such a board would result in a "surrender of power" and decreased ability to respond to emergencies. Such a concern could be dealt with by specifically articulating the responsibilities of the board, a task that has become more feasible due to the development of theories of policing and the realities of the New York experience.

Although this chapter has focused on aggressive tactics as organizational or official policy, it does not mean that individual officers are not responsible for abuses of power. On a micro level or individual officer level, it has been noted that there are few corrective measures that can be effective deterrents due to vague standards of legality, qualified immunity, administrative indifference, and the like. Motivations for police abuse range from discriminatory animus to monetary benefits from overtime. Assuming the findings in *Floyd* are correct and the NYPD implemented aggressive police tactics and encouraged or were deliberately indifferent to police violations of the Fourth Amendment, it is easy to see how this would translate into individual instances of police officer misconduct. Removal of this policy will undoubtedly go a long way toward reducing individual misconduct. Greater community participation in policy making and empowering institutions such as the Civilian Complaint Review Board would be significant restraints as would the newly created office of inspector general.

An agency that takes seriously its obligation to assure legal enforcement and due process as well as effective policing should have the tools to monitor its success. As with any other priority such an endeavor requires resources and a commitment. Unfortunately, success in such an endeavor will not be as measurable as crime reduction strategies. There is no model to measure satisfaction with police service. There is, however, a model to measure crimes not reported to the police, the National Crime Victimization Survey (NCVS).

Concern over the accuracy of the uniform crime rate as well as recognition that the crime victim is an important component of the crime paradigm led to the institution of the NCVS in 1973. Expanding the NCVS to include a survey of police citizen satisfaction or developing a similar periodic measure would fill an important performance measurement gap. The benefit would be that it would put police departments in competition with each other for citizen satisfaction ratings. For example, if an increase in the crime rate occurs simultaneously with a decrease in citizen satisfaction, conclusions can be drawn from the data and meaningful strategies based on community compliance can be developed. It would also give a basis for corrective action: an increase in citizen and community satisfaction. To be effective the survey would have to be somewhat sophisticated and complex; however, the benefits would be transformative. In light of the cost of the administration of justice in America, the survey cost would be negligible.

Another approach to officer abuse is to apply principles of restorative justice to the problem. Restorative justice is an alternative to adversarial and punitive justice by returning the conflict to the community for resolution. By involving the offender, the victim, and the community (the three parties with ownership over the criminal event), restorative justice seeks meaningful resolution of the event and diversion from the criminal justice system. If an acceptable model could be developed based on restorative justice principles, it would benefit all parties.

3.7 Conclusion

The NYPD (and the police institution) has undergone significant change over the past 47 years. Since the *President's Commission on Law Enforcement and the Administration of Justice* (1967) report, the department has grown to 30,000 members, shrunk to under 20,000 members, and increased again to almost 40,000 members. Its operations have gone from periods of organized corruption, to passive reactive policing, to community policing, and ultimately to "effective" policing where crime reduction has become an agency obsession. Simultaneously, rules of criminal procedure have shifted from local to a federal constitutional set of standards and rules with the U.S. Supreme Court formulating a national body of criminal procedure law.

Stop-and-frisk policies in New York are a hot-button topic due to the seemingly invasive nature of these encounters. The issue of racial profiling in high crime areas became evident from the sheer magnitude of the stop-and-frisk policy. The stop-and-frisk program was intended to remove threats to public safety from the streets of New York and targeted high crime areas in order to reduce crime rates and remove illegal weapons. And although it may be argued that without the authority to conduct stop and frisks, street-level crime prevention efforts might well become impossible, the *Floyd* decision indicates that the program violates the Fourth and Fourteenth Amendments to the U.S. Constitution and as such violates fundamental American concepts of privacy and liberty and thoroughly damages police legitimacy.

Targeting high crime areas with adequate policing resources and applying stop and frisk in a constitutionally appropriate manner may or may not enable the police to protect the public and uphold the constitutional rights of U.S. citizens. If constitutional practices are inadequate, the problem must be addressed through a full legal process, not by the adoption of policies that alienate large sections of the community and demean the Constitution as being subservient to the greater good of crime control. Such single strategies are notorious for being nearsighted and precursors of greater evils. Theoretical models provide an extensive array of options. In fact there may well be too many options and competing models to be considered. And it must be remembered that artificially empowering the police to solve society's problems simply temporarily masks those problems.

The issues are truly complex and serious. Whether they can be resolved with an injunction, the establishment of an office of inspector general, judicial appointment of a referee as a remedy to an equal protection violation, or a temporary change in policy may be the most pressing question facing policing in the twenty-first century.

Aggressive policing is not the only problem facing the criminal justice system today. Terrorism, school shootings, local gun control, arrest policies, and prison overcrowding are just a few of the priorities facing the system and collectively they represent a daunting agenda. The last time there was concern over the operation of the criminal justice system, President Johnson convened the President's Crime Commission. At that time there were few experts available to address or even understand the criminal justice system. Today, there is a consensus that streets are safe, disorder is low, and the police can be highly effective in crime control. There is a growing consensus that incarceration rates are excessive and that minority communities are overpoliced. The commission did a commendable job and was successful in establishing an academic interest and significant research. It may well be time to revisit the concept of a national commission to examine the function of the criminal justice system, 50 years after this noble effort.

References

10 U.S. Const. amend.

14 U.S. Const. amend.

42 U.S. Code § 1983.

Barron v. Baltimore, 32 U.S. 243 (1833).

Benton v. Maryland, 395 U.S. 784 (1969).

Charney, D., Gonzalez, J., Kennedy, D., Leader, N., & Perry, R. (2010). Suspect fits description: Responses to racial profiling in New York City. 14 N.Y. City L. Rev. 57.

Fagan, J., Davies, G., & Carlis, A. (2012). Race and selective enforcement in public housing. Journal of Empirical Legal Studies. 9, 697.

Federal Bureau of Investigation. (2012). Crime reported by New York City Police Dept., New York. Retrieved from http://www.ucrdatatool.gov/Search/Crime/Local/RunCrimeJurisbyJuris.cfm

Floyd v. New York City, 08 Civ. 1034 (SAS). (2011).

Floyd v. New York City, 813 F. Supp. 2d 457. (2012).

Floyd v. New York City, 08 Civ. 1034. (2013).

Gideon v. Wainwright, 372 U.S. 335 (1963).

Gitlow v. New York, 268 U.S. 652 (1925).

Goldstein, H. (1979). Improving policing: A problem oriented approach. *Crime and Delinquency,* 25, 236–258.

Kabakova, D. (2012). The lack of accountability for the New York police department's investigative stops. 10 *Cardozo Pub. L. Pol'y & Ethics J.* 539.

Katz v. U.S., 389 U.S. 347 (1967).

Mapp v. Ohio, 367 U.S 643 (1961).

Meares, T. (2013). The good cop: Knowing the difference between lawful or effective policing and rightful policing—and why it matters. *Faculty Scholarship Series.* Paper 4661.

Miranda v. Arizona, 384 U.S. 436 (1966).

Near v. Minnesota, 283 U.S. 697 (1931).

Palko v. Connecticut, 302 U.S. 319 (1937).

People v. DeBour, 40 NY2d 210 (1976).

People v. Hollman, 79 N.Y. 2d. 181 (1992).

President's Commission on Law Enforcement and Administration of Justice. (1967). *Task Force Report: The Police.* Washington, DC: U. S. Government Printing Office.

Rosmarin, A. (2012). The phantom defense: The unavailability of the entrapment defense in New York City "plain view" marijuana arrests. 21 *J.L. & Pol'y* 189.

Segal, J. (2012). Note: All of the myticism of police expertise: Legalizing stop-and-frisk in New York, 1961–1968. 47 *Harv. C.R.-C.L. L. Rev.* 573.

Starkey, B.S. (2012). A failure of the Fourth Amendment and equal protection's promise: How the equal protection clause can change discriminatory stop and frisk policies. 18 *Mich. J. Race & L.* 131.

Terry v. Ohio, 392 U.S. 1 (1968).

Washington v. Davis. 246 U. S. 229 (1976).

Wilson, J. Q., & Kelling, G. (1982, March). Broken windows: The police and neighborhood safety. *Atlantic Monthly,* 29–38.

Wolf v. Colorado, 338 U.S. 25 (1949).

Zeidman, S. (2012/2013). Whither the criminal court: Confronting stop-and-frisks. 76 *Albany Law Review,* 1187.

Endnote

1. The departmental form used to record street encounters is referred to as a UF 250. A police officer is required to complete a UF 250 each time the officer conducts a stop or a stop and frisk (two separate events). UF 250 information is maintained in an NYPD database and it was these data which were analyzed and provided significant information in *Floyd. v. NYC,* 08 Civ. 1034 (SAS).

Evaluating How the NYPD Handles Crime Victims

Judgments Based on Statistical Performance Measures

4

ANDREW KARMEN

Contents

4.1   Introduction

This is the age of ratings and rankings. A growing number of agencies, institutions, companies, groups, products, and services earn or are assigned numerical scores that place them on lists of the 10 best or 10 worst in their fields. Sports teams, restaurants, hospitals, high schools, high school teachers, universities, college professors, cars, airlines, even airports receive rankings. Why not rate police departments too?

The NYPD has long been referred to as "New York's Finest." But is it the nation's finest police force and perhaps even the world's best department? What would be the appropriate criteria for evaluation? Performance measures could indicate progress and mastery along a number of dimensions: protecting the public from ordinary street crime as well as terrorist attacks, spending taxpayers' money wisely and efficiently, preventing or rooting out corruption in the ranks, using force (and especially deadly force) with restraint, respecting the civil liberties of the citizenry, keeping traffic flowing smoothly, taking charge of emergencies, educating residents about crime prevention tips, disseminating important information via a user-friendly website, and effectively addressing the needs of their most immediate "customers," "consumers of their services," or direct "clients" whom they pledge to protect and serve: crime victims.

Victimization rates across the country have been falling steadily over the past several decades and, by the end of 2013, had tumbled to roughly the same levels as they were in the 1960s, when the issue of victims' rights emerged for the first time in U.S. history. Consequently, with each passing year, fewer Americans joined the ranks of crime victims. This favorable trend was especially true for the inhabitants of New York City, where the crime problem receded more dramatically than in other major cities in all the major categories of interpersonal violence and theft (murders, aggravated assaults, robberies, forcible rapes, burglaries, larcenies, and vehicle thefts were all committed far less frequently). Because the sheer number of victims has diminished, perhaps the remaining ones can be handled with greater care.

Ever since the mid-1990s, New York City's two mayors and four police commissioners have insisted that the suddenly safer city was almost entirely the result of revamped NYPD policies that were "smarter" (e.g., CompStat) and tougher (e.g., more stopping-and-frisking and more arresting for minor infractions), even though many criminologists argued that the jury was still out on this question of how much credit the police deserve for the plunging crime rates (e.g., see Karmen, 2006). Over the past 20 years since 1993, the mayor's and the police commissioner's public relations units repeatedly have directed the media's attention to this ebbing of the crime wave that had gripped the city from the mid-1960s until the start of the 1990s. The NYPD continually reminds the public about all the crimes that have not taken place. But what about the crimes that have been committed? How did the department respond to the real flesh-and-blood victims of these violations of law that weren't "prevented" by their improved operations? Even after the "crime crash," thousands of New Yorkers still inform the NYPD each year that they have been harmed by criminals. For example, during 2012, according to the CompStat system's statistical report on the NYPD website, almost 20,000 persons reported that they had been feloniously assaulted, over 20,000 complained that they had been robbed, and nearly 20,000 told detectives that their homes had been burglarized.

4.2   "Satisfied Customers"?

Were these tens of thousands of crime victims generally pleased with the way the NYPD handled their cases?

A journalistic approach to explore this issue would be to tell the story of a particular individual's experiences in depth. In an article entitled, "Burglary Victim, and Satisfied Customer of the NYPD" (Wei, 2012), a young woman told the reporter, "I really didn't expect the NYPD to care as much as they did." Finding her apartment in disarray and some valuables missing, she called 911. Within five minutes, two uniformed officers arrived, followed shortly thereafter by two more, and then members of the crime scene unit to take photos and search for fingerprints and other forensic evidence, and finally a detective in a trench coat who interviewed her and some neighbors. Within a week, she received a picture message of a necklace (which was similar but not hers) and a personalized security survey with some burglary prevention tips. On the basis of her personal experience, she concluded, "Call me overly optimistic, but I actually have faith in the system now. The police don't pull out all the stops just for the big crime scenes. They don't just care about the stories that make the news. The reality is that they're just as thorough with all crimes, petty as they may be." The implication of this highly favorable newspaper coverage was, "What more could a victim ask for?" (The obvious rejoinders would be, "How about catching the burglar?" and "What about recovering the stolen property?")

Criminologists and victimologists could carry out research in a number of ways to see if this individual's VIP treatment represented standard operating procedure or was atypical. An exploratory study could be based on interviews with victims who sought help by filing complaints at their local precincts. More generalizable empirically based findings could be derived from a survey of a representative sample of the tens of thousands of persons who told desk sergeants and detectives each year that they had sustained injuries or suffered thefts.*

A quantitative indicator, "level of victim satisfaction," was calculated for a number of different cities just once, in a 1998 study conducted by the Bureau of Justice Statistics (BJS) of the U.S. Department of Justice. The findings were derived from that year's National Crime Victimization Survey (NCVS), which the BJS has carried out annually since 1973. The analysis of the survey of a larger than usual sample discovered that individuals who suffered acts of interpersonal violence had a considerably lower level of satisfaction with the way the police department handled their cases in New York than in any of the other 11 cities. (See the percentages in column two of Table 4.1.)

Table 4.1   Satisfaction Scores for Victims of Violent Crimes, 12 Cities, 1998

City	Percentage of Violent Crime Victims Who Were "Satisfied"
Chicago	75
Kansas City	72
Knoxville	74
Los Angeles	74
Madison	92
New York City	61
San Diego	81
Savannah	69
Spokane	74
Springfield	69
Tucson	70
Washington, DC	69
Total, All 12 Cities	69

Source: Adapted from Smith, S., Steadman, G., & Minton, T., Criminal Victimization and Perceptions of Community Safety in 12 Cities, 1998 BJS Report, U.S. Department of Justice, Washington, DC, 1999, Table 35, p. 26.

Note: Wording of the question: "How satisfied are you with the police, Are you very satisfied, satisfied, dissatisfied, or very dissatisfied?" Combining of categories: Satisfied = very satisfied plus satisfied.

---

* About 400 officers have been issued smartphones that are capable of listing the names of all residents who have been victims of crimes at any given street address in New York City (Ruderman, 2013). Therefore, it appears that the names and addresses of all recent complainants are readily available in some NYPD database. It is not known whether the NYPD would grant researchers access to this database.

Clearly, this type of survey of comparative satisfaction levels needs to be replicated on a regular basis. But the 1998 results provide an empirical foundation for the hypothesis that victim dissatisfaction with NYPD handling might still be a problem, many years later.

Victim satisfaction and dissatisfaction are rather vague terms that could be influenced by many different aspects of police operations. The 1998 expanded BJS survey did not delve deeply into this matter. What would be ideal service? What could victims want, and what might they expect? A list of what all police departments should strive to deliver to their residents who were harmed by offenders could include the following:

1. Make the reporting system "victim-friendly" so that injured parties will anticipate that their calls for help will be fielded efficiently and sensitively and will be properly investigated.
2. When summoned in an emergency, arrive as rapidly as possible at the scene of a crime in progress.
3. Solve the crime by making an arrest; prepare a solid case that will stand up in court and lead to a conviction.
4. Recover stolen property and return it to its rightful owner.

In addition to conducting interviews with victims or surveying them, a third empirical approach would be to compile certain official statistics that are made public by the department itself in various reports, and treat these disclosures as performance measures. That is the approach to be adopted here, in order to assemble the "big picture" of how the NYPD responds to New Yorkers who file complaints that they have been harmed physically, emotionally, or financially by offenders.

Data from official sources is presented to answer the following questions:

A. "How often do crime victims turn to the NYPD for help?"
   Estimated reporting rates address this issue.
B. "How quickly do officers arrive when summoned?"
   Computations of response times to emergency calls for help suggest what the typical waiting time might be.
C. "How often do victims experience the satisfaction of finding out that someone was taken into custody and charged with harming them?
   Published figures about the proportion of cases that are "cleared" by an arrest are the appropriate indicators.
D. "How often do victims get their cash and valuables back?"
   Information about stolen property recovery rates would shed some light on this matter.

4.2.1 (A) Tell Them What Happened

4.2.1.1 *Performance Measure: Reporting Crimes to the Police*

In order to receive help and support from the justice system, a crime victim in any jurisdiction must come forward and formally file a complaint. Whether the victim is seeking treatment and rehabilitation of the offender, or restitution from the wrongdoer for out-of-pocket expenses, or—more commonly—punishment and retribution, no assistance from government agencies will be forthcoming unless a written report sets the machinery of justice into motion. A department can be considered "victim-friendly" if a very large proportion of persons harmed by criminals share their problems with the authorities. Conversely, if many innocent law-abiding people whom this branch of government is supposed to serve and protect are reluctant to have any dealings with it, that is a sign of serious strains within police–community relations. Reporting rates are the statistical performance measures that can shed light on this very fundamental aspect of police operations. The goal of any community-oriented and service-oriented department should be to maximize reporting rates.*

Every year, the BJS publishes a national estimate of the proportion of victims who say that they reported to their local police the same incident which they were willing to disclose on the NCVS. An analysis of the NCVS findings over the years reveals that victims are most likely to report crimes involving the use of weapons, the infliction of physical injuries, or the imposition of substantial financial losses. Of the violent crimes, aggravated assaults are reported at the highest rates; rapes and simple assaults by intimates are brought to the attention of the authorities the least often. Acts of interpersonal violence generally are reported more frequently than property crimes, but completed (not attempted) vehicle thefts are reported at the highest rate of all. Of the various social groups, lower-income people, urban residents, and Black victims were more inclined to seek police assistance than other demographic categories; seniors are the most likely, and teens are the least likely to call the cops, according to the annual findings of the NCVS (Hart & Rennison, 2003; also see Karmen, 2013 for trends).

4.2.1.2 *How Does the NYPD Compare to Other Departments in Terms of Getting Victims to Seek Their Help?*

Rarely have the relative successes and failures of various police departments to get victims to come forward been investigated. Over the years, just two

---

* Even if that means, in the short run, that there will be an apparent increase in crime rates when in reality there is merely an increase in reporting rates. Police chiefs and commissioners across the country sometimes explain a spike as merely the result of improved reporting. However, they never raise the possibility that observed decreases are due to diminishing reporting rates.

studies have yielded some evidence about the degree of cooperation from victims that the NYPD and other police departments have been able to achieve.

One was the 1998 study cited above. It might be considered a one-of-a-kind comparative analysis or perhaps a spot-check of how 12 departments functioned during that year. The analysis, based on an NCVS sample that was expanded enough to permit city-level comparisons, confirmed the suspicion that some police departments learned about a much greater proportion of victimizations than others. The NYPD ranked near the bottom in terms of the proportion of victims who shared their troubles with the authorities. Only the police department in Spokane, Washington was notified about a smaller percentage of acts of interpersonal violence. Only the San Diego police force learned about a smaller fraction of the property crimes its residents experienced during 1998. (See the percentages in columns two and three in Table 4.2.)

One other study yielded some evidence that the NYPD has not fared well in a match-up of reporting rates with other departments. This study calculated overall reporting rates by victimized New Yorkers for the years 1980 to 1999. (See Table 4.3.) These reporting rates to the NYPD for selected crimes averaged out over a 20-year span can be compared to the average reporting rates to all local law enforcement agencies across the country, derived from

Table 4.2   Percentage of Victims Who Reported Crimes Committed Against Them to Their Local Police Department in 12 Cities During 1998

City	Percentage of Violent Crimes Reported to the Local Police	Percentage of Property Crimes Reported to the Local Police
Chicago	38	37
Kansas City	44	45
Knoxville	41	43
Los Angeles	34	33
Madison	36	37
New York City	32	29
San Diego	36	28
Savannah	40	47
Spokane	31	38
Springfield	58	41
Tucson	42	44
Washington, DC	50	41
Total, All 12 Cities	35	34

Source: Adapted from Smith, S., Steadman, G., & Minton, T., Criminal Victimization and Perceptions of Community Safety in 12 Cities, 1998 BJS Report, U.S. Department of Justice, Washington, DC, 1999, Table 2, p. 3.

Note: Violent crimes include rape/sexual assault, robbery, and aggravated/simple assault. Property crimes include household burglary, motor vehicle theft, household larceny, and personal larceny without contact.

Table 4.3   Proportion of Victims Reporting Their Misfortunes to the Police, for New York City, 1980–1999; for the Entire United States, 1992–2000

Type of Crime	Robbery (%)	Aggravated Assault (%)	Burglary (%)	Larceny (%)	Vehicle Theft (%)
Average reporting rate to the NYPD, 1980–1998	49	51	55	23	70
Average reporting rate to all U.S. police departments, 1992–2000	57	55	53[a]	29[a]	81[a]

Sources: New York data = Langan & Durose, 2004; national data = Hart & Rennison, 2003.
Note: Both New York and national figures include only offenses against persons and exclude crimes against commercial entities.
[a]   Only available figure is for 2000, not 1992 to 2000.

an NCVS study that merged survey findings for the years 1992 to 2000 (this is the closest available matching time period).

The data reveal that in New York victims of robberies, aggravated assaults, larcenies, and vehicle thefts were less inclined to report their suffering to the police than similar victims in other jurisdictions scattered across the country. (See Table 4.3.) Only burglary victims were slightly more willing to file complaints in New York than in other places (55% compared to 53%).

4.2.1.3   Does the NYPD Encourage Victims to Disclose Their Troubles or Discourage Them From Filing Official Complaints, or Even Disregard Their First-Person Accounts?

Ever since crime rates in New York City began their dramatic decline from their record-setting levels in 1990, reports have circulated in the news media and in the scholarly literature that NYPD statistics might be "fudged" or "massaged" to keep them artificially low for some ulterior purposes.

If there is some truth to these charges, then genuine victims might be subjected to needless additional suffering imposed by departmental practices. If the severity of the accounts of victims of violence is downplayed and downgraded, or disbelieved and dismissed entirely, then these individuals will not receive the support and assistance to which they are entitled (e.g., financial reimbursement from the New York State Crime Victims Compensation Board). Also, they might not be able to exercise their recently gained legal rights in court (for instance, to voice their views in a victim impact statement at a sentencing hearing). Downward statistical manipulation not only hurts victims, but it also endangers the general public. To be effective, police forces must have accurate, complete, and timely data in order to detect patterns of criminal activity and subsequently to act to put a stop to these depredations.

Whether a systematic disregarding of victims' accounts by the NYPD constitutes a serious problem remains unresolved because the available evidence points in different directions.

A comparison of crimes known to the NYPD with NCVS-based estimates of the actual number of incidents in the five boroughs was carried out for the years 1980 to 1999 by BJS researchers to "put NYPD statistics to the test." This study (cited above) discovered that for the seven index crimes (with the exception of aggravated assaults), the correlation between the two data sets was high and became even higher, not lower, during the years following 1993, when pressures on precinct commanders by higher-ups became intense: to show at each subsequent CompStat meeting that public safety had improved even further. The study's authors (Langan & Durose, 2004, p. 21) concluded, "In short, crime fell in New York City probably for lots of reasons, but rising reticence to report crime to the NYPD was not one of them." However, these government statisticians also stated, "Still, we cannot rule out the possibility that on occasion, some of the 75 precincts in New York City may have downgraded or concealed crimes to make their statistics look better" (p. 19). Indeed, over the past two decades, some precinct commanders have gotten into trouble for "cooking the books" to reduce artificially the number of reported crimes in their jurisdiction (e.g., see Blau, 2006; Butterfield, 1998).

Because this accusation flares up periodically, the NYPD's brass has responded by ordering quality assurance audits (see Blau, 2006; Hoffer, 2012). These internal reviews of 911 logs, incident reports, and CompStat tallies conclude that the official statistics are very accurate (see Smith & Purtell, 2006).[†]

The controversy over whether the NYPD welcomes complaints or has adopted unfriendly protocols remains unresolved. A steady stream of accusations has appeared in the news media in recent years about a reticence on the part of the department to accept, record, and act upon some of the complaints. As two reporters (Baker & Goldstein, 2011) characterized the problem after citing some real-life examples, "Crime victims in New York sometimes struggle to persuade the police to write down what happened on an official report" (p. A16).

---

[*] The NCVS has suffered periodic cutbacks in its funding, necessitating repeated trimming of the size of its nationwide sample. For example, in 1980, the NCVS carried out close to 250,000 interviews, of which nearly 7,400 persons (about 3%) lived in the five boroughs (counties) of New York City. By 1995, the countrywide sample had decreased to about 180,000 people, of which roughly 4,500 (about 2.5%) were New York City residents (Langan & Durose, 2004, p. 9).

[†] To try to dispel these lingering charges of systemic undercounting, the police commissioner empaneled a group to investigate whether the department's statistics were being manipulated. Its report urged the NYPD to do more to hold supervisors accountable for egregious mistakes in classifications (Goldstein, 2013).

Researchers have verified that these improprieties were not aberrations but represent the institutionalization of a manipulative "numbers game" (see Eterno & Silverman, 2012). A survey in 2008 of retired police captains and other supervisors unearthed evidence that more than 50% of them were aware of instances in which statistical reports were altered in ways that the majority felt was "unethical" (Eterno & Silverman, 2012). A follow-up survey in 2012 revealed that a little more than half of the nearly 2,000 retirees (of varying ranks) had observed the intentional misclassification of serious crimes as mere petty offenses, along with other unethical practices. The respondents confirmed that the pressures to artificially depress the number of reported index crimes (which are closely monitored) intensified in the years following a change of mayors and police commissioners in 2002 (Silverman, Eterno, & Levine, 2012).*

Some of the most compelling charges about a reluctance to accept complaints at face value have emanated from whistleblowers. As one patrolman explained, an assault could be downgraded to a mere violation such as harassment. A sergeant cited how shots fired at a cab driver might be classified as just reckless endangerment rather than as a felonious assault (Hoffer, 2012).† A city councilman usually regarded as a staunch defender of the department against its critics asserted that fudging does indeed take place, declaring, "I have spoken to many current and former police officers who unfortunately refused to go on the record but have corroborated that fact. And I've spoken to many civilians whose valid complaints were not accepted by the Police Department" (quoted in Baker & Rashbaum, 2011). One of the most believable sources for this accusation has been the voice of the rank-and-file officers, the Patrolmen's Benevolent Association (PBA). As one posting on the PBA's website revealed (quoted in Moses, 2005):

> So how do you fake a crime decrease? It's pretty simple. Don't file reports, misclassify crimes from felonies to misdemeanors, under-value the property lost to crime so it's not a felony, and report a series as a single event.
>
> A particularly insidious way to fudge the numbers is to make it difficult or impossible for people to report crimes—in other words, make the victims feel like criminals so they walk away just to spare themselves further pain and suffering.
>
> We're asking every PBA member to share with their delegates the hard evidence of crimes being downgraded so we can save this department from itself.

---

* One respondent wrote, "… and the average person that wants to make a legitimate complaint is totally discouraged and a report will be taken to placate them only until they leave and another report will be [sic] done downgrading the original report to a lesser crime …" (Silverman, Eterno, & Levine, 2012).

† Similarly, a grand larceny can be written up as a petit larceny; and burglary as criminal trespass; also, several break-ins in the same building could be consolidated into just one case of burglary (see Silverman, Eterno, & Levine, 2012).

Victims should not have to suffer in silence, nor should they have to resort to retaliatory justice. In order to counteract this vote of "no confidence in the criminal justice system", and to improve reporting rates and thereby enhance public safety, it is necessary to determine the leading causes of nonreporting. A survey similar to the annual NCVS should be carried out periodically in New York City to discover the reasons some victims do share their woes with the NYPD and others don't (e.g., due to a fear of reprisals or a belief that the police won't be able to rectify the situation, or that the criminal justice process is too time-consuming and hence costly, or that the victim lacks proof to substantiate the charges). Once the barriers to reporting have been identified, victim-friendly procedures can be developed to elicit a higher degree of cooperation from the public.

Furthermore, complainants ought to be entitled to find out the NYPD's response to the charges they are lodging against suspects. The police department could provide a complainant with an official receipt that explains what actions the department will take, if any, and why.*

4.2.2   (B) Come Quickly!

4.2.2.1   *Performance Measure: Response Time to Urgent Calls for Help*

Strict gun-control laws make New Yorkers especially dependent upon officers to rescue them when they are under attack. Therefore, the police department has a responsibility to do all it can to reduce its average response time to 911 calls that are classified as critical because of impending violence.

Minimizing response time is of utmost importance to victims in the throes of a crisis for a number of reasons. The arrival of an officer can save the person from further harm. The officer can administer immediate medical and psychological first aid. First responders also can secure the crime scene, preserving crucial evidence and locating eyewitnesses before they disperse. Ideally the officer might even be able to catch the culprit red-handed.

Since 1991, the City Council has required the NYPD to calculate and disclose its response times to crimes in progress, and to critical calls where violence is impending or already has been unleashed. Responding to emergencies quickly is one of the NYPD's stated goals in the annual agency report

---

* Victimizations reported to the police can be deemed to be: Founded = the complainant's version of events is accepted. Unfounded = detectives reject the account and disbelieve the person claiming to be a victim. Some small proportions of complaints surely are untrue and are lodged by individuals with ulterior motives (such as filing a false claim of vehicle theft for insurance reimbursement). Defounded = detectives believe a crime occurred but the incident was not as serious as the victim described it.

card called the Mayor's Management Report (MMR).* Data tracking this performance measure since 1999 appear in Table 4.4. Additional rows indicate response times for other agencies that are summoned in crises: the Fire Department of New York (FDNY) and its Emergency Medical Service (EMS) ambulances.†

The performance indicators assembled from the annual MMRs show that the shortest elapsed time from receiving a 911 call to racing through city streets to the scene of an emergency is about four minutes flat. The FDNY has just about achieved that rapid arrival time to put out blazes frequently in recent years (row three). The FDNY has maintained a similar excellent record getting to the kinds of medical emergencies they handle (row four). The NYPD has improved its response time to critical 911 calls about serious violence (such as aggravated assaults or the sounds of shots fired) almost as quickly (around 30 seconds longer) as the FDNY. EMS ambulances tend to arrive to assist injured parties about two or three minutes later, on average, during most years.

A broad measure of police response time also appears in the annual MMRs for "All crimes in progress." The MMR defines this category to include not only racing to "critical" calls for help, but also arriving as soon as possible to the scenes of "serious" crimes (including larceny directly from a person, such as a purse or chain snatching; vehicle theft; and an unarmed assault) as well as speeding to "noncritical" situations (that don't involve the threat of an injury). Trends in this broader measure appear in Table 4.5.

The data assembled in Table 4.5 reveal a somewhat different trend than in Table 4.4. The response time to all kinds of crimes in progress improved during the first half of the 1990s and then slipped back during the second half. It improved again during the 21st century and dipped to its best level (less than seven minutes) in 2007. Since then, it has crept back upward by more than two minutes and was no better in 2012 than it had been in 1996 (row 2). Over the years, NYPD spokespersons have blamed delays on nonemergency calls (which should be phoned in to 311) flooding the 911 system, time lost notifying dispatchers about the arrival of a squad car, shortages of patrol units, and traffic jams. Even though some studies have questioned the importance of

---

* When expected improvements did not materialize in the mid-1990s, Mayor Giuliani asserted that monitoring response time was an outmoded approach: "…indicators that are 3, 4, 5, maybe 10 years old as a way of measuring police performance" (quoted in Topousis, 1997, p. 22).

† The clock starts running when a 911 operator fields a call for help and stops when an officer or firefighter or EMS technician leaps out of a vehicle at the scene. The specific definitions from the Mayor's Management Report are as follows: NYPD critical crimes in progress include assaults with a weapon, gunfire, and robberies. FDNY fires are structural blazes. FDNY medical emergencies include life-threatening problems such as major burns, cardiac arrest, and choking. EMS ambulance runs are responses to life-threatening emergencies.

TABLE 4.4 Response Times to Emergencies: NYPD and FDNY, 1999–2012

Year	1999	2000	2001	2002	2003	2004	2005	2006	2007	2008	2009	2010	2011	2012
NYPD critical calls	6.3	6.4	6	4.8	5	5	4.4	4.3	4.2	4.3	4.3	4.4	4.6	4.6
Min. FDNY fires	4.2	4.2	4.2	4.1	4.2	4.2	4.3	4.3	4.3	4.2	4.1	4.0	4.0	4.1
FDNY medical emergencies	4.3	4.3	4.2	4.2	4.3	4.3	4.5	4.3	4.2	4.2	4.1	4.2	4.2	4.1
Ambulances EMS	7.5	7.5	7	6.5	6.5	7	6.5	6.4	6.4	6.4	6.4	7.0	7.0	6.3

Source: Mayor's Management Reports, 1999–2012.
Note: All times are in minutes.

TABLE 4.5 Response Times to All Crimes in Progress: NYPD, 1992–2012

Year	1992	1993	1994	1995	1996	1997	1998	1999	2000	2001	2002	2003	2004	2005	2006	2007	2008	2009	2010	2011	2012
Time	9.9	8.0	7.9	7.7	9.1	9.2	9.8	10.3	10.1	10.1	7.2	7.5	7.7	7.2	7.1	6.9	7.3	7.3	7.5	8.4	9.1

Source: Mayor's Management Reports, 1992–2012.
Note: All times are in minutes.

cutting response time, whenever a 10–13 call ("officer needs help") is broadcast across the police radio band, nearby officers drop what they are doing and race to the scene as fast as they can (Karmen, 2013).

To victims under attack, a rapid response can be a matter of life-and-death.[*] The data show that there is room for improvement. The department must continually devise ways to arrive at the scenes of violent crimes as quickly as possible.

4.2.3 (C) Catch the Culprit!

4.2.3.1 Performance Measure: Clearance Rates

Clearance rates are traditional measures of police performance. These statistics indicate how well a department is accomplishing its basic job of solving cases brought to its attention by injured parties (or, in the case of homicides, by the discovery of a corpse).

A case is cleared when an arrest is made and someone is charged with the crime. An exceptional clearance takes place if the suspect can't be arrested (e.g., is deceased). A cleared case does not necessarily lead to a conviction in court. Successful conclusions depend upon the strength of the underlying evidence and the skills of the prosecutor, and the ultimate outcomes of the legal process are not factored into the calculation of a solution rate.

The proportions of investigations that lead to arrests are indicators of the effectiveness of the police to apprehend suspects. Clearance rates can also be interpreted as one determinant of "degree of satisfaction": the proportion of victims who might feel that the police "did their job effectively" by making an arrest and charging someone with a crime.

4.2.3.2 What Is the NYPD's Track Record?

The percentage of cases of violence and theft that patrol officers and detectives closed each year by making an arrest was a performance measure that appeared in the annual statistical report by the Office of Management Analysis and Planning (OMAP), entitled "Complaints and Arrests." Citywide clearance percentages for all seven index crimes for the years 1990 to 2001 appear in Table 4.6.[†]

Victims of interpersonal violence (and their loved ones if they perished) were more likely to be satisfied with the department's performance as the

---

[*] How crucial emergency first aid can be was dramatized when a Brooklyn woman whose throat was slashed by her boyfriend bled to death during a 15-minute delay when her 911 call got mishandled (Kemp & Otis, 2013).

[†] Breakdowns of complaints and arrests for each precinct and each borough were also available. Arson was added by Congress as the eighth index crime in 1978 but it is usually excluded from any analyses because so many fires are classified as "of undetermined origin."

Table 4.6   NYPD Clearance Rates, All Seven Index Crimes, 1990–2001

Year	1990	1991	1992	1993	1994	1995	1996	1997	1998	1999	2000	2001
Murders	62	59	59	62	64	73	87	88	87	82	78	67
Rapes	49	57	49	44	51	61	52	51	59	59	53	53
Robberies	22	22	21	21	25	29	30	31	34	33	33	34
Aggravated assaults	50	51	50	47	53	56	55	64	69	65	65	67
Burglaries	9	9	8	8	9	12	13	14	16	14	14	15
Grand larcenies	7	7	6	6	7	9	9	9	10	10	10	10
Vehicle thefts	7	7	6	5	5	7	7	7	7	7	8	8

Source: OMAP's annual statistical reports, "Complaints and Arrests" for 1990 to 2001.

years wore on. Clearance rates for murders and manslaughters bottomed out when slayings peaked at the start of the 1990s (row two). More than 40% of all killers "got away with murder" in those "bad old days." But then the NYPD's ability to solve homicide cases improved dramatically during the second half of the decade. Impressive solution rates of 87% and 88% were achieved with the help of a cold case squad that brought killers to justice who thought they had escaped the long arm of the law.* (However, a disappointing drop materialized at the start of the 21st century.) Felonious assaults (row three) and robberies (row four) also were solved at a much better rate by the second half of the 1990s, presumably pleasing those victims. Arrests in cases of forcible rape did not rise as consistently (interpreting clearances rates are complicated in cases of sexual assaults because acquaintance rapes are by definition "solved" if and when they are reported).

As for victims of crimes against their property, the findings displayed in Table 4.6 present a disappointing picture. During the latter part of the 1990s compared to the early years of the decade, a substantially larger proportion of New Yorkers who reported that their homes (and stores and offices) were broken into were satisfied to learn that an arrest was made in their case. However, even after this improvement took place, the vast majority of burglary victims (85%) would wind up frustrated that no one was charged with entering their premises to steal things (row six). Similarly, an improvement was registered in the NYPD's ability to solve grand larcenies over the 11-year span (row seven). And still, by the start of the new century, the overwhelming majority (90%) of victims of major thefts (of possessions worth $1,000

---

* Unfortunately, the possibility exists that some cases are "solved" by arresting—or worse yet, convicting and punishing—an innocent person. Victims suffer when old wounds are reopened when miscarriages of justice are being rectified. For example, the Brooklyn district attorney's office was forced to review 50 homicide convictions because of questionable confessions and witness statements obtained by a single detective over his career (see Clines, 2013).

or more) would not get any closure from an arrest of a suspect. Victims of vehicle theft (grand larceny auto, GLA) experienced no significant improvements at all during the 1990s (row eight). Car thieves drove off in their stolen vehicles in over 90% of all reported incidents (including the fraction of those cases that were just attempted thefts; still no one was caught).

In sum, the handling of cases involving victims of violence improved considerably during the decade, whereas the solving of cases of victims of thefts also improved somewhat but remained at frustratingly low levels. Because acts of theft are much more common than acts of violence, the majority of victimized New Yorkers were unable to experience the satisfaction of knowing that someone had been arrested and charged with harming them.

Unfortunately, the disclosure of this performance measure in the yearly statistical compendium, "Complaints and Arrests," ended in 2001, when a new mayor and police commissioner took office. Furthermore, the NYPD has not sent comprehensive data (on forms called "Return A's") about its clearance rates to the FBI's Uniform Crime Reporting division for inclusion in the bureau's well-known Uniform Crime Report (UCR) since early 2002 when the NYPD reportedly changed its computer programming.[*] The only sources of post-2001 data about NYPD clearance rates in more recent years appear in articles in newspapers, based on internal leaks or from disclosures from the Public Information Office to journalists, sometimes in compliance with a Freedom of Information Act request. As two reporters wrote, "The NYPD closely guards its performance figures, unlike crime stats ..." (Blau & Hamilton, 2010). The data released by the Deputy Commissioner for Public Information (DCPI) in 2010 appear in Table 4.7.

Table 4.7   NYPD Clearance Rates Compared to National Averages, 2008 and 2009

Crime Category	All PDs (%) 2008	NYPD (%) 2008	All PDs (%) 2009	NYPD (%) 2009
Murders	64	67	67	59
Forcible rapes	40	70	40	75
Robberies	27	35	28	42
Aggravated assaults	55	55	55	54
Burglaries	13	16	12	18
Larcenies	20	19	22	25
Vehicle thefts	12	7	11	9

Sources: NYPD figures: Blau & Hamilton, 2010; all police departments: FBI's UCRs for 2008, 2009.

---

[*] Return A databases are available to researchers and journalists on request from the FBI.

The NYPD's clearance rates for forcible rapes and robberies in 2008 and 2009 were higher than the national averages for these crimes (rows four and five). As for aggravated assaults, New Yorkers who brought their injuries or near-death experiences to the attention of the NYPD were as likely as other Americans to have their cases solved (row six). Murder investigations are always assigned a high priority, and consequently result in the best clearance rates of all. Homicide cases were closed successfully more often in New York than in the rest of the country in 2008, but less often in 2009 (row three). (In 2009, homicide squads in San Jose, Denver, Washington DC, Jacksonville, Las Vegas, Oklahoma City, Philadelphia, Memphis, San Antonio, Milwaukee, and Seattle all did better than the NYPD, solving 70% or more of the slayings in their cities [see Karmen, 2013, p. 180]).

As for property crimes, burglaries were cleared by an arrest more often by the NYPD than by other departments in both 2008 and 2009 (row seven). However, vehicle thefts were solved less often by NYPD officers, auto squad investigators, and other detectives than by police forces nationwide.[*] Patterns in larcenies are more difficult to discern because NYPD statistics focus only on grand larcenies, not all thefts including petty larcenies.

In 2013, in response to a journalist's inquiry, the DCPI stated that the NYPD's homicide clearance rate for 2012 was 75% (Gardiner, 2013). The comparable figure for the entire country was substantially worse, just 63% (in 2012), according to the FBI's UCR. Note that much more impressive homicide clearance rates were achieved by the NYPD during the late 1990s (as high as 88%; see Table 4.6) than in 2012. (Perhaps that explains the desire of the department to keep these figures confidential.) The DCPI pledged that the NYPD would make its clearance rates public on a regular basis in the future (Gardiner, 2013).

New Yorkers who come forward and report offenses committed against them should not be kept in the dark. They ought to be informed of the NYPD's track record for various categories of crime so they will have realistic expectations about the "odds" that their kind of case will be solved. And the fortunate complainants whose cases are cleared by an arrest ought to get an official notification right away, so they can monitor how "their" case is handled by their borough's district attorney's office.

---

[*] And yet, the problem of car stealing decreased further and faster in New York than in the rest of the country, and more so in the city than any other index crime, even though the perpetrators were caught less often than elsewhere. This has led some criminologists to question whether crime "crashed" solely due to re-engineered police operations (inasmuch as auto theft investigations were subpar in New York City), or because of a confluence of some other factors (see Karmen, 2006, pp. 112–113).

4.2.4 (D) Return the Stolen Goods!

4.2.4.1 *Performance Measure: Recovery Rates*

Victims want their possessions back. If an arrest is made, the possibility arises that any goods stolen by robbers, burglars, pickpockets, chain-snatchers, and car thieves can be retrieved once they are no longer needed as evidence. Even if the case is not solved, the fruits of crime might be abandoned or be seized from a fencing operation.

Two sets of data reveal stolen property recovery rates on a national basis. The NCVS asks victims if they got back some or all of what was taken from them, either thanks to police investigations or through their own efforts. The problem is that recovery rates are generally very low. Stolen property usually is not returned to its rightful owner, according to the NCVS. For example, in 2008 (the latest figures available), only 24% of all robbery victims and merely 7% of all burglary victims got back some or all of their stolen goods. Only victims of car theft (58%) have a good chance of regaining their prized possessions (see Karmen, 2013, p. 184).

The other indicator of stolen property recovery rates appears in the annual UCR. Police departments are asked to estimate the value of property stolen and recovered for various categories. For example, in 2011, police nationwide seized only 5% of the value of all stolen jewelry and another 5% of the value of all stolen electronic goods, and 52% of the depreciated value of all stolen vehicles (FBI, 2012).

Certainly, recovery rates for two often-stolen items would not be too difficult to operationalize, track, and make public: automobiles and smartphones. Victims of completed motor vehicle thefts report their losses to the police at a very high rate, for insurance purposes, to avoid liability for subsequent accidents or crimes, and in the hope of getting their abandoned vehicles returned to them in drivable condition. The NYPD carries out many traffic stops and issues a great many tickets, and routinely uses surveillance cameras and license plate readers for antiterrorism as well as anticrime operations, so there are reasons for victims to be optimistic. Insurance companies maintain their own independent and accurate databases of losses and recoveries organized by serial numbers (vehicle identification numbers or VINs), so the recovery statistics could be double-checked for accuracy.

Similarly, efforts are underway to set up databases of stolen smartphones and similar electronic goods. Currently, smartphones are taken in about 33% of all robberies nationwide and 40% in New York City (AP, 2013). The precision of this figure indicates that NYPD files already contain notations about smartphones. It should not be too difficult to determine their recovery rate, along with methods to return seized electronic goods to their rightful owners before they became outdated.

Departments ought to grant victims the right to a good faith effort to locate and retrieve their stolen property. It is well known that many agencies, including the NYPD, auction off unclaimed stolen property seized from offenders. More victims could identify and reclaim their stolen goods if a better system were devised. The NYPD might consider setting up a user-friendly online inventory of recovered stolen property before it is auctioned off.[*]

4.3 Summary of Findings

According to the performance measures and statistical benchmarks presented above, it seems that the NYPD ranks well above the national average in its ability to solve rapes, robberies, and burglaries, as well as murders (during certain years). But its daily operations are substandard when it comes to catching car thieves.

The NYPD's response times to critical calls for help lag behind the FDNY's ability to get to the scene of a blaze or a medical emergency, but are better than the average time it takes for ambulances to arrive. Unfortunately, response times to all crimes in progress used to be speedier than they were in 2011 and 2012.

Currently, it is not known whether victimized New Yorkers are more or less willing to report offenses committed against them than are other Americans, and whether they are more or less "satisfied" with how they were handled because NCVS-like surveys are not carried out routinely. It is also unclear whether the department is above average or subpar in its ability to retrieve stolen goods because it does not release the kinds of mathematical breakdowns other police forces do about "percent of value recovered" which appear in the FBI's annual UCR.

Surely, there is plenty of room for improvement in the department's efforts to provide immediate assistance and to furnish other forms of help to get victims back on track in the aftermath of a crime.

4.4 Policy Recommendations: Make the Department More Victim-Oriented

Several policy recommendations flow directly from this review of the available data that can enhance accountability, transparency, and receptivity to reform.

---

[*] One model could be the independent website http://www.stolen911.com.

The first is that the NYPD ought to post an annual report card on its website, disclosing how well it did on these four victim-oriented performance measures: reporting rate, response times, clearance rates, and stolen property recovery rates. These dimensions of standard operating procedures that are so crucial to victims should be monitored by the CompStat system as closely as other indicators such as crime rates and summonses issued.

Another recommendation would be to implement a procedure whereby officers or detectives would "read victims their rights" after filing a complaint, certainly not to dissuade them but rather to inform them about what they need to know. These would include a right to information about developments in their cases (whether an arrest was made, if stolen property was seized as evidence, whether the suspect was jailed or released on bail, the dates of hearings and other court proceedings, opportunities for input such as a victim impact statement, the outcome in terms of a negotiated plea or a verdict after a trial, and the whereabouts of a convict: returned to the community on probation, incarcerated, granted a furlough or work release, out on parole). The reading of rights should also include information about social programs offering assistance (such as the services furnished by Safe Horizons, domestic violence shelters, or rape crisis centers), as well as avenues to pursue for reimbursement (via court-ordered restitution, compensation from the state board, or a lawsuit in civil court). Furthermore, complainants need to be told about their obligations as a witness for the prosecution and the possibility of protection from intimidation and reprisals, and intercession on their behalf by the prosecutor with employers, landlords, and creditors.

A final policy recommendation would be to institutionalize victim advocacy. In every precinct, a civilian could be assigned the task of contacting victims to review their rights and obligations, and to collect data as part of a "consumer satisfaction" survey about whether they were accorded the "courtesy, professionalism, and respect" that the department pledges in its mission statement. Ever since the 1970s, a nationwide victims rights movement has been educating and sensitizing police professionals about the needs, fears, and desires of people who have been harmed by criminals. Advocates at precinct houses could ensure that progress is underway and improvements are being implemented.*

---

* Most victims will never get to exercise their other important rights (to attend bail proceedings and trials, to have input into sentencing, to ask judges to order restitution, to appear before parole boards) because their cases are not reported, will not be solved, won't be prosecuted, or don't lead to convictions on serious counts.

4.5 Suggestions for Further Research: Interview and Survey Victims

It is highly likely that the quality of the service provided by the NYPD to victims varies substantially by the type of crime. It is also possible, even probable, that the NYPD's response is influenced to some degree by the characteristics of the complainants (especially their social class, occupation, race/ethnicity, native language,* gender, age, and prior contacts with the police, including past arrests and convictions). Out-of-towners visiting the city on business or as tourists might be handled differently from residents. Also, certain groups with special problems, such as individuals who have suffered sexual assaults or molestations, or intimate partner violence, or near-death experiences might not be getting the extra-sensitive care that they require. Some precincts might be delivering much better services than others; an in-depth, narrowly focused comparative study could reveal "best practices."

Trying to infer how victims in general are routinely handled by interpreting impersonal statistical performance measures is an important first step. These judgments contribute to an overview, or what might be called the "big picture" which can dispel misimpressions or atypical characterizations derived from anecdotal evidence and journalistic accounts, whether favorable or unfavorable. How the NYPD ranks on various benchmarks provides context or fills in the background, but the information lacks sufficient details to make an informed judgment. Only interviewing some injured parties up-close and personal and then regularly surveying a representative sample of victims can provide definitive answers to the questions: "How well does the NYPD handle victims?" and "How does it rate compared to other big city departments?"

References

AP (Associated Press). (2013, June 13). *Prosecutors push for anti-phone theft measures*. Retrieved June 15, 2013 from http://www.npr.org/templates/story/story.php?storyId=191208244

Baker, A., & Goldstein, J. (2011, December 30). Police tactic: Keeping crime reports off the books. *New York Times*, p. A16.

---

* The NYPD is proud of the diversity within its ranks and the number of officers who are fluent in foreign languages. But a review by the Justice Department's Office for Civil Rights concluded that the department often fails to ensure that New Yorkers who do not speak English have access to certified interpreters when seeking police assistance (Rivera & Zraick, 2010).

Baker, A., & Rashbaum, W. (2011, January 6). New York City to examine reliability of its crime reports. *New York Times*, A16.

Blau, R. (2006, November 10). Call NYPD stats true blue: Skeptics question findings. *The Chief*, p. 3.

Blau, R., & Hamilton, B. (2010, April 25). This job is murder: NYPD solved 59% of 2009 slayings. *New York Post*. Retrieved June 15, 2013 from http://www.nypost.com/p/news/local/this_job_is_murder_Io0fUMUyvKjq8r9zSH1a6L

Butterfield, F. (1998, August 3). As crime falls, pressure rises to alter data. *New York Times*, pp. A1, A16.

Clines, F. (2013, June 15). A song for the exonerated. *New York Times*, p. A16.

Eterno, J., & Silverman, E. (2010). The NYPD's Compstat: Compare statistics or compose statistics? *International Journal of Police Science and Management*, 12(3), 426–449.

Eterno, J., & Silverman, E. (2012). *The Crime Numbers Game: Management by Manipulation*. Boca Raton, FL: CRC Press.

Federal Bureau of Investigation (FBI). (2013). Uniform Crime Report, 2012. Retrieved October 30, 2013 from http://www.fbi.gov/ about-us/cjis/ucr/crime-in-the-u.s/2012/crime-in-the-u.s.-2012/offenses-known-to-law-enforcement/clearances.

Gardiner, S. (2013, February 15). Data will show crime-solving rates: NYPD to resume sending figures on "cleared" felonies to FBI. *Wall Street Journal*, p. B1.

Goldstein, J. (2013, July 3). Audit of crime statistics finds mistakes by police. *New York Times*, A18.

Hart, T., & Rennison, C. (2003). Reporting crime to the police, 1992-2000. BJS Special Report. Washington, DC: U.S. Department of Justice.

Hoffer, J. (2012, March 26). Investigation into under reported crime rates. *WABC Eyewitness News*. Retrieved April 2, 2012 from http://abclocal.go.com/wabc/story?section=news/investigators&id=8596098&pt=print.

Karmen, A. (2006). *New York Murder Mystery: The True Story Behind the Crime Crash of the 1990s*. New York: NYU Press.

Karmen, A. (2013). *Crime Victims: An Introduction to Victimology*. Belmont, CA: Wadsworth/Cengage.

Kemp, J., & Otis, G. (2013, May 20). Slow 911 cost a bid to survive. *New York Daily News*, p. 10.

Langan, P., & Durose, M. (2004). The remarkable drop in crime in New York City. Paper delivered at the International Conference on Crime, Rome, December 3–5.

Matarese, (2012).

Moses, P. (2005, March 29). Corruption: It figures. NY Police Department crime stats and the art of manipulation. *Village Voice*, pp. 4–6.

Rivera, R., & Zraick, K. (2010, November 18). Audit says police fall short in providing interpreters. *New York Times*, p. A14.

Ruderman, W. (2013, April 12). New tool for police officers: Records at their fingertips. *New York Times*, p. A17.

Silverman, E., Eterno, J., & Levine, J. (2012, August 13). Manufacturing low crime rates at the NYPD: Reputation vs. safety under Bloomberg and Kelly. *The Huffington Post*. Retrieved April 5, 2013 from http://www.huffingtonpost.com/eli-b-silverman/low-crime-rates-nypd-eli-b-silverman-john-a-eterno-b_1772489.html.

Smith, D., & Purtell, R. (2006, August). *Managing crime counts: Occasional papers.* New York University School of Law, Center For Research on Crime and Justice. Retrieved June 16, 2013 from http://wagner.nyu.edu/news/crimedata.pdf

Smith, S., Steadman, G., & Minton, T. (1999, May). Criminal victimization and perceptions of community safety in 12 cities, 1998. BJS Report. Washington, DC: U.S. Department of Justice.

Topousis, T. (1997, August 15). Cops take their time responding to fewer crimes. *New York Post*, p. 22.

Wei, C. (2012, February 28). Burglary victim, and satisfied customer of the NYPD. *New York Times*, p. B1.

The New Corruption
Overwhelming Evidence of the NYPD's Crime Report Manipulation

5

JOHN A. ETERNO
ELI B. SILVERMAN

Contents

Policy makers who promote performance incentives and accountability seem mostly oblivious to the extensive literature in economics and management theory, documenting the inevitable corruption of quantitative indicators and the perverse consequences of performance incentives which rely on such indicators.

Rothstein (2008, p. 79)

5.1   Introduction

Over the years prudent investors have learned to be cautious especially when something appears too good to be true. Bernard Madoff ran a Ponzi scheme with billions of dollars of investors' money for many years. He is now serving a 150-year sentence in federal prison. Whistleblowers shouted warnings but the Securities and Exchange Commission (SEC) failed to heed the dire warnings in any significant way. As the Office of the Inspector General's report reads,

> ... despite numerous credible and detailed complaints, the SEC never properly examined or investigated Madoff's trading and never took the necessary, but basic, steps to determine if Madoff was operating a Ponzi scheme. Had these efforts been made with appropriate follow-up at any time beginning in June of 1992 until December 2008, the SEC could have uncovered the Ponzi scheme well before Madoff confessed. (U.S. SEC Office of Investigations, 2009, p. 41)

Certainly there were failures at the SEC. These are now well known because the SEC has an Inspector General (IG) who has true oversight and independence. The IG office, which also has oversight of the Federal Bureau of Investigation, helps to maintain integrity and assure transparency of government operations.

The New York City Police Department (NYPD) is one government organization that has never had an independent IG with basic powers of immunity and subpoena nor is there any direct meaningful outside agency solely responsible for oversight of the department. Even the current IG bill places the IG under the mayor and does not grant it power of immunity. Placing an IG under the mayor is weak, at best. If history is any indicator, then such an IG may be worthless, depending on the mayor. Mayor Bloomberg, for example, effectively rendered a mayoral agency, the Commission to Combat Police Corruption, useless. Mark Pomerantz, a respected former federal prosecutor, headed the agency and questioned the crime statistics. When

Pomerantz requested crime statistics from the department, the commissioner refused and the mayor concurred. The commission was immobilized and Pomerantz resigned. In subsequent years, the budget for the commission was slashed (Eterno & Silverman, 2012). Larger than many armies of the world, the NYPD is the largest police organization in the United States with enormous worldwide influence, yet oversight is weak. Bayley (1994) labels the NYPD a flagship department because its practices are emulated by many police agencies.

Evidence continues to mount that the NYPD is manipulating its crime reports to ensure that reported crime numbers look good. Specifically, the NYPD manipulates the seven major felonies reported to the FBI (changes to the definitions of these crimes by the FBI do occur): murder/nonnegligent manslaughter, forcible rape, burglary, grand larceny, robbery, aggravated assault, and motor vehicle theft (also arson but the NYPD does not count that crime). These index crimes (divided into violent and property crimes) are used to gauge the level of crime in New York City as throughout the United States much as the Dow Jones Industrial is used as a gauge of the stock market. While Bernard Madoff schemed with his investor's money, there is clear evidence that the NYPD is playing with the lives of crime victims (see also Andrew Karmen's chapter). The evidence for cooking the books is so overwhelming that even the inept SEC investigators examining Bernie Madoff might have been able to find this one.

5.2 Spinning the Truth

With great fanfare the NYPD has trumpeted its so-called "success" by repeatedly telling the public it has decreased crime by 80% since 1990 (e.g., NYPD press release, 2007). This has been called the "Guinness Book of World Records" crime drop (Zimring, 2011). Such claims lead the prudent person to question, inquire, and evaluate the accuracy of the boast.

The spin created by the New York City Police Department and those who concur is that crime is down 80% in New York City due entirely to the agency's efforts. They attribute this crime drop to aggressive policing tactics such as stop and frisk and a management system called CompStat (short for compare statistics; e.g., Mac Donald, 2013) Such spin has little merit in the scientific world. There are simply no methodologically sound studies by value-neutral researchers that either fully support or totally contradict the NYPD. The scientific literature on the influence of NYPD strategies is decidedly mixed and generally counters NYPD boasting (e.g., Bowling, 1999; Conklin, 2003; Harcourt, 2001; Karmen, 2000; Messner et al., 2007; Rosenfeld, Fornango, & Rengifo, 2007). The consensus, with which we agree, is that the NYPD has some influence but certainly is not totally responsible for the entire crime decrease.

In this chapter we examine NYPD management practices that place enormous pressures on its officers to reach artificially created target numbers that may, in fact, have little or no bearing on actual crime reduction. We outline the overwhelming evidence that the NYPD is playing with crime reports effectively making the decrease in crime appear larger than it actually is. At the time of publication we are left trusting NYPD management that what they are doing is successful, yet little or nothing scientific suggests that is the case. Again, the bulk of evidence suggests the police have some influence on crime but not to the extent they claim. When spin rather than legitimately grounded facts becomes the organizational compass, it is clear that the direction the agency is taking is not only wrong but dangerous. Are NYPD crime numbers accurate or have they been corrupted?

5.3　Just the Facts, Ma'am

This chapter outlines the strong case that the NYPD manipulates its major crime reports. We review some of our previous work published in several articles (see especially Eterno & Silverman, 2010a) and our book *The Crime Numbers Game* (Eterno & Silverman, 2012). We then add more recent and powerful evidence including a second survey that replicates the results of our first survey with a different sample of officers, a Quality Assurance Division memorandum unearthed by a reporter proving the NYPD not only knew that some of these allegations were true but hid those facts from public scrutiny, additional open-ended and unsolicited comments from officers taking the new survey, and more. We now present the facts.

5.3.1　Union Press Release

One of the most salient revelations appeared on May 23, 2004, when the Patrolmen's Benevolent Association and the Sergeant's Benevolent Association (the NYPD's unions for officers and sergeants, respectively) issued a joint press release reporting widespread downgrading of reports. These are the police themselves stating this, not Eterno and Silverman. The release boldly states

> Our own members tell us that they have been conditioned to write crime complaints to misdemeanors rather than felonies because of the abuse they receive from superior officers worried about their careers. The case of the 10th precinct where a 7% decrease became a 50% increase is a shocking example of what is occurring throughout the city in many station houses. It is a truth that is widely known by members of the department and now we have to see if the

police commissioner has the courage to face the truth and do what is right for the city. (PBA/SBA Press Release, 2004)

A PBA article by then treasurer Robert Zink goes even further and states quite specifically what is occurring. Zink (2004, n.p.) writes, "The department's middle managers will do anything to avoid being dragged onto the carpet at the weekly CompStat meetings. They are, by nature, ambitious people who lust for promotions, and rising crime rates won't help anybody's career."

He goes into great detail explaining how the crime drop was accomplished.

So how do you fake a crime decrease? It's pretty simple. Don't file reports, misclassify crimes from felonies to misdemeanors, under-value the property lost to crime so it's not a felony, and report a series of crimes as a single event. A particularly insidious way to fudge the numbers is to make it difficult or impossible for people to report crimes—in other words, make the victims feel like criminals ....

What could be more revealing? When two police unions state, quite emphatically, that their members are engaged and have reported these unethical activities, any reasonable person would take notice. Indeed, Mark Pomerantz, a former federal prosecutor who headed the mayoral Committee to Combat Police Corruption at the time, perceived the importance of such public statements. He attempted to investigate the department's crime reporting practices but his investigation was immediately thwarted by the NYPD's refusal to grant access. Pomerantz's appeal to the mayor was rebuffed, effectively making the commission powerless. Pomerantz soon resigned from his impotent position.

5.3.2   Substantial Decrease in Officers

While the NYPD is claiming continuous crime declines, they have been profusely bleeding out police officers working the streets. There were approximately 40,800 officers on the streets in 2001. The number has steadily decreased under Mayor Bloomberg to staggering lows of fewer than 35,000. In 1995 the NYPD merged with the former Transit and Housing Police Departments, meaning they have added more duties. Additionally, under Commissioner Kelly thousands of officers have been reassigned to terrorism, intelligence, overseas, and other duties that have little to nothing to do with crime fighting. These shifts and a lack of manpower leave precincts and other crime fighting units depleted. It is simply a major stretch to think that the police can continue to bring down crime without manipulating the crime numbers. When their resources have simply been radically depleted, it seems implausible. In addition, there is a debate as to whether the police have an influence on crime. At this point, it is safe to assume that if the agency is using its resources properly, they can have an effect (Silverman, 2001). Furthermore, scant research does indicate that agency manpower also can have an influence (Sherman & Weisburd, 1995). Although we do not argue that simplistic agency size is highly correlated with crime rate, we do argue that drastically reducing headcount and concurrently claiming a major crime rate reduction due exclusively to the police seems illogical, at best. As suggested by Karmen (2000), a variety of factors more likely influences the crime rate, assuming the police are not covertly (and even overtly) playing with the crime reports.

We also note that police playing with the crime numbers can influence their actual headcount in a negative way. Mayor Bloomberg, for example, has made it known that there is no need to hire more officers because crime continues to record continuous declines (Weiss, 2012, para. 15). Indeed, there is not one year in which there is a dramatic increase in any index crime category since the mayor took office. This seems incredulous inasmuch as he has failed to hire officers in any significant amount other than to replace retirees.

5.4   Our First Study

Without going into great detail, our research on crime manipulation first went public on February 7, 2010, with a Sunday front page article in the *New York Times* (Rashbaum, 2010). We have since published two peer-reviewed articles (Eterno & Silverman, 2010a, 2010b) and a book (Eterno & Silverman, 2012) based on this earlier study. This chapter provides in layperson's terms a number of significant updates and a consolidation of numerous papers and talks on the topic.

Our first scientific study was conducted in 2008. It is a survey of over 400 retirees who worked both in the pre-CompStat (before 1995; 1995 was the first full year of CompStat) and post-CompStat periods (1995 and after) in the ranks of captain and above. We secured the assistance of the Captain's Endowment Association who provided access to their retired members. In return we provided the funding for the project, inserted several of their questions in the instrument, and supplied them with a full report on the project.

Using the pre-CompStat period as a baseline, we are able to compare the answers from both periods. Overall the survey clearly indicated that pressures to downgrade crime reports, decrease index crime, and get promoted based on crime numbers greatly increased in the CompStat era (after 1994). Additionally, the pressures to ensure integrity in the crime reporting system were significantly less in the CompStat period. This lethal combination of pressures—greater pressure to reduce crime and lesser pressures for integrity in crime numbers—led to unethical manipulation of the crime reports.

In fact, over 75% of captains and above who were aware of manipulation indicated that the manipulations were at least moderately unethical. We also note that over 50% of those aware of manipulations felt they were highly unethical. This means that over 100 commanders were aware of unethical crime report manipulations in the CompStat period. This result floored us and for readers, who want more information, we refer them to our book and our articles (see References section).

5.5   Stop-and-Frisk Trends: Two Viewpoints

The police in the United States cannot forcibly stop anyone they please. To legally conduct a forcible stop, officers must have some evidence. The level needed is called reasonable suspicion (see U.S. Supreme Court case *Terry v. Ohio* 1968). This level is less than probable cause, the amount of proof needed to make an arrest, but more than mere suspicion. As a general guideline we can think of probable cause as an officer being about 50% sure the alleged perpetrator did the crime. Mere suspicion is simply a gut feeling that someone did a crime. This means there is little or no evidence to support the hunch. Reasonable suspicion is somewhere around, say, 25% sure the suspect did a criminal act.

The NYPD has placed itself in a completely illogical position. The NYPD claims that crime is down 80%. This should mean there are fewer criminal suspects on the streets of the city. However, just the opposite has occurred. As crime has decreased, the number of criminal suspects on the streets reported by police has drastically increased. Indeed the increase is so dramatic that one cannot help but be awed. In 2011, the high point of NYPD forcible stops of suspects, they recorded nearly 700,000 criminal suspects stopped by police. In 2002 the NYPD made fewer than 100,000 such stops. This translates into a whopping 600% increase in the number of criminal suspects on the streets (see Figure 5.1).

Thus, the incongruence of the two trends is difficult, if not impossible, to reconcile. One way to attempt to reconcile the numbers, without resorting to manipulation, is to suggest that police need to conduct huge numbers of stops (perhaps violating the law; see *Floyd v. City of New York*) to bring crime down. The major problem with this argument is that crime was markedly trending down when the NYPD was conducting fewer than 100,000 stops in 2002. In fact, crime was already down 60% (in 2002) from 1990 and still trending down without the drastic increases in forcible stops.

A second, more recent, explanation by the NYPD is that they have more efficient recordkeeping. This explanation fails for at least two reasons. First, there is no way that recordkeeping explains an increase of 500,000 stops in a few short years. It is far too drastic a rise. Second, and more important, NYPD

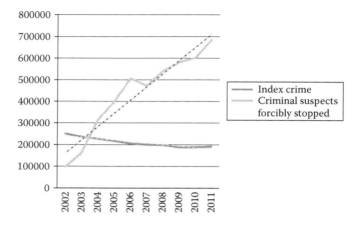

Figure 5.1 Index crime versus criminal suspects in New York City, 2002–2011.

officers have been recording all reasonable suspicion stops since January 1, 2001 (see Eterno, 2003). Every officer was trained on this by the Legal Bureau and the Office of Management, Analysis and Planning. This means it is highly unlikely that better recordkeeping was responsible for increases from 2002 to 2011, inasmuch as maximum efforts and improvements had already been enacted a year before Commissioner Kelly even came into office.

We are left with little or no plausible explanation other than report manipulation. That is, as crime trends down, there should be fewer criminal suspects on the streets. The trends should be similar but because they are totally dissimilar, this strongly suggests crime report manipulation and perhaps even illegal stops on the part of the police.

A second way in which to view stop-and-frisk trends with respect to crime report manipulation is to focus on the pressures officers face. We conducted two surveys (discussed in more detail later in the chapter) that measure the pressures on officers in the 1980s and early 1990s before CompStat began, during the early CompStat era, and during the Kelly/Bloomberg era. Focusing on these pressures with respect to stop and frisk we found that only 9.1% of officers surveyed felt high pressure to write stop-and-frisk reports in the pre-CompStat era. Moving forward to the early CompStat era—1995 to 2001—there was an increase in pressure but not extreme. That is, 19.1% of officers who retired in this period felt high pressure to write stop-and-frisk reports. It is important to note that in the most recent period, 2002 to 2012, 35.1% of officers felt high pressures to write stop-and-frisk reports. So comparing these pressures to the number of stop-and-frisk reports we find that, as the pressures increased more and more reports were written with a high point in 2011 of nearly 700,000 stop-and-frisk reports.

The stop-and-frisk pressures can be seen as an indicator of how pressure manifested itself among the officers serving on the NYPD, that is, the more pressure, the more reports. Next, we examine the pressures to downgrade crime reports.

In the pre-CompStat period only 15.8% of officers felt high pressure to downgrade reports. More recently, in the Kelly/Bloomberg era the numbers more than doubled to 37.9% feeling high pressure to downgrade. We clearly see a similar trend in pressures to downgrade crime reports that we see in stop-and-frisk reports. That is, pressures increase dramatically. What this means then is that the marked increase in pressure to downgrade likely led to numerous downgraded crime reports, just as the increase in pressure led to numerous stop-and-frisk reports. We further elaborate on this issue when we specifically discuss our second survey. Regardless of the interpretation one takes, they all point to crime report manipulation drastically increasing after 2002.

5.6 Misdemeanor Crime Trend

The seven major felonies (not including arson) that make up the violent and property crimes are often called index crimes and are generally used to gauge crime trends in an area. This is based on crime reports, which are crimes known and recorded by police departments and then reported to the FBI. The seven major violent and property crimes are supposed to be a quick gauge of how all crimes in a jurisdiction are trending. Consequently, if crime numbers are accurately recorded, then one should logically expect misdemeanor crime to trend in the same direction as the seven major index crimes. That is, if crime is actually decreasing in a jurisdiction, misdemeanor crimes as well as the violent and property crimes should be markedly decreasing.

Raymond Kelly re-entered the commissioner's office in 2002. Examining index crime we note a huge decrease since 2002. Index crime has essentially been down since 2002 falling from 154,809 index crimes to 111,147 index crimes in 2012. This translates into a 28% decrease. Assuming the books are not being cooked, we expect similar trends in misdemeanor crimes.

However, there is no discernible trend in misdemeanor crime from 2002 to 2012 (see Figure 5.2). Indeed, misdemeanor crime is essentially flat during the entire time period going from 379,026 to 374,364 crimes, a small 1.2% decrease. Inspecting the trend line, however, we see that overall throughout the period misdemeanor crime actually trends up. There is some slight fluctuation as might be expected if crime is remaining about the same over the period. The trends in misdemeanor crime and index crimes are, therefore, anything but similar.

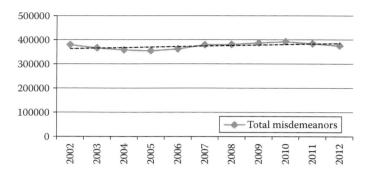

Figure 5.2 Misdemeanor crime in New York City, 2002–2012.

5.7   Criminal Trespass

Even more of a concern is criminal trespass trending up. Criminal trespass is knowingly used to hide downgraded index crimes. Criminal trespass trends much higher (see Figure 5.3). The graph clearly shows marked increases in criminal trespass with some decreases—but not nearly reaching 2002 levels—in more recent years. We note that our research went public at nearly the same time that the trend line for criminal trespass began to go down. Our research was widely reported in the New York area including a front page *New York Times* article on February 6, 2010 (Rashbaum, 2010). The percentage increase from 2002 to 2012 is 37%. If we calculate to the high point, the increase in criminal trespass until 2009 is a whopping 83%.

Criminal trespass can be used to downgrade numerous crimes. Perhaps the most obvious is burglary because burglary is simply a criminal trespass combined with another crime committed while doing the trespass. Of course, if criminal trespass (a nonindex crime) is up so markedly, we expect

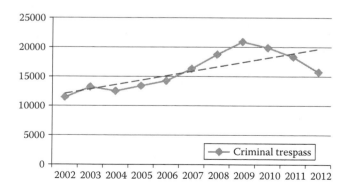

Figure 5.3 Criminal trespass in New York City, 2002–2012.

similar upward trends in burglary, if the books are not cooked. In 2002 there were 31,275 recorded burglaries and in 2012 there were 19,168. This is a huge 39% decrease. Comparing the 39% decrease to the 37% increase in criminal trespass, the trends are in the exact opposite direction.

These are not our numbers but the crime numbers reported by the NYPD. Such trends are highly suspicious. Regardless of the explanations the NYPD may suggest, this is clearly a major concern for any competent investigator. The experiences of whistleblower Detective Harold Hernandez heighten the concerns regarding criminal trespass.

5.7.1 Detective Harold Hernandez

It is clear that criminal trespass is trending in the exact opposite direction from crime in the city. Is this coincidence or is it possible that something more disturbing is at work? *Village Voice* reporter, Graham Rayman, exposed what is obviously the downgrading of sex crimes. Retired first-grade detective (the highest rank of detective the NYPD has; only the most elite receive it) Harold Hernandez came forward to report on a case he was working on in the 33rd Precinct. The case involved a serial rapist. It was solved after someone spotted the perpetrator pushing a victim into an apartment. Police came and made an arrest. During interrogation of the perpetrator, Detective Hernandez became aware of six other forcible rapes committed by the suspect. As any good detective should, he searched the complaint file for the other rapes hoping to close out all of them. What he found was staggering: all the other rapes that the perpetrator admitted to had been recorded as lesser crimes, most being criminal trespass. These were sexual assaults clearly downgraded to criminal trespass.

As any good officer would do, Detective Hernandez reported that the patrol supervisors were apparently downgrading. In Hernandez's own words, "They look to eliminate certain elements in the narrative. One word or two words can make the change to a misdemeanor" (Rayman, 2010).

This is a tragedy. Had these reports been taken properly, a pattern could have been developed and a rapist stopped before he struck seven times. Furthermore, with each sexual assault the perpetrator become more violent. Recently, the perpetrator was convicted and is now serving a 50-year sentence (Rayman, 2010).

There are several issues here confirming our research. First, the downgrading is apparent. Second, regardless of the level of oversight from headquarters, the paperwork is sufficiently doctored to prevent other units from properly classifying the report. For example, the Data Integrity Unit will read the report at headquarters as will the Quality Assurance Division, but the report is not properly classified because the wording has been changed. It is unlikely that a department accounting or audit will capture this; it requires more intrusive methods of detection. Third, and most important, how many others are out there? How many more victims must suffer? Fourth, why is this case exposed by a reporter and not the NYPD? Detective Hernandez informed appropriate authority in the police department. He expected what every good officer would. At a minimum a full investigation with the parties responsible being disciplined should have taken place. What happened here? Nothing apparently happened in response to Detective Hernandez's allegations. No public report has ever been issued. The NYPD fears of embarrassment and damage to its public image trumped what needed to be done, countering a culture of downgrading that had developed over time. Just as with Bernie Madoff, all the warning signs are there. Did anyone else blow the whistle?

5.8 Brave Whistleblowers

To blow the whistle on such sinister activities is not easy. The blue wall of silence is a powerful deterrent. Even with that wall, some officers have bravely come forward. What makes their coming forward critically important is that some of them have audiotapes clearly supporting their allegations. Some of these officers, like Detective Hernandez, tried to go through proper channels. Unfortunately, rather than these officers being rewarded for bravely coming forward, nearly all of them were disciplined for their efforts: some suspended, some transferred, and some had their identities exposed. A short list of some sworn NYPD officers who have come forward specifically about crime report manipulation includes Robert Borelli, Frank Polestro, Adhyl Polanco, and Adrian Schoolcraft.

5.8.1 Robert Borelli

Sergeant Robert Borelli worked in the 100th Precinct in Queens for nearly 10 years when he blew the whistle. Sergeant Borelli initially went through the proper NYPD channels to report the downgrading of crime reports. He gave to investigators dozens of reports such as shootings changed from assault 1 (an index crime) to reckless endangerment and burglaries changed to criminal mischief after officers on the scene coached the victim. He reported that officers were leaving out specific details of crimes such that the reported crime would be downgraded. He has some audiotapes of a victim and Quality Assurance confirming at least some of his allegations. This was aired by investigative reporter Jim Hoffer on *ABC News* in New York City. Hoffer (2012) reports,

[L]ast May, Borrelli started handing over dozens of crime reports to the NYPD's Quality Assurance Division, whose job it is to ensure the accuracy of crime stats. The reports, he claims, amounted to smoking gun—evidence of intentional, routine downgrading of crimes. "They're constantly changing the classification to downgrade crimes so they're not tracked," he said. "It goes under the radar according to the FBI crime stats."

Sergeant Borrelli for his troubles was transferred to a midnight shift at a Bronx courthouse. This is the NYPD equivalent of being sent to Siberia. They also hit him with disciplinary charges for arguing with an officer.

5.8.2   Frank Polestro

Officer Polestro was the union delegate in the 42nd Precinct in the Bronx. He went to the Internal Affairs Bureau (IAB) without any fanfare to report a lieutenant who was fudging the crime numbers among other allegations. For his troubles he was somehow discovered as having gone to IAB and a mousetrap with his name on it was found inside the stationhouse (a rat is one who exposes something going on in a precinct, breaking the code of silence; see Parascandola & Marzulli, 2010). The department transferred him for "his protection." How officers found out about his allegations to IAB is not known but clearly something went wrong with the internal system aimed at rooting out corruption.

5.8.3   Adhyl Polanco

Officer Polanco is a whistleblower from yet another precinct, the 41st Precinct in the Bronx. Officer Polanco, like Sergeant Borrelli, has audiotapes to support him. In a report aired by *ABC News*, investigative reporter Jim Hoffer (2010) stated, "Officer Polanco says One Police Plaza's obsession with keeping crime stats down has gotten out of control. He advises that Precinct Commanders relentlessly pressure cops on the street to make more arrests, and give out more summonses, all to show headquarters they have a tight grip on their neighborhoods."

The department has retaliated in the guise of longstanding charges stemming from writing false summonses, which he contends supervisors ordered him to write. These supervisory pressures to write summonses, make stop and frisks, and make arrests are likely emanating from the same top-down management style responsible for report manipulation. For the record, at least three other officers who have not specifically alleged crime report manipulation have blown the whistle on quota pressures: Vanessa Hicks, Craig Matthews, and Pedro Serrano.

5.8.4   Adrian Schoolcraft

The granddaddy of them all is Officer Adrian Schoolcraft. His audiotapes of Brooklyn's 81st Precinct is, at first, simply unbelievable. When we first heard them we realized they were authentic and accurate. They floored both of us confirming every aspect of this research. The tapes are very powerful evidence that crime report manipulation is simply routine. The supervisors on the tapes think their behaviors are normal. They are anything but.

The Schoolcraft tapes clearly contain verbiage from supervisors telling patrol officers how to handle complaints in order to minimize the number of reports. One of the most egregious discussions involves not taking complaint reports (i.e., 61s) if victims of robberies do not return to the station house to talk to the detective squad. This is heard at several roll calls. At the roll call of October 12, 2009, for example, the supervisor is heard stating, "You know we been popping up with those robberies, whatever. The best thing I can say … if the complainant does not want to go back to the squad [detectives], then there is no 61 [complaint report] taken. That's it." (Schoolcraft, 2009). At this roll call the supervisor is clearly telling the officers not to take reports for robberies unless the victims go back to the station house to talk to the precinct detectives. The concern is that the victim may be making a false complaint. Regardless, the officer should still take the report and seasoned investigators should make that determination later. A preliminary investigation should be done but a report should always be taken. Requiring a complainant to go to the station house not only discourages the complainant from making a report, but is clearly contrary to proper police procedure. Officers are supposed to take the reports at the scene. A complainant should never be sent elsewhere. The police department has ignored police science, victim care, and criminology.

Failure to take the report has serious consequences including preventing detectives from doing their jobs properly. For example, detectives will lack information necessary to establish a possible pattern (as was seen previously in statements made by Detective Harold Hernandez). Many people may be robbed yet may not be willing to visit the station house. In these cases, no report will be taken resulting in the police being left in the dark about numerous robberies.

Another audiotape reveals similar practices. The roll call of October 4, 2009, is particularly revealing. At this roll call officers are instructed to question victims, that callbacks are being made by supervisors, and that officers should not take reports if they think the district attorney will not prosecute.

> *Supervisor:* … If you got a robbery and the squad's working, which they're usually working the day tour, the squad should be notified and they should do the complaint report. If you any problems with that, talk to a [boss] …

Supervisor 2: Yeah, we had a robbery. Guy sounded totally believable. He said he got yoked up at Myrtle and Lewis. And he was yoked up from behind by a couple of guys who took his wallet and some money, and went to the squad for a debrief, and they were questioning him, where was this, where was that, and he finally admitted he was full of shit. I didn't get the rest of the story. ... It's a common tale. ... Commercial guys xxxxxx stole it himself, sold it or whatever the case is and he's trying to cover his tracks. Don't be afraid to question a robbery suspect. If it's a little old lady and I got my bag stolen, then she's probably telling the truth, all right. If it's some young guy who looks strong and healthy and can maybe defend himself and he got yoked up, and he's not injured, he's perfectly fine, question that. *It's not about squashing numbers* [italics added]. You all know if it is what it is, if it smells like a rotten fish, then that's what it is. But question it. On the burglaries as well.

Other supervisor: On that note too, because, uh, whether it's CO, [or other lieutenants (their names were removed)], *they always do callbacks* [italics added]. So, a lot of time we get early information and they do callbacks.

Sgt: And then we look silly. .... A domestic violence victim, woman, says, "Hey, my boyfriend stole my phone." He didn't really steal the phone. It's his phone, and he was taking it. Did he snatch it out of her hand? Yeah. Is it a grand larceny? No, because I'm telling you right now *the DA [District Attorney] is not going to entertain that* [italics added].

Other supervisor: Exactly. (Schoolcraft, 2009)

There are so many questionable practices that it is difficult to enumerate them. First, why do the supervisors instruct police officers to question the veracity of robbery victims? It is not because they are interested in fighting crime but because robbery is an index crime that will be reflected at CompStat meetings and subsequently in FBI statistics. It will make the commander and the NYPD look bad. Second, when we hear "it's not about squashing numbers," unfortunately, it comes across as exactly that, squashing numbers. These supervisors are, with great ease as if this were normal (and we think it now has morphed into common practice), telling officers to do activities in which officers should not be engaged.

Third, callbacks to victims by the CO and lieutenants are among the most disturbing issues here. Victims are not being called back in an attempt to find a suspect. These are not detectives contacting victims, but relatively high-ranking personnel at the precinct level. Why? Clearly they are doing everything possible, everything, to lower the index crime numbers.

Fourth, a supervisor states it's not a grand larceny because the "DA is not going to entertain that." This is highly questionable behavior. Precinct personnel are not in a position to decide what the district attorney will "entertain." District attorneys often lower charges made by police for many reasons. Police should not be taking initial reports based on what they think the district attorney will do. Again, why is this done? It should be clear at this point, to lower index crime numbers due to CompStat pressures.

The audiotapes reveal how headquarters' bean counting has been interpreted by lower-level precinct supervisors and even precinct commanders. CompStat's extreme pressure is translated into not taking reports, questioning the veracity of victims, downgrading reports, haranguing officers about callbacks by supervisors, attempting to figure out what a district attorney will do, and in general, keeping the numbers of index crimes down in any way possible, regardless of consequences.

There are numerous other tapes and many other disturbing aspects to Officer Schoolcraft's situation. Officer Schoolcraft like the other whistleblowers was disciplined. His situation, however, is something we did not believe when first told. The entire episode is on audiotape.

Officer Schoolcraft, like his fellow whistleblowers, was trying to go through normal channels by talking to the units responsible for quality assurance. After a supervisor at the precinct closely inspected his activity log (a written record of all he does and where Officer Schoolcraft wrote notes about many unethical practices he was reporting) Officer Schoolcraft felt that someone had compromised his identity. Among other suspicious actions occurring at the precinct, Officer Schoolcraft was in fear for his safety. He then advised a supervisor he was going sick and went home. NYPD supervisors then tracked Officer Schoolcraft to his apartment. After gaining admission into the apartment by someone with a key, they observed Officer Schoolcraft relaxing. Numerous officers remained in the apartment and the entire exchange between Officer Schoolcraft and the highest uniformed member at the scene, Chief Marino, was captured on audiotape. Chief Marino eventually orders Officer Schoolcraft to be forcibly taken out of his home to a mental hospital where he is detained for six days. A tape recorder hidden on Officer Schoolcraft was found when he was subdued and then mysteriously disappeared. Officer Schoolcraft had another recorder taping the incident so that we were still able to listen to the entire episode. Once at the hospital, police were required to notify his next of kin immediately. However, also mysteriously, they were not immediately notified of his hospital admission. To hear some of the tape recordings of this event, we refer readers to the radio program *This American Life* (see Glass, 2010).

As if this were not bizarre enough, the Quality Assurance Division (QUAD) wrote a report on Schoolcraft's allegations of crime downgrading in the 81st Precinct. This report remained hidden from the public until reporter Graham Rayman discovered it in 2012. It was dated June 2010; the exact time the police department was attempting to sugarcoat and even suppress our first study. This QUAD report confirms nearly all of Schoolcraft's allegations and our findings (see Rayman, 2012).

As a final note, we have talked to many officers. Most are in fear of coming forward with any allegations. They are afraid of being "Schoolcrafted." His name is now used to mean retaliation by NYPD brass for whistleblowing.

5.9   Sex Crime Victims and Sex Crime Victim's Groups Come Forward

There are numerous victims who have come forward. In this chapter, however, we focus on the most egregious: sex crimes victims. First, we discuss the case of attempted rape victim Debbie Nathan. She represents the type of horror that victims can experience due to police behavior. Her account has now been publicized in the *Village Voice* and the *New York Times* among other outlets. She contacted us after our research went public early in 2010. This is her story in her own words,

> I am a freelance journalist, formerly an editor at *City Limits* magazine, who was sexually assaulted in February of this year [2010] in Inwood Hill Park. I was overpowered by a man and pushed/dragged into a wooded area. The man told me he wanted to have sex with me. Continuing to push me, he masturbated against me until he made a noise as though he was having an orgasm. Only then did he let me go, and he ran off into the woods.
>
> As soon as I was free I called the police. It took them two hours to respond. When they did, six officers came to my home. They spent almost two hours talking with me about what had happened. Toward the end of that period some of them stepped out into the hall of my apartment building and called SVU, the Special Victims Unit, the NYPD police unit that specializes in identifying and investigating sex crimes. After relaying questions from SVU to me, and my answers to SVU, the officers told me that—at the behest of SVU—they were classifying the crime as misdemeanor "forcible touching." As far as I was concerned, it was clear that what had happened to me was a felony attempted rape. I argued with the officers but they insisted on maintaining their classification.
>
> Next morning I complained about what had happened to me on an online, community public safety site. The people running that site notified my state assemblyman and by early afternoon the misdemeanor classification had been upgraded to felony attempted rape. A community meeting was called to discuss what had happened to me, and at that meeting, I told the precinct commander for my neighborhood that I wanted to see my incident report. When I got the report several days later, I discovered that all the details I had given the officers about the perpetrator—the color of his clothing, what he'd said to me, how he touched me physically, and how he pushed me into the woods—were missing. Further, the report falsely stated that no sexual contact had occurred.

A few days after the assault against me, I contacted Harriet Lessel of NYC Against Rape. She told me that her organization had become aware during the past year and a half of systemic misclassification and downgrading, in all the boroughs of New York City. Subsequently I got a call from Lisa Friel, head of the sexual assault unit at the Manhattan DA's office. Before she learned from our conversation that I was a journalist, she, too, told me that the NYPD was deliberately or at least systematically downgrading sexual assault reports. She said she had repeatedly complained about this to higher-ups in the NYPD. She later told me that she called all six officers who were in my house into her office and questioned them about why they misreported my report. They all simply shrugged, she said. I certainly can't prove this. But oddly, while I was embroiled in the controversy and it became a public issue among anti-rape activists, I got calls from people who volunteer as counselors at hospitals which provide rape crisis services to sexual assault victims. I was told that SVU agents are some of the worst minimizers at the hospitals, when they come to take reports.

... I am feeling increasingly troubled that the NYPD might be pulling a fast one on the press.... (personal communication from Debbie Nathan, dated 12/26/2010)

Her words are disheartening, discouraging, and debilitating. One can only imagine the horror that Ms. Nathan went through. Moreover, she was clearly victimized again by those charged to help her. Forcible touching is the lowest criminal charge, a misdemeanor. Had she not been a journalist who is politically savvy, her report would be buried with, we fear, countless others. At a minimum, this case appears to be an attempted rape first degree and possibly sexual abuse first degree, both felonies. Why forcible touching and not attempted rape? Attempted rape is an index offense counted in CompStat figures. Although we do not know for sure, a plausible explanation for this is downgrading due to fear of CompStat. Are there others?

Making Ms. Nathan's story even more disturbing is the public outcry from victims' groups and rape counselors. Ms. Nathan's story was occurring throughout the city. These groups came forward in April 2010 just after we released our study in February. They argued that reports of sex crimes were not being taken. After these groups confronted Mr. Kelly, he quietly formed the "Sex Crimes Working Group" to examine the NYPD's reporting of sex crimes. This lends enormous credibility to Ms. Nathan's communication. Furthermore, it strongly corroborates our position of downgrading.

Ultimately, some minor changes were made as a result of the Working Group. Gardiner (2010) reports that one of the most important is that "... all sexual-assault complaints be assigned to Special Victims Division (SVD) detectives who are specially trained in sex-crime investigations. Currently, sexual-assault complaints are handled by patrol officers." Although this may seem appropriate, it is merely window dressing, a superficial change.

Any changes must address top-down management pressures reflected in CompStat meetings. Rape and other index crimes are downgraded due to this pressure. In addition, as Ms. Nathan advises, SVD detectives may not be appropriate for determining the classification, as they apparently misclassified her case, and may be equally likely to downgrade. Most important, Ms. Nathan was politically savvy. What about those from disenfranchised populations such as Blacks, Hispanics, lesbian, gay, and transgender populations? How about prostitutes who are raped? Such victims may be left powerless by a bureaucracy focused on numbers and not caring for victims. How many more victims will go unheard?

5.10   Hospital Data

As if this were not enough, there are even more indicators of manipulation. The New York City Department of Health and Mental Hygiene maintain detailed statistics on patients who come to the hospital. Their data are publicly available (although they have not been updated; what we cite are the most recent publicly available data) and, although not directly comparable to NYPD data, they do provide insight into important city trends. If NYPD numbers are accurate, they should show trends similar to the hospital data.

The trends are anything but similar. This strongly suggests manipulation of crime statistics by the NYPD. This is seen throughout the data. We examine four separate indicators in data collected by hospitals. None is consistent with NYPD records.

The hospital data for emergency department visits for assaults are completely at variance with NYPD figures. NYPD data show a huge decrease approaching 50%; however, hospital records show an enormous increase. Figure 5.4 indicates a steady rise in emergency room visits for assault for

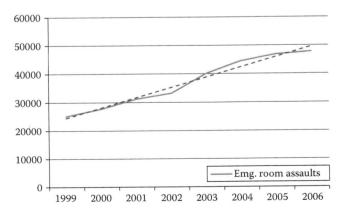

Figure 5.4 Emergency department visits: assaults.

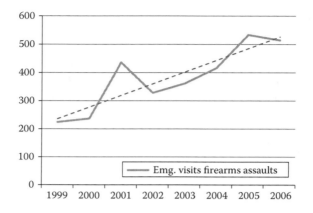

Figure 5.5 Emergency department visits: firearms assaults.

every year that statistics are available. In 1999 there were 25,181 visits for assault and in 2006 there are 47,779 visits. This represents a whopping 90% increase in emergency room visits for assaults. These numbers are not even close! This is a very strong indicator of manipulation by the NYPD, possibly even turning victims away.

Second, emergency room visits for firearms assaults have also skyrocketed. Figure 5.5 shows a fairly steady increase in emergency room visits for firearms assaults. In 1999 there were 224 visits and in 2006 there were 514 visits. This represents a huge 129% increase in visits. This is yet another indicator completely in the opposite direction of the NYPD's crime report data. We note that by law these firearms assaults must be reported to the police by hospital authorities (see New York State Penal Law Section 265.25). We have no indication that medical personnel are commonly not following the law. So, where are the police reports?

Two other hospital indicators are also available supporting the position of NYPD manipulation. Intentional injury hospitalization statistics also show an increasing trend. From 1999 until 2006 there is a 15% increase of hospitalizations for assault. Although less pronounced, the trend is again nothing close to the NYPD data. Yet another indicator, firearms assault hospitalizations, was basically unchanged from 1999 to 2006. What does all this mean? Absolutely none of the hospital data demonstrated the marked decrease in assaults that the NYPD claims. These data are in stark contrast to the NYPD's and clearly are evidence of manipulation.

5.11   Drug Use in New York City Compared to NYPD Complaints

Illicit drug use in New York City is higher compared to the rest of the nation. The New York City Department of Health and Mental Hygiene (NYCHMH,

2010, p. 1) report is unequivocal: "Nearly one million New Yorkers report using illicit drugs in the past year (16%). The national rate is 14%." Additionally, they write, "Excluding marijuana, New Yorkers are more likely to use illicit drugs than Americans overall (9.1% vs. 8.5%)" (NYCHMH, 2010). This is not only completely at odds with NYPD data but it is an indication that the New York spin being the "safest large city in America" is mistaken.

Furthermore, illicit drug use appears to be rising. "From 1999 to 2006, the proportion of hospitalizations that were drug-related increased by 14%" (NYCHMH, 2010, p. 2); NYPD data, however, show enormous declines in illegal drug use in the city. The NYPD recorded 38,088 felony dangerous drug complaints in 2000 (the last year available on the NYPD website). In 2006, they recorded 29,516 (we use 2006 merely to compare with other data. The 2009 percentage decreases are in the last paragraph of this section). This represents a 22.5% decrease. Misdemeanor dangerous drugs show a similar trend. In 2000 there were 96,590 misdemeanor complaints for dangerous drugs and in 2006 there were only 65,945 complaints. This represents a 31.7% decrease. This downward trend, however, is completely at odds with the New York City Department of Health and Mental Hygiene report.

Based on NYPD statistics, the trend down for illicit drug complaints continues through 2009 with nearly a 40% decrease in complaints for felony dangerous drugs compared to 2000. The trend for misdemeanors is also down from 2000 with a 17.3% decrease. The incompatible trends are likely due to the mimicking of CompStat-like management throughout the department. Narco-Stat or other pressures emanating from headquarters are the likely cause of the lack of congruity between HMRH data and NYPD complaint reports.

5.12 NYPD'S Known Problems With Manipulation

The NYPD is aware of crime report manipulation within its ranks. The QUAD report substantiating nearly all of whistleblower Officer Adrian Schoolcraft's allegations, which was kept hidden from public scrutiny, is one example (see Rayman, 2012). Beyond this the NYPD has admitted and disciplined staff for manipulation. That is, they admit to identifying a few "rotten apples" who have played with the numbers. At least four commanders (with another one pending) and seven others (with three more pending) have been accused and convicted of manipulation of crime statistics. This, in itself, is very disturbing. The NYPD claims these acts are few and tries to scapegoat an exceedingly small number of commanders identified by the department's weak and self-regulated internal system of integrity. The evidence, however, indicates that cooking the books is now the cultural norm at the NYPD. It appears to have become an informal mechanism of dealing with the inordinate pressures from headquarters' bean counters who want to show, at any cost, the crime numbers declining. Thus, the de facto way of handling complaints from victims is to downgrade them or discourage victims from making a report when NYPD staff members think they can get away with it.

Even the NYPD's Data Integrity Unit (DIU), which reviews only the computerized reports that were actually taken, admits that it tends to raise the crimes charged to a higher level on audited complaint reports rather lowering them. This is when they manage to find errors on reports that have already passed precinct muster. That is, in correcting complaint reports that have already been thoroughly inspected at the precinct, the DIU more frequently upgrades the classifications on the crime reports. A 2005 Quality Assurance Division memorandum advises that complaint reports from 1999 until the time of the memorandum were corrected upward for 2% of the corrections and down for only 0.4% (Smith & Purtell, 2006, p. 18). In fact, if there is no cooking of the books, the numbers being corrected up and down should be about equal. That is, if honest, random mistakes are being made in interpretation of the law or incidents, the distribution of errors being upgraded and downgraded should be about equal.

The NYPD claims that the upgrading concern is due to "strict interpretation bias" (Kelley & McCarthy, 2013, p. 13). Strict interpretation as defined by NYPD headquarters means that complaints should be classified by the highest charge leading to classifications that are too high. The department claims strict interpretation bias leads to higher charges, when, in fact, it could go either way. Kelley and McCarthy explain the NYPD position:

> This means that crime reporting generally reflects the *most serious view of crime, as opposed to a more nuanced and a potentially more realistic view* [italics added]. In addition, the strict-interpretation bias also affects error rates. Because of this bias, the theory is that, as more individuals review an incident recorded on a complaint report, there is an increased probability that a reviewer may believe that a complaint report should be upgraded.

The NYPD interpretation is fatally flawed. Crime reporting should reflect the facts not "the most serious view of crime, as opposed to a more nuanced and a potentially more realistic view." The facts dictate the charge. Honest mistakes can be made classifying the highest charge, either too high or too low. Strict interpretation of facts means that DIU should be finding a 50/50 ratio of errors, some classifying too high and some classifying too low. For example, let's say they are auditing grand larceny complaints. Assuming there are only honest classification errors, about 50% of the errors should be upgrading to, for example, robbery and the other 50% should call for downgrading to, say, petit larceny. Strict interpretation should never, assuming honest error, lead to a higher level of upgrading by DIU.

Even if we assume the NYPD argument is correct, it fails miserably when faced with basic logic. To that end, we dispute their fatally flawed logic. Our rationale is simple; because precinct staff and supervision (with countless levels of review and checks including crime analysis officers, supervisors, self-audits, the integrity control officer, the executive officer, even the CO in most commands, and much more) have already carefully scrutinized the reports, strict interpretation bias would mean that by the time the reports reach DIU, the reports must necessarily now be overclassified into "higher categories." If their argument were in any way accurate, DIU should actually be downgrading more than upgrading! Their explanation is clearly discreditable and illogical. Strict interpretation bias is no excuse or even a decent explanation for DIU doing more upgrading compared to downgrading of the reports.

Furthermore, DIU is making fewer changes than in the past (Mac Donald, 2010). This is a strong indication that, as suggested by Detective Hernandez, a few words are being changed to have the report pass muster both in the field and at DIU so it is not considered an index crime (Rayman, 2010).

5.12.1 NYPD, Lack of Transparency

The NYPD has not allowed scrutiny of its data. Why? If everything is so clean, there should be no problem allowing outside scrutiny. American corporations are held to far greater standards compared to our police. The disproportionate number of Freedom of Information law (FOIL) requests denied by the NYPD, the lawsuits needed to unearth easily obtainable data, and the mysterious disappearance of lost property numbers are some examples.

A recent report by Public Advocate Bill de Blasio found that the NYPD is one of the worst city agencies when it comes to responding to Freedom of Information law requests. Two agencies received failing grades, one being the NYPD. The Public Advocate's comments on the NYPD's response time to FOIL requests: "28% of answered requests took more than 60 days to process" (NYC Public Advocate, 2013, p. 13). Furthermore, a whopping "31% of requests received no response." This comports well with others we know who have placed requests with the NYPD (p. 13).

The debacle with lost property is a good example. Lost property figures were recently released after many years of stalling despite numerous FOIL requests. We now know why they had a problem. They were released with great fanfare as a NYPD-friendly newspaper was given a scoop (see Gardiner, 2011, January 11). Interestingly, we also note that as of this writing the NYPD has once again mysteriously removed them from their website. There was no publicity over this: just there one day and gone the next. On again, off again. This is typical of the NYPD crisis de jour mentality. In the case of lost property statistics, there were major concerns. Once released, we find it highly disturbing that the lost property numbers go directly down every single year since Paul Moses penned a critical report showing the numbers drastically increasing as burglary and other crimes were going down (see Moses, 2005). One must be suspicious of such a linear decrease year after year. Why? Did people suddenly stop losing property? Did the NYPD do a lost property initiative? Why do the numbers go down without any normal statistical fluctuations? Perhaps, the NYPD focused enormous time and effort into making sure the lost property numbers went in a direction favorable to them after the embarrassment exposed in Moses' story. One can only ponder. However, when numbers decrease like this for no apparent reason, it is very strong evidence, yet again, of manipulation.

What the NYPD calls "historical data" (i.e., basic crime data including misdemeanors) was not released until the *New York Times* sued the NYPD for the data (Barron, 2010). These data are collected with taxpayer money. There is nothing secretive about them. In fact, every other jurisdiction in New York State except Newburgh was reporting them regularly. The NYPD ceased reporting about the time Commissioner Kelly re-entered office and only resumed in 2010 after being sued.

5.12.2 Defensive NYPD Obsessed With Public Image Rather Than Public Service

We have many concerns that the NYPD is simply protecting its public image rather than serving the public, for example, claims of stopping numerous terrorists through NYPD efforts (e.g., Levitt, 2013); denials of Commissioner Kelly appearing in an anti-Muslim biased video, even denying the existence of the video (e.g., Democracy Now!, 2012); denial of spying on Muslims (e.g., Levitt, 2013); and the exposure of the QUAD memorandum on Officer Schoolcraft years after it was completed (see Rayman, 2012). Recently, the Central Intelligence Agency's Inspector General's Report revealed that four CIA agents were assigned to the NYPD. The NYPD's track record in this area would make any rational person skeptical.

The NYPD is also exceedingly defensive when it comes to crime reporting. They constantly deny any downgrading (even though their own QUAD report indicates it was taking place in the 81st Precinct). Despite the mountains of other evidence we report, the department fails to allow serious outside scrutiny. The department points to reports by a handful of academics who did not conduct actual audits, scientifically examine responses to surveys of officers in the field, and address the overwhelming amount of evidence, much of it contained in this work. Zimring (2011), for example, argues: "The best way to verify trends is with independent data" (p. 10). We have no disagreement with crime trends in New York City. We have consistently stated that we believe crime is down. It is the extent of the decrease that is open to serious question. Zimring simply does not address the evidence. Similarly, a study by Smith and Purtell, frequently cited by the NYPD, is equally weak. They admit in a hidden footnote in their unpublished paper,

> Our conclusions are based on conversations with senior command staff and a review of written materials. We neither observed the actual sampling or auditing processes nor did we test the accuracy of the sampling procedures used by the Department in its audits. We can only infer how the written procedures were implemented in practice …. (Smith & Purtell, 2006, p. 5)

A third group was set up by the defensive NYPD after our research went public and the department was faced with enormous and building criticism. The creation of this panel to examine the auditing system at the NYPD was likely an attempt to put off any true investigation. The panel consisted of three former U.S. attorneys. Not surprisingly, the press release setting up the panel indicates the department is taking the issue seriously,

> Police Commissioner Raymond W. Kelly today announced the appointment of three prominent attorneys and former Federal prosecutors—David Kelley, Sharon McCarthy, and Robert Morvillo—to serve as members of a newly established Crime Reporting Review Committee.
> 'The integrity of our crime reporting system is of the utmost importance to the Department," Commissioner Kelly said. "It is essential not only for maintaining the confidence of the people we serve, but reliable crime statistics are necessary for the effective planning and evaluation of crime reduction strategies. I know of none better or more qualified than these three highly regarded professionals to review how well our crime reporting functions.… The Committee has been asked to complete its work over the next three to six months, with the full cooperation of all units in the Police Department." (NYPD press release, 2011)

The press release is dated January 11, 2011. The only public report released by the panel was eventually released just before Independence Day on July 3, 2013, over two years overdue. In addition, the report is dated April 8, 2013 which means the NYPD had it for over two months before releasing it. Given past issues with the police department carefully vetting such reports and changing them to their benefit, this report is also likely carefully nuanced (see, e.g., the Center for Constitutional Rights website which references the RAND study on stop and frisks in the *Floyd v. City of New York* case; numerous e-mails between the NYPD and RAND effectively changed the entire complexion of the RAND report). Furthermore, the press was given less than one hour's notice of the impending release of the panel's findings. Interestingly, Graham Rayman, a reporter who is cited numerous times in the panel's report, was denied entry into the press conference (Rayman, 2013).

The panel is filled with weaknesses. It was set up by the police department itself and lacked subpoena power, the ability to grant immunity from prosecution, a budget, and a staff, with essentially nothing but a request from the police commissioner. Thus, the committee had little ability to uncover the truth. Yet even this impotent committee managed to find many issues with the NYPD's current system of auditing.

The methodology is little more than what Smith and Purtell did. The panel essentially talked to a few hand-picked NYPD members, a few supporters of the NYPD including Smith and Purtell and Zimring, and the local district attorney's offices; examined some media coverage; and spoke to only two outspoken critics of NYPD's system—the authors of this chapter—Eterno and Silverman. They examined the auditing system in place during a very limited time frame, from 2009 to 2011. We note that our research went public in early 2010 making such a time frame weak, at best, because during the time period they were looking at nearly everyone in the NYPD was aware of our criticisms for two out of the three years being examined. The committee, in fact, notes this in a buried footnote, "During the Committee's interviews, NYPD personnel indicated that recent press coverage of crime reporting issues had raised awareness and served as a deterrent to misconduct" (Kelley & McCarthy, 2013, fn. 124). In addition, they visited four precincts and talk to members of the NYPD. We note that the NYPD cherry-picked the four precincts (the panel did not pick the precincts, either at random or in any other scientific way). They examined no transit districts or police service areas.

Overall, we can say with confidence that this was neither an audit nor a comprehensive investigation of the NYPD; rather, it was a cursory exposure to the NYPD mostly from its supporter's viewpoints. The panel itself writes, "The committee was not appointed to review or audit the crime statistics reported by the NYPD, but rather to assess the auditing processes that are now in place" (Kelley & McCarthy, 2013, p. 1).

The report is 60 pages long. About half of the report is dedicated to explaining the auditing process which is already well known. The department has boasted about it for years, and it was widely circulated in Smith and Purtell (2006). The remainder of the report, and buried in it, describes the panel's findings regarding the auditing process. They essentially find some major weaknesses in the auditing system such as a lack of transparency in the process, no written audit procedures, and no follow-up on egregious violators regarding discipline, and they also find that crime reports, to some extent, are being manipulated and may have an influence on the crime rate.

We also note that the panel went out of its way to say that we were wrong about CompStat pressures. Kelley and McCarthy (2013, fn. 51) write, "The opinions expressed by the current precinct commanders [selected by NYPD headquarters] stand in marked contrast to the opinions of anonymous and retired survey respondents obtained by Eterno and Silverman." Such a claim should never be made in a report such as this. First, it is not part of their stated mission but more important, it cannot be supported by the evidence. Even they admit that the commanders were selected by the NYPD but, without protections, any rational person should not expect these commanders to say anything but the NYPD line. We note here for the record just some of our concerns with this report:

- No budget
- No power to grant immunity
- No subpoena power
- No staff
- Failure to examine our book and its evidence
- Failure to examine our second study (see later in this chapter)
- Examination of only four hand-picked precincts
- No scholarly studies reviewed except our first peer-reviewed article
- Use of a newspaper's op-ed to suggest our scientific study is not accurate
- Never attending a CompStat meeting
- Never talking to a commander who received a "beating" at CompStat
- No anonymity or even confidentiality given to those they questioned
- No motivation explaining why NYPD staff would bother to manipulate the crime reports, assuming, as they suggest, there is no pressure from CompStat
- No examination of victims of crimes or victims' groups
- No personal discussion with the whistleblowers
- Only 2009 to 2011
- No baseline to compare to previous time periods

They also make the astounding claim that the NYPD was responsible for the historic crime decline. Again this is not within their stated mission and such a claim cannot remotely be supported by their exceedingly limited report. Numerous scientific studies directly on this issue contradict this suggestion (e.g., Bowling, 1999; Conklin, 2003; Harcourt, 2001; Karmen 2000; Messner et al., 2007; Rosenfeld et al., 2007).

Overall, this study, although not a whitewash, is a bleak attempt at a fig leaf for weaknesses in the NYPD's unwritten management policies. In addition, there is not a shred of respectable evidence in the Kelley and McCarthy (2013) anecdotal examination of the NYPD to suggest that our research—confirmed in two scientific surveys—is incorrect. Our research shows that the NYPD places undue pressures on their own supervisors and officers which lead to problematic behaviors toward victims and others. We confidently stand by our research; some of it is synopsized in this chapter.

5.12.3   National and International Examples of Manipulation

NYPD operational practices are emulated throughout the United States and, indeed, the world (Bayley, 1994). The CompStat, top-down style of management is now practiced throughout the democratic world (Eterno & Silverman, 2012). Nationally and internationally allegations and examples of crime report manipulation from agencies who have copied the NYPD continue to mount. A partial listing of agencies throughout the nation where reports about gaming the crime numbers include Atlanta, Baltimore, Broward County (Florida), Dallas, Milwaukee, Mobile (Alabama), New Orleans, and Philadelphia (Bernstein & Isackson, 2014; Eterno & Silverman, 2012; McClendon, 2013; Poston, 2012). We note that several of these agencies had former NYPD commanders in positions of authority. Internationally, gaming the crime numbers has been reported in numerous countries: Australia (e.g., Wallace, 2009), France (e.g., Mattelley & Mouhanna, 2007), Sweden (e.g., Holgersson & Knutsson, 2011), and the United Kingdom (e.g., Patrick, 2011; see also Eterno & Silverman, 2012).

A recent conference of investigative reporters discussed the issue of the crime reports in the United States and how they can be gamed. They point out that each state has different reporting requirements and that the FBI's uniform crime reporting is a voluntary system; agencies do not have to cooperate. They further point out that agencies often brag about their jurisdictions using these numbers. Departments may compare to one another but this is clearly questionable. The investigative reporters correctly argue that "It's next to impossible to accurately compare crime statistics between cities and states" (Matson & Turk, 2013, n.p.).

The NYPD is notorious for its bragging, every chance they get. The NYPD's website offered a good example: "Mayor Michael R. Bloomberg and Police Commissioner Raymond W. Kelly today announced that New York City remains the safest big city in America, according to the FBI's Crime in the United States, the preliminary Uniform Crime Report for 2009" (NYPD Website, 2013). Such statements are totally disingenuous. The fact is that the FBI itself writes,

> Each year when Crime in the United States is published, some entities use reported figures to compile rankings of cities and counties. These rough rankings provide no insight into the numerous variables that mold crime in a particular town, city, county, state, or region. Consequently, they lead to simplistic

and/or incomplete analyses that often create misleading perceptions adversely affecting communities and their residents. Valid assessments are possible only with careful study and analysis of the range of unique conditions affecting each local law enforcement jurisdiction. *The data user is, therefore, cautioned against comparing statistical data of individual reporting units from cities, metropolitan areas, states, or colleges or universities solely on the basis of their population coverage or student enrollment.* "VariablesAffectingCrime" in Crime in the United States has more information on this topic. (FBI, 2013)

The NYPD has no footnote in its bragging.

It is clear that there are issues with crime reporting in the United States and throughout the democratic world. Of concern here is not simply the crime numbers but the victims.

Because police are the gatekeepers of the criminal justice system, they determine when the law will be invoked. By not taking reports, the system does not get intelligence information that is needed to actually fight crime, victims do not get the help that they need, investigators will not be able to develop patterns (e.g., Detective Hernandez), and social policy will be based on faulty data.

A recent report on how sex crime victims are handled in Victoria, Australia is an example of how a department can, at times, fail to help those who need it most. Taylor, Muldoon, Norma, and Bradley (2012) write a very thorough scientific report that, including appendices, is 411 pages long. One reporter refers to the study, "Police refused to take statements from four victims of a serial rapist who was later jailed years after abusing 20 women" (Ainsworth, 2013). The similarities to the NYPD are apparent, that is, Detective Harold Hernandez's experiences.

The report also outlines various strategies that officers may use at times to rebuff reports or discourage victims from reporting. For example, they indicate that in offering options to victims, officers may manipulate the situation:

Differences in responses were detected when dealing with certain types of offences. Police officers raised the issue of resourcing constraints or a belief that certain types of cases were less likely to succeed at trial, or victim credibility issues and in these instances some police used the "options talk" to dissuade victims from continuing with a report. Police viewed historical offences as particularly problematic and often targeted these cases for non-recording by dissuading victims from reporting in the first instance. In essence, police attitudes at various times drove their decision making. (Taylor et al., 2013, p. 10)

This report has very specific recommendations including police encouraging victims to make a report. Unfortunately, CompStat-like management systems are not likely to encourage police to seek out victims for fear of creating another crime number. Of course, police should always take a report (unless impossible) even where the victims do not want to prosecute. At a minimum, this information will be intelligence gathering.

5.13   Our Second Study

As discussed earlier, our first study uses a sample of retired captains and above who are members of the Captain's Endowment Association. Using the pre-CompStat retirees as a baseline, we compared responses to various questions in the two time periods: pre- and post-CompStat eras. We found that those who worked during the CompStat period felt far more pressure to make sure the crime numbers look good. Simultaneously, respondents during the CompStat era felt less pressure to ensure accuracy in the crime numbers. This combination led to a significant difference in the level of manipulation of crime reports. Namely, those who worked during the CompStat period were aware of far more manipulation of the crime numbers.

That survey is very powerful. However, we wanted to be absolutely sure our results were accurate. To do so, we did another study with a completely different sample. If the results from this sample replicated the first, we could be very confident that our first survey was correct. If the results did not comport well with the first, then we would have had to rethink our hypotheses using the new results.

Using Internet-based techniques, we sent the survey in March 2012 to all retired officers who identified themselves as "actively retired" with the NYPD. This means they are willing to help the NYPD in an emergency and want to remain in touch with the department. The officers on this NYPD-maintained website are much more likely to be favorable to the NYPD, inasmuch as they had to indicate a willingness to remain active. Most officers, who retire, then, do not opt for remaining active because only 4,069 retirees with good e-mail addresses are on the website. In total, there are approximately 43,000 retirees of the NYPD so only about 10% remain active. We reiterate, however, that if any social bias exists in the sampling frame, it is likely in favor of the NYPD because these officers must affirmatively register and maintain membership on the NYPD official website. This sampling frame is the best we can do without NYPD support (which is impossible for anyone trying to gain access; e.g., see earlier discussion on FOIL requests); therefore, we went forward.

The instrument was sent via e-mail to all 4,069 active retirees with 1,962 responses. This indicates a return rate of 48.2% which corresponds well with our previous postal mail survey suggesting few, if any, differences between the modes of administration. Crawford, Couper, and Lamias (2001), for example, indicate that when well-designed procedures are used, response rates with Internet surveys are equivalent to mail surveys.

Does the sample reflect NYPD retirees? First, the fairly large sample size adds assurance that the findings accurately reflect the experiences of retired officers. Second, the range of respondents' dates of retirement is from 1941 to 2012. This wide range with hundreds in each time period indicates the sample is somewhat representative and, importantly, allows comparisons over three key periods (pre-CompStat, before 1995 (562 respondents); early CompStat 1995–2001 (382 respondents); the Kelly/Bloomberg era 2002–2012 (871 respondents); with the remainder not giving a retirement year). A further indication of the sample's representativeness is the characteristics comporting with what we would expect from known distributions. That is, the pyramidal structure of the ranks of retirees is congruent with known distributions. This survey includes all ranks and those who responded include 10 chiefs, 36 inspectors, 63 captains, 262 lieutenants, 382 sergeants, 1,154 police officers/detectives, and 3 other (52 did not indicate their rank). The number of retirees in each rank comports well with known rank distributions of the NYPD. Thus, police officers/detectives are the largest group with descending counts as one goes up the ranks. Therefore, as expected, there are fewer sergeants compared to police officers/detectives and so forth. Education level is also as expected: 8% with a high school only education (NYPD now has a two-year education/military requirement to join), 44% with some college, 30% with a college degree, 7% with some graduate education, and 11% with an advanced degree. Gender too comports with expectations with far more males than females; the NYPD is currently about 18% female but over its history it has hired more and more in recent years. Thus, the gender gap is entirely expected. Because we do not have access to the NYPD, we cannot give exact numbers but these figures certainly comport well with what is publicly known about the NYPD.

5.13.1 Results

5.13.1.1 Crime Statistics

Results indicate that the majority of retirees (60%) lacked confidence in the accuracy of official NYPD index crime statistics which proclaim a huge decrease of about 80% since 1990. Most of these respondents (89.2%) felt that crime did decrease but not to the extent claimed by NYPD management. Those who indicated crime declined but not as precipitously as the NYPD suggests, on average, felt it was about one-half of what the NYPD claims. Specifically, on average, these officers felt that crime actually went down 42% in New York City. Interestingly, this comports almost exactly with the nationwide drop in crime during the same period.

5.13.1.2 Pressure From Management/Supervisors

Officers were also asked to gauge the levels of pressure they felt from management/supervisors. They were asked to base their answers on their personal experiences/knowledge. With respect to pressure to increase summonses, increase stop and frisk, increase arrests, decrease index crime, and downgrade index to nonindex crime, there is a clear pattern that completely corresponds with our previous research (see Table 5.1). Namely, pressures were greatest for every variable mentioned above for officers who worked during the CompStat era. Thus, results indicate that pressures significantly increased from 1995 to 2001 (the Giuliani years). In this study we were able to parse out the effect of those who worked 2002 and onward. It is important to note that we also found that the pressure markedly increases from 2002 onward to much higher levels. Thus there is increasing pressure in the CompStat era and then significantly added pressure in the current era. This is clearly demonstrable throughout the data.

We also note that the pattern is similar when it comes to protecting Constitutional rights and ensuring crime statistics are accurate. For these variables, however, we see the least pressure to obey the law and accurately report statistics in the current era (the Bloomberg/Kelly years). We do note that initially during CompStat's first years, these percentages were favorable. This precisely substantiates our long-standing position that CompStat was

Table 5.1 With Respect to the Following Criteria and Based on Your Personal Experience Knowledge ... How Much Pressure Did Precinct (Patrol) Personnel Receive From Management/Supervisors to ...[a,b]

	Retired Before 1995 (%)	Retired 1995–2001 (%)	Retired 2002+ (%)
Increase summonses	37.3	49.2	61.6
Increase stop and frisk	9.1	19.1	35.1
Increase arrests	18.4	35.3	49.3
Decrease index crime	19.9	33.0	43.2
Downgrade index crime to nonindex crime	15.8	21.8	37.9
Accurately report crime statistics	29.1	35	27.9
Obey legal/Constitutional restrictions	44.6	46.9	35.7

Source: Eterno, J.A., & Silverman, E.B., 2012, survey.

[a] Numbers in cells represent percentage of respondents who indicated that the pressure on them was high (answered 8–10 on a 10-point scale).

[b] These differences were all statistically significant meaning that it is highly unlikely that these results are due to chance alone.

initially a positive development but morphed into a "numbers game." Every indicator supports our basic theme.

Note that we observe the increase in stop and frisks is particularly strong ranging from about 9% before CompStat to over 35% feeling high pressures in the current Kelly/Bloomberg era. Additionally, we note that downgrading is itself suspect activity. Although there was a modest increase at the beginning of CompStat, it appears that the bulk of downgrading pressures are more current. The large percentage indicating high pressure to downgrade has grown astoundingly to nearly 40% in the current era. This is a major concern. Combined with these facts are the weakest pressures to report crime statistics accurately and obey legal restrictions in the current era. We now specifically examine crime report manipulation.

5.13.1.3 Crime Report Manipulation
We also asked officers a variety of questions inquiring if they had personal knowledge of crime report manipulation. Again, a clear pattern emerged with the most recent era (2002 and onward) showing the highest personal knowledge by officers of such manipulation, by far (see Table 5.2). Approximately 50% of officers who retired in 2002 and after had personal knowledge of crime report manipulation. This is clear evidence that this is systemic throughout the NYPD.

Overall, our second study, using a different sampling frame, replicated our first study. This is very strong evidence that our interpretations regarding crime report manipulations are absolutely accurate. The second study also suggests that the majority of the manipulations are occurring after 2002.

5.13.1.4 Comments of Interviewees
In our surveys we asked respondents to "… make any comments that you feel are important to understanding the NYPD based on your experiences." We did not specifically solicit any comments about crime numbers or manipulation. Retired officers could say whatever they liked.

TABLE 5.2 Crime Report Manipulation

	Retired Before 1995 (%)	Retired 1995–2001 (%)	Retired 2002+ (%)
… changed to make numbers look better	30.2	34.9	55.6
… not taking reports when should have	28.2	32.2	46.7
… changing words … to downgrade …	25.3	28	50.8

Source: Eterno, J.A., & Silverman, E.B., 2012, survey.

We have publicized some of the negative comments from our first survey in our first book and elsewhere. However, our most recent 2012 survey of all ranks has not yet been published. The 2012 survey takes an additional step of conducting a content analysis of all the unsolicited statements.

That content analysis indicates that with respect to crime report manipulations there were 164 unsolicited comments in 1995 (the first full year of CompStat) and after. Of these, over 84% (138) were decidedly negative. Table 5.3 shows, in their own words, small samples of these unsolicited negative comments, all from different respondents.

5.13.2   Comparing Apples and Oranges

Understanding of how the NYPD operates is critical to comprehending the crime numbers. Commanders, for better or worse, are very concerned about how their crime numbers look. At times, this consumes them. We are aware of commanders who had the numbers with them every day. They would call the precinct for regular updates. Why? Because it is how they are judged.

The unrelenting pressures of CompStat clearly had an influence on how complaint reports were processed and handled. Without a doubt a microscope was placed over reports (especially index crime reports) and they were examined as never before. In and of itself this will have an enormous influence on crime numbers because it leads to a different way of counting compared to the past: enforcing the letter of the law on each report as it is carefully vetted through teams of officers and supervisors dedicated to trying to somehow, anyway they can, get the report reclassified to a nonindex crime. Using the letter of the law is a completely different standard of counting compared to the past when the victim's word would essentially be accepted. We believe these citywide behaviors are at least partially responsible for some of the huge crime drop (see Eterno, 2003 p. 114).

For the skeptic who still does not believe, even the most ardent supporter of the NYPD will agree: the NYPD has changed its accounting practices midstream. Some may argue it's better; some may argue worse: that does not matter. What matters is this, it is different. You cannot compare the crime figures using today's new accounting methods with those of the past; it is apples and oranges!

In the past, the officer in the field would essentially take a crime report and it would be entered into the complaint reporting system. There was some review—a desk officer or supervisor—but very little oversight. Today, teams of officers are dedicated to attempting to change the status of the crime report in any way possible. Some will claim it is for the accuracy of the numbers; others will say they are fudging. Our evidence indicates both are happening.

TABLE 5.3   Various Unsolicited Comments Regarding Crime Manipulations[a]

Year Retired	Comment
2011	This is systematic corruption extending from the top down. Those in the position to stop it rather insure they don't step on toes. The corruption is not in the form of graft, drugs, etc. It is a willingness to fudge numbers, and spiteful punishments against those that defy the system
2006	…When CompStat took effect precinct commanding officers were only promoted by how well they reduced felony crimes in their pct. So what you had is competition between Boro COs on who can reduce the seven major crimes during that month, so when they had to attend CompStat, they would look good in the eyes of the Boro CO, which in turn would put that pct. CO on the fast track for promotion… the job of the Crime Statistic Sergeant (a newly created position when CompStat started just for the purpose of downgrading crime stats when possible). I could go on and on, but in the ending, CompStat is a good tool, but it's used the wrong way by pct. commanding officers. I believe that if the police commissioner changes the way pct. commanding officers are promoted from how well their crime stats measure up against other COs, then the good and proper use of CompStat will be fruitful all over the city.
2005	Years ago, the 61s [complaint reports] were done by the police officer on the street and turned into the 124 room [administrative personnel] for entry into the system; they were only looked at for errors and omissions. Now before they are turned in they are looked at to see how the crime can be downgraded, and as such sometimes the report that is entered into the system is not what the street officer had written and it is changed without knowledge or consent of the officer. Many times the 61 was totally rewritten and the officer's name and signature were photocopied on to a new report and a copy of the whole report was filed and the original was never to be seen again. The statistics game has changed the way we do policing but not for the good, and the average person who wants to make a legitimate complaint is totally discouraged and a report will be taken to placate them only until they leave and another report will be done, downgrading the original report to a lesser crime thus making it seem like things are better, when in reality it is just the opposite.
2003	Was in a [detective] squad [during CompStat years]. We did a lot of grand larceny cases. Many times the complaints were changed or we just made them forgeries or criminal impersonation as the highest charge because of the flack I took from precincts…. Sometimes went days before we got 61s [complaint reports] because the precinct CompStat Unit had to call and interview complainants to see if the complaint was properly classified or if they could change it to another crime (not one of the category). Lots of crimes became lost property complaints.
2005	… I saw firsthand how precinct commanders and their underlings downgraded crimes for their own benefit….

continued

TABLE 5.3 (continued)   Various Unsolicited Comments Regarding Crime Manipulations[a]

Year Retired	Comment
2002	The systematic downgrading of crime reports and crime statistics did not begin in earnest until the Safir administration. During the Bratton administration the message was continually communicated that the numbers must be accurate.... I do not believe they directly ordered any manipulation of the crime statistics, but they certainly took no affirmative steps (as Bratton and Jack Maple had) to prevent the manipulation and tacitly permitted manipulation to take place. Careerist precinct commanders who engage in manipulation in the hope of currying favor and receiving promotion, not the PC or the super-chiefs, are held (somewhat) accountable when manipulation is discovered. With regard to the PC and the super-chiefs, I'm sure they are shocked—shocked!—to find that manipulation is going on...
2006	... Commanders are no longer empowered, but still held accountable, so the rationale is to control the numbers as much as possible, so you can't get in trouble. That's why the numbers are managed [the way] they are.
2008	In terms of downgrading, it was happening everywhere in the department. Even when IAB was notified about downgrading, nothing was done about it. If the CO was liked in the dept., the downgrading was explained away as a minor mistake with retraining for those involved.
2004	... The precinct commander is pressured from every rank above him, up to and including the Chief of Department to further reduce crime. I believe the greatest pressure comes from the Deputy Commissioner of Operations. I was there in the beginning when it was XXXXX, and it really hasn't let up. There comes a time I believe that it can be reduced no further. The precinct commanders and the CompStat sergeant are left with no alternatives other than to "massage" the numbers. Felony crime complaints are thoroughly reviewed not for accuracy, but to find a reason to reduce the crime classification to a misdemeanor. Patrol officers are sometimes coaxed to leave out certain words which might influence the classification. Most precinct commanders would rather see a grand larceny than a robbery complaint. Simply by removing the use or threatened use of force from an incident is the difference between a robbery and grand larceny. The other frequent downgrading that I saw was the misclassification of felony assault vs. misdemeanor assault reports. Many times the reporting officer failed to accurately record the injury suffered by the C/W and/or failed to mention that a weapon was used in the commission of the crime. In almost all instances the officers felt that they were doing the "right" thing and that the CO was a gentleman. The root cause for this was, and still is the same. The unreasonable expectation for the precinct CO to maintain further reductions in index crime....
2001	CompStat meetings were the biggest cause of COs downgrading crimes. COs did not want to be ostracized for crime increasing. Therefore, complaints were looked at with a fine tooth comb to see how they could be downgraded.

TABLE 5.3 (continued)   Various Unsolicited Comments Regarding Crime Manipulations[a]

Year Retired	Comment
2004	The CompStat theory put such pressure on COs that complaint reports were changed from grand larceny to petit larceny numerous times. Robberies were changed to larcenies. Some larcenies were changed to lost property. Burglaries were also changed to larcenies. I have witnessed all of these acts. I also have witnessed 61s being held in the command blotter and being instructed not to sign off on them, because the command had already reached their numbers for that period…. I witnessed these acts….
2002	The heightened emphasis by COs on "crime reduction" (or underreporting) occurred mainly due to the implementation of CompStat meetings, whereby pct. COs were belittled, humiliated, ambushed, and confronted with crime patterns of which they were unaware, and embarrassed in front of (and by) the brass (XXXX, XXXX, XXXX). After one beating, you'd have to be a consummate idiot to report higher crime stats the next time. …
2006	The start of Impact Zones was a great opportunity to cook the books… [The boss] had the scruples of a used car salesman, and an obsession with getting steady days off. [He has a] deal. Keep the crime down in the impact zone, and you will have the days off/flexibility you need. We were averaging 18 index crimes PER WEEK in the impact zone. With our new "proactive" lieutenant, we had ZERO index crimes for the … month. We had to ease up on the reductions. That is just one example of many. The methods used to cook the books were easy…. The problem as I see it today is that the public is prevented from having reports taken by sectors who ask for the most ridiculous documentation BEFORE taking a report, such as receipts. …The books are still being cooked.
2000	Bottom line, it is a politically sensitive organization and when the numbers become the priority then people become creative in addressing them.
2004	The fact that the NYPD was using accounting depreciation principles to lower the value of stolen goods was at minimum unethical. Therefore, a stolen laptop that was two years old was no longer valued at over a thousand dollars and thus the crime was downgraded to a misdemeanor. Meanwhile, that the cost to replace the stolen item was over a thousand dollars did not affect the crime classification. The most common change that I observed was that stolen property was reclassified as lost property because no one witnessed the theft.

Source: Eterno, J.A., & Silverman, E.B., 2012, survey.

[a] These are edited for brevity, pertinence, and maintaining anonymity.

However, even if there is absolutely no fudging, the new standard is the letter of the law. Commanders and others are assigned to do anything possible, including callback to victims, to classify the crime as something other than one of the seven major felonies that CompStat examines. Very stringent preliminary investigations are now conducted that were never previously done to this extent. Victims are questioned vociferously as never before to ensure that the crime must be classified as a critical felony. Crime reports for serious crimes may eventually be taken but the desk officer will not be happy about it, eventually giving up the concerted effort to reclassify the crime. Of course, the attempt to reclassify does not end there as numerous officers will read it and again try to reclassify.

Teams of officers are dedicated to reading crime reports. Entire bureaucracies are dedicated to examining the written report, calling back complainants, and ensuring that the proper crime is listed. The Data Integrity Unit that the NYPD touts as a watchdog for crime numbers did not exist until after CompStat. There is no question about this. It was likely precisely created due to the concerns raised in this chapter.

There are at least two key problems with such efforts. The first is that more and more layers of bureaucracy are created to examine these reports. This has been the experience in the United Kingdom as documented in our book (Eterno & Silverman, 2012). The recent crime committee appointed by the commissioner falls into this trap and attempts to solve the issues by creating more and more bureaucracy.

The second issue is that by examining the letter of the law, the NYPD has adopted new and creative accounting procedures that in no way compare to the past; again, it is apples and oranges. One example of this can be seen in how auto crime reports are now taken. Around 1999 there was an enormous policy shift by the NYPD in which they began to require victims of auto theft to sign supporting depositions. Victims are now questioned much more extensively and are required to go back to the scene for a full investigation. The decrease in auto theft is at least partially due to how the NYPD now treats victims differently. This is an earth-shattering policy shift which is documented in the *NYPD Patrol Guide 207-11*.

5.14   Recommendations

In sum, the overwhelming evidence indicates that the NYPD engages in corrupt practices with respect to its crime numbers. This evidence cannot be ignored: front-line unions indicate their members are involved in downgrading; substantial decreases in the number of New York City police officers; our first study indicating enormous pressures on commanders and over 100 of them aware of crime report manipulation; the number of reported criminal suspects supposedly walking the streets skyrocketing; a flat misdemeanor crime trend; complaints for criminal trespass (a favorite to downgrade) dramatically increasing; Detective Harold Hernandez whistleblowing regarding a serial rapist arrested and confessing to several others rapes (all the crime reports were downgraded to criminal trespass or other minor crimes and no one in the NYPD would do anything); other brave whistleblowers, all of them punished for their troubles, some with audiotapes, screaming that crime report manipulations are occurring; sex crime victims and sex crime victims' groups confronting Mr. Kelly complaining about difficulties in getting their reports recorded by NYPD officers; hospital data showing trends in assaults and firearms assaults dramatically increasing; drug use in New York City higher than the national average (and crime reports for drugs going down); the NYPD's known problems with manipulation including four commanders and other officers; the NYPD's lack of transparency failing to respond in any reasonable way to numerous requests for information; a defensive NYPD constantly denying report manipulation (even its own impotent crime reporting committee found some evidence of manipulation); national and international examples of manipulation mostly in jurisdictions that have adopted the NYPD management style; quantitative analysis of our second study using previous eras as a baseline finding marked increases in crime report manipulations personally seen by hundreds of officers as well as increased pressure to manipulate such reports and less pressure to maintain the integrity of the crime reports; qualitative analysis of our second study with 138 unsolicited comments by respondents who worked after 1995 indicated report manipulation; and a different way of counting compared to the past as seen in NYPD documents.

Would a prudent investor put money on the NYPD's crime numbers? Absolutely not! The NYPD is clearly playing with the crime reports and victims of crime. It is equally clear that crime has declined in New York City but, unfortunately, the extent of that decrease may have much to do with creative accounting, manipulation, and a failure of the system (perhaps willfully) to supervise officers properly. The pressures on officers are great enough such that many officers are no longer concerned about criminals, the community, or even service; rather they are concerned about pleasing their supervisor whose main concern is numbers. The message is clear: even if it means manipulation, the numbers must look good.

To ameliorate these problems we have some very specific recommendations that can be summarized as increased transparency and community partnerships. Without these two components of democratic policing, the NYPD and any other department emulating its management style will inevitably devolve into corruption of its numbers.

We specifically recommend the following:

1. Develop and regularly conduct integrity tests to address the problem of crime manipulation. This may include undercover officers, the use of fake radio runs, and developing lists of precincts that are problems. There is nothing unusual about integrity testing. The NYPD currently uses these tests with corruption and more recently with

ticket-fixing. In this way, much more thorough audits should be conducted on those precincts that fail or are doing poorly on the tests. This must be done in conjunction with our other recommendation so as to not simply increase pressures on line officers.

2. Ironically, by following recommendation number 1—targeted auditing—the enormous gain in efficiency will allow the NYPD radically to diminish its staff dedicated to auditing. Such staff at headquarters and at the precinct level should immediately be transferred to more appropriate duties.

3. Adopt the mission statement on its website as the new narrative. Again, this statement reads: "The Mission of the New York City Police Department is to enhance the quality of life in our City by working in partnership with the community and in accordance with constitutional rights to enforce the laws, preserve the peace, reduce fear, and provide for a safe environment (NYPD, 2011, para. I).

4. Immediately stop the unrelenting focus on numbers at CompStat. Develop a more comprehensive approach that takes into account the multifaceted aspects of policing.

5. Allow commanders to work more closely with communities, focusing on local conditions and not following mindless directives from headquarters units who may have little understanding of local conditions. Closer community cooperation will provide the NYPD with enhanced intelligence thereby strengthening their anticrime and antiterrorism efforts.

6. Focus far more attention on protecting rights. Hundreds of thousands of forcible stops of innocent people need to be something headquarters questions, not promotes. How is it possible that crime was brought down for years without such aggressive behavior by police?

7. End the micromanagement. Iron control from headquarters stifles efficiency and effectiveness.

8. Immediately, stop the bullying. Think collaboration. Headquarters must support the field not demand mindless numbers from them. This will mean, for example, immediately transferring many of the bloated units at headquarters devoted to CompStat. There will be no need for detectives and other staff to be part of a chief's personal squad. The "gotcha" game must end. Headquarters must learn to delegate power to the commanders they place in the field. This means leadership, not iron control.

9. Legislation at the state level to force police departments to be more transparent must be penned. The press as well as taxpayers are entitled to basic information without having to initiate lawsuits. Oversight of this may be required.

10. Legislation for outside oversight of all police agencies in the state should be approved. The agency should be permanent, have subpoena power, and the ability to grant immunity from prosecution when warranted.

11. Legislation regarding decertification of police officers should be done at the state level. If officers are convicted of felonies and fired by a department, they should be decertified and not allowed to work in the state as an officer. New York is only one of six states that does not have this (see Goldman & Puro, 2001).

12. Even without legislation, the NYPD must become more transparent. This means, at a minimum, responding promptly and fully to FOIL requests, providing access to redesigned CompStat meetings, providing press access to all personnel without first securing DCPI's permission, not selectively releasing easily obtainable data; allowing local commanders authority to release data based on local conditions. Allow commanders to talk freely to the press and allow the press access to nearly every command with very few exceptions. The deputy commissioner for public information's job should be to help create access not as spin control over events.

13. The NYPD's upper echelon must be leaders.

14. The NYPD should immediately begin the process of accreditation through the Committee on Accreditation of Law Enforcement Agencies (CALEA). This is a good first step toward a new and improved department.

15. An oversight body outside the department (not under the mayor) should be created with sufficient independent oversight powers.

These remedies are not meant to be all inclusive. Rather, they are simply the beginnings of developing a more professional department. If democratic policing is to thrive, these recommendations offer the best hope.

References

Ainsworth, M. (2013). Victoria Police has frequently failed rape victims, report finds. *Herald Sun*. Retrieved from http://www.heraldsun.com.au/news/law-order/victoria-police-has-frequently-failed-rape-victims-report-finds/story-fni0ffnk-1226668455432

Barron, J. (2010, December 21). *Times* sues city police, saying information has been illegally withheld. *The New York Times*. Retrieved from http://www.nytimes.com/2010/12/22/nyregion/22nypd.html

Bayley, D. (1994). *Police for the Future*. New York: Oxford University Press.

Bernstein, D., & Isackson, N. The truth about Chicago crime rates part II. *Chicago Magazine*. Retrieved from http://www.chicagomag.com

Bowling, B. (1999). The rise and fall of New York murder: Zero tolerance or crack's decline? *British Journal of Criminology*, 34, 4, 531–554.

Conklin, J. (2003). *Why Crime Rates Fell?* Boston: Allyn & Bacon.

Crawford, S.D., Couper, M.P., & Lamias, M.J. (2001). Web surveys: Perceptions of burden. *Social Science Computer Review*, 19, 2, 146–162.

Democracy Now! (2012, January 27). *NYPD commissioner urged to resign after police conceal role in anti-Muslim documentary*. Retrieved from http://www.democracynow.org/2012/1/27/nypd_commissioner_ray_kelly_urged_to

Eterno, J. A. (2003). *Policing within the Law*. Westport, CT: Praeger.

Eterno, J.A., & Silverman, E.B. (2010a). The NYPD's Compstat: Compare statistics or compose statistics? *International Journal of Police Science & Management*, 12, 3, 426–449.

Eterno J.A., & Silverman E.B. (2010b). Understanding police management: A typology of the underside of CompStat. *Professional Issues in Criminal Justice*. 5, 2&3, 11–28.

Eterno, J.A., & Silverman, E.B. (2012). *The Crime Numbers Game: Management by Manipulation*. Boca Raton, FL: CRC Press.

Floyd v. City of New York. Order on liability. (2013). Retrieved from http://ccrjustice.org/files/Floyd-Liability-Opinon-8-12-13.pdf

Gardiner, S. (2010, December 22). New focus in sex-assault cases. *The Wall Street Journal*. Retrieved from http://online.wsj.com/article/SB10001424052748703581204576033873467370478.html

Gardiner, S. (2011, January 11). NYPD's long war over crime stats. *Wall Street Journal*. Retrieved from http://online.wsj.com/article/SB10001424052748704698004576104203869313630.html

Glass, I. (2010, September 10). The right to remain silent. *This American Life* radio program on NPR. Retrieved from: http://www.thisamericanlife.org/radio-archives/episode/414/right-to-remain-silent

Goldman, R., & Puro, S. (2001). Revocation of police officer certification: A viable remedy for police misconduct. *St. Louis University Law Journal*, 45, 541.

Harcourt, B.F. (2001). *Illusion of Order: The False Promise of Broken Windows Policing*. Cambridge, MA: Harvard University Press.

Hoffer, J. (2010, March 2). NYPD officer claims pressure to make arrests. ABC Television News. Retrieved from http://7online.com/archive/7305356.

Hoffer, J. (2012, March 26). Sergeant says NYPD manipulating crime stats. *ABC Television News*. Retrieved from http://abclocal.go.com/wabc/story?section=news/local/new_york&id=8594984

Holgersson, S., and Knuttson J. (2011) *Policing Narcotics, Risspolisstyrelsens utvarderigsfunktion*, Rapport, Stockholm: Rikspolisstyrelsen.

Karmen, A. (2000). *New York Murder Mystery: The True Story Behind the Crime Crash of the 1990s*. New York: NYU Press.

Kelley, D.N., & McCarthy, S.L. (2013, April 8). The report of the Crime Reporting Review Committee to Commissioner Raymond W. Kelly concerning Compstat auditing. Unpublished report retrieved from http://www.nyc.gov/html/nypd/downloads/pdf/public_information/crime_reporting_review_committee_final_report_2013.pdf

Levitt, L. (2013, June 24). The NYPD's Muslim spying: Kelly's lame game. *NYPD Confidential.* Retrieved from http://nypdconfidential.com/

Mac Donald, H. (2010, February 17). Compstat and its enemies. *City Journal,* n.p. Retrieved from http://www.city-journal.org/2010/eon0217hm.html.

Mac Donald, H. (2013, June 11). How to increase the crime rate nationwide. *The Wall Street Journal.* Retrieved from http://online.wsj.com/article/SB10001424127887 324063304578525850909628878.html

Mapp v. Ohio 367 U. S. 643. (1961).

Matson, Z., & Turk, M. (2013, June 20). Delving into crime data and finding flaws. *Investigative Reporters Conference* blog. Retrieved from http://ire.org/blog/ ire-conference-blog/2013/06/20/delving-crime-data-and-finding-flaws/ #.UcQSOSac3qo.email

Mattelley, J.H., & Mouhanna, C. (2007) *Police des chiffres et des doutes,* Paris: Michalon.

McClendon, R. (2013). Mobile's altered crime reports not limited to a single officer, unidentified fellow officers say. *AL.COM.* Retrieved from http://blog.al.com/ live/2013/06/mobiles_altered_crime_reports.html

Messner, S.F., Galea, S., Tardiff, K.J., Tracy, M., Bucciaelli, A., Piper, T.M., Frye, V., & Vlahov, D. (2007). Policing, drugs, and the homicide decline in New York City in the 1990s. *Criminology,* 45, 385–413.

Mirsky, S. (2011, August 9). The city that became safe: What New York teaches about urban crime and its control. *Scientific American.* Retrieved from http:// www.scientificamerican.com/podcast/episode.cfm?id=the-city-that-became- safe-what-new-11-08-09

Moses, P. (2005, December 20), Something's missing. *Village Voice.* Retrieved from http://www.villagevoice.com/2005-12-20/news/something-s-mnp

New York City Department of Health and Mental Hygiene (NYCHMH) (2010). *NYC vital signs,* February, 9, 1. Retrieved from http://www.nyc.gov/html/doh/down- loads/pdf/survey/survey-2009drugod.pdf

New York City Department of Health and Mental Hygiene (NYCHMH). (2013). Illicit drug use in New York City. *NYC Vital Signs,* 9, 1, 1–4. Retrieved from http://www.nyc.gov/html/doh/downloads/pdf/survey/survey-2009drugod.pdf.

New York City Public Advocate. (2013). *Breaking through bureaucracy: Evaluating government responsiveness to information requests in New York City (Bill de Blasio).* Retrieved from http://advocate.nyc.gov/sites/advocate.nyc.gov/files/ deBlasioFOILReport_0.pdf

NYPD Press Release (2007, December 26) *Mayor Bloomberg and Commissioner Kelly announce that city is on course to set a new record in crime reduction— fewest murders since records have been kept.* Retrieved from http://www.nyc. gov/portal/site/nycgov/menuitem.c0935b9a57bb4ef3daf2f1c701c789a0/index. jsp?pageID=mayor_press_release&catID=1194&doc_name=http%3A%2F%2Fwww. nyc.gov%2Fhtml%2Fom%2Fhtml%2F2007b%2Fpr473-07.html&cc= unused1978&rc=1194&ndi=1

NYPD Press Release (2011, January 5). *Police Commissioner Raymond W. Kelly announces Crime Reporting Review Panel.* Retrieved from http://www.nyc.gov/ cgi-bin/misc/pfprinter.cgi?action=print&sitename=DOH

NYPD website. (2011). About us: Mission statement. Retrieved from http://www.nyc. gov/html/nypd/html/adminstration/mission.shtml

NYPD website (2013). *Mayor Bloomberg and Police Commissioner Kelly announce New York City remains the safest big city in America according to FBI crime report.* Retrieved from http://www.nypdrecruit.com/news/mayor-bloomberg-and-police-commissioner-kelly-announce-new-york-city-remains-safest-big-city

Parascandola, R., & Marzulli, J. (2010, February 23). NYPD whistleblower Palestro reports alleged corruption at 42nd Precinct—and he was union delegate. *New York Daily News.* Retrieved from http://www.nydailynews.com/news/nypd-whistleblower-palestro-reports-alleged-corruption-42nd-precinct-union-delegate-article-1.194881

Patrick, R. (2011). A nod and a wink: Do gaming practices provide an insight into the organisational nature of police corruption? *The Police Journal.* 84, 3, 199–221.

PBA/SBA Press Release (2004). *Unions call for crime stat audit and crime reporting policy change.* (2004, March 23). Retrieved from http://www.nycpba.org/archive/releases/04/pr040323-stats.html

Poston, B. (2012). Hundreds of assault cases misreported by Milwaukee Police Department. *Journal Sentinel.* Retrieved from http://www.jsonline.com/watchdog/watchdogreports/hundreds-of-assault-cases-misreported-by-milwaukee-police-department-v44ce4p-152862135.html

Rashbaum, W.K. (2010, February 6). Retired officers raise questions on crime data. *The New York Times*, p. A1.

Rayman, G. (2010, June 8). NYPD tapes 3: A detective comes forward about downgraded sexual assaults, *The Village Voice*, n.p. Retrieved from http://www.villagevoice.com/2010-06-08/news/nypd-tapes-3-detective-comes-forward-downgrading-rape/

Rayman, G. (2012, March 7). The NYPD tapes confirmed. *The Village Voice.* Retrieved from http://www.villagevoice.com/2012-03-07/news/the-nypd-tapes-confirmed/

Rayman, G. (2013, July 3). NYPD tapes update: Kelly's crime stats panel finally releases its report, things not all rosy for the commish. *The Village Voice.* Retrieved from http://blogs.villagevoice.com/runninscared/2013/07/nypd_tapes_upda_1.php

Rosenfeld, R., Fornango, R., & Rengifo, A. (2007). The impact of order-maintenance policing on New York City homicide and robbery rates: 1988–2001. *Criminology,* 45, 355–384.

Rothstein, R. (2008). *Holding Accountability to Account.* Nashville, TN: National Center on Performance Incentives.

Schoolcraft, A. (2009). *Schoolcraft tapes* [Tape Recordings 81Precinct Roll Call on October 12] from Rayman, G. (2010, May 4). NYPD Tapes Series. Retrieved from http://img.villagevoice.com/player/?i=4767701

Sherman, L.W., & Weisburd, D. (1995). General deterrent effects of police patrol in crime "hot spots": A randomized, controlled trial. *Justice Quarterly,* 12, 4, 625–648.

Silverman, E.B. (2001). *NYPD Battles Crime.* Boston: Northeastern University Press.

Smith, D.C., & Purtell, R. (2006, August). Managing crime counts: An assessment of the quality control of NYPD crime data. (Occasional paper). *New York University School of Law.*

Taylor, S.C., Muldoon, S., Norma, C., & Bradley, D. (2012) *Policing just outcomes: Improving the police response to adults reporting sexual assault.* Social Justice Research Centre, Edith Cowan University, Western Australia. Retrieved from http://www.ecu.edu.au/__data/assets/pdf_file/0004/483016/Policing-Just-Outcomes-in-Sexual-Assault-Final-Report.pdf

U.S. Securities and Exchange Commission. (2009, August 31). *Investigation of failure of the SEC to uncover Bernard Madoff's Ponzi scheme—public version. Case No. OIG 509.* Retrieved from http://www.sec.gov/news/studies/2009/oig-509.pdf

Wallace, R. (2009). Police manipulation skews crime statistics. *The Australian.* Retrieved from http://www.theaustralian.com.au/news/police-manipulation-skews-statistics/story-e6frg6of-1111119104767

Weiss, M. (2012, September 19). NYPD to lose thousands of cops to retirement over next few years. *DNAinfo.* Retrieved from http://www.dnainfo.com/new-york/20120919/new-york-city/nypd-could-lose-thousands-of-cops-retirement-over-next-few-years

Zimring, F. (2011). *The city that became safe: New York and the future of crime control.* Unpublished article retrieved from http://www.scribd.com/doc/48102346/Zimring-Journal-Article

Zink, R. (2004, summer). The trouble with Compstat. *PBA Magazine.* Retrieved December 29, 2010 from http://www.nycpba.org/publications/mag-04-summer/compstat.html

Marijuana Madness
The Scandal of New York City's Racist Marijuana Possession Arrests

HARRY G. LEVINE
LOREN SIEGEL

Contents

6.1 Introduction

There are five basic things to understand about the scandal of marijuana possession arrests in New York City. From these all other questions follow.

First, simple possession of less than an ounce of marijuana is not a crime in New York State. Since 1977 and passage of the Marijuana Reform Act, state law has made simple possession of 25 grams or less of marijuana (or less than seventh-eighths of an ounce) a violation, similar in some ways to a traffic infraction. A person found by the police to be possessing a small amount of marijuana in a pocket or belongings can be given a criminal court summons and fined $100 plus court costs, and may suffer other consequences, some quite serious.[1] But at least initially, violations and summonses rarely include arrests, fingerprints, criminal records, and jailings.[2] For over 30 years, New York State has formally, legally decriminalized possession of marijuana.

Second, despite that law, for more than a decade the New York Police Department has arrested, prosecuted, and jailed more people for marijuana possession than for any other crime whatsoever (see Figure 6.1.). From 1997 through 2012 (and into 2013) the New York City Police Department made more than 600,000 arrests and jailings of people for possessing small amounts of marijuana, mostly teenagers and young people in their 20s. In 2011, the NYPD made more than 50,000 arrests of people who possessed only a small amount of marijuana. In just that one year, the NYPD made more marijuana arrests than it did in the 19 years from 1978 through 1996. These arrests have been carried out under two mayors (Giuliani and Bloomberg) and three police commissioners (Safir, Kerik, and Kelly). These simple marijuana possession arrests have skyrocketed even though marijuana use has remained much the same. As numerous news stories have pointed out, these extraordinary numbers of arrests and jailings have made New York City the marijuana arrest capital of the world.

Third, most people arrested were not smoking marijuana. Usually they just carried a bit of it in a pocket. The police most commonly found the marijuana in the course of a stop and frisk in which they searched (often illegally) the person's pockets and belongings. The people arrested were handcuffed, taken to a police station, fingerprinted, photographed, eye-scanned, and usually held for 24 hours in the city's jails. They were spit out the next day into the criminal arraignment court where, if it was a first offense, they usually received a year of probation and a life-time, permanent, inexpungeable criminal record.

Fourth, these marijuana possession arrests have targeted young people. Nearly 70% of the people arrested are younger than 30, about 56% are younger than 25, and nearly a quarter are teenagers. The possession arrests also target people who have never been convicted or even arrested before.[3] The youngest people, the great majority of those arrested for marijuana, are the least likely to have criminal convictions; 94% of the teenagers (age 16 to 19) arrested for marijuana possession and 77% of the young people age 20 to 24 arrested for marijuana possession had never been convicted of even one misdemeanor. The arrests are not capturing career criminals; they are ensnaring young people, overwhelmingly without any criminal convictions. For many of the young people, this is their first arrest.[4]

Fifth, these arrests have targeted young Blacks and Latinos even though U.S. government studies have consistently found that young Blacks and Latinos use marijuana at lower rates than young Whites.[5]

About 77% of the arrests have been made in the NYPD precincts where the majority of the residents are Black and Latino (half the city's neighborhood precincts). Although Blacks and Latinos together make up about 53% of the city's residents, for more than a decade they have been 87% of the people arrested for possessing marijuana. In the last 10 years, Blacks constituted about 25% of New York's residents, but 54% of the people arrested for marijuana possession. Latinos constituted about 27% of the city's residents, but 33% of the people arrested. Whites (non-Hispanic Whites) made up about 35% of the city's population but about 11% of the people arrested.

The police have arrested Blacks at seven times the rate of Whites and Latinos at nearly four times the rate of Whites, even though, as stated above, many years of U.S. government studies have found that young Blacks and Latinos use marijuana at lower rates than young Whites.[6]

There are prejudiced and bigoted people in any large organization, but these many racially skewed or biased marijuana arrests have not been the result of individual prejudice or racism of some police officers. These arrests have been carried out by tens of thousands of officers, every day for more than 15 years. The arrests are not racist in their intent, but very much so in their effects. The arrests are precisely what is meant by the term "institutional racism," or what some have termed "racism without racists."

NYPD commanders concentrate police patrols in only certain neighborhoods, designated high crime areas, where residents are largely Blacks and Latinos, disproportionately from low-income families. That is where the police do most stop and frisks, write most criminal court summonses, and make most misdemeanor arrests including for possession of marijuana. In addition, as several studies have found, police are more likely to stop, frisk, and search Blacks in any neighborhood, including predominately White ones. The police catch so many more of one kind of "fish" because they are mostly searching in certain waters, looking mainly for certain kinds of fish.

The marijuana possession arrests are carried out at the command and instruction of individuals at the highest levels of the NYPD and the mayor's office. They find it fair and reasonable to continue making these arrests even though they fall most heavily on people who use marijuana at lower rates, and who are among the most vulnerable people in New York City. The patrol and narcotics officers' arrests of mainly Blacks and Latinos for marijuana possession are driven not primarily by racial or ethnic animosity, but by a systemic focus within the police department on Black and Latino young men. And the effects are clearly racially biased, discriminatory, unfair, and unjust. They are racist.

With several colleagues, we have been researching these arrests since 2005.[7] We have obtained arrest data from New York State and the FBI. In conferences, academic settings, and private meetings, we have learned much from current and former police officers from New York and other big cities in the United States, Canada, the United Kingdom, and elsewhere. We also have learned about the arrests from experienced public defenders and private attorneys who have handled literally thousands of these cases, from judges and former prosecutors, from people who work in New York's jails and courts, and from many young people arrested for marijuana possession. Our research, reports, and testimony have helped make the marijuana arrests a major news and political issue in New York City and to some extent nationally. Very good reporters, journalists, and researchers have documented extensively the way the arrests are carried out, the use of illegal searches, and the racial, age, and gender skewing of the arrests (which are nearly 90% males).[8]

We regard New York City's marijuana possession arrests as a scandal, similar to Love Canal and the Ford Pinto. Love Canal, filled with 20,000 tons of deadly chemicals, was the first toxic waste scandal. The Pinto and its exploding gas tank is still the most famous car-design scandal. These kinds of scandals are of horrific situations, harming many people, that go on for years before being revealed. Important institutions including Hooker Chemical and Ford had long benefited and did not want the conditions exposed or the practices stopped.

New York City's marijuana possession arrests are the same kind of scandal. They have gone on for years and harmed millions of people, but two mayors and three police commissioners have continued making the arrests and resisted all efforts to end them. And until recently the NYPD has been remarkably successful at keeping the arrests out of the public eye. The NYPD started and has continued this marijuana arrest crusade on their own, and they could end it, but Mayor Bloomberg and Police Commissioner Kelly were unwilling to do so. As a result members of the state legislature and the governor have sought to change New York State's marijuana law to stop the NYPD from making these possession arrests.[9]

This chapter summarizes what we have learned about how these arrests are made, and about why the NYPD has made and continues to make them, despite what is now a large, vocal, and broadly based opposition to the arrests. It answers questions we have been asked many times.[10] First it uses a series of graphs to show the rise of the marijuana possession arrests from a few thousand a year for 19 years (1978–1996) to averaging 35,000 arrests a year since 1997, and their racial bias. Second, it focuses on how police usually find the marijuana: by searching the pockets and possessions of people they stop, often illegally. Third, it discusses the marijuana arrests and stop and frisks as a way for the NYPD to deploy officers in a time of a nationwide decline in serious crime beginning about 1990. Fourth, it describes the usefulness of the marijuana possession arrests to specific groups within the NYPD including supervisors at all levels, as well as many patrol and narcotics police. Fifth, it briefly discusses the extraordinary rise of public opposition to the stop and frisks, the marijuana arrests, and policing as it has been carried out in New York City for nearly two decades.

6.2   Rise of the Marijuana Arrest Crusade

Some of what has been happening can best be seen graphically.[11] The five graphs shown in Figures 6.1 though 6.5 summarize well the major developments and themes in the story of New York City's marijuana arrests. The

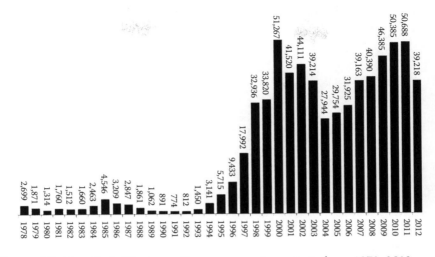

Figure 6.1 New York City's marijuana possession arrests from 1978–2012.

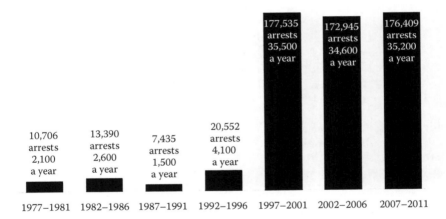

Figure 6.2 New York City's marijuana possession arrests in five-year periods. These are lowest-level arrests, age 16 and older, charged under NYSPL 221.10. (From New York State Division of Criminal Justice Services, Albany, New York.)

first two graphs show the total number of marijuana arrests by year and by five-year blocks revealing the extraordinary increase in marijuana arrests beginning in the mid-1990s. The next two graphs show the marijuana use of young Whites, Blacks, and Latinos, and the marijuana arrests by race for each group over 16 years. The graphs show that, as *New York Times* columnist Jim Dwyer once put it, "Whites Use Pot, but Blacks Are Arrested."[12]

The final graph shows the 15 precincts with the lowest per capita rate of marijuana arrests and the 15 NYPD precincts with the highest rates

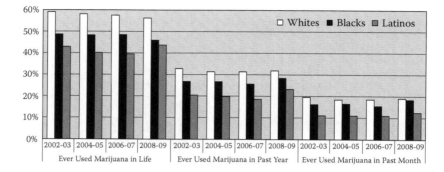

Figure 6.3 Marijuana use by Whites, Blacks, and Latinos, ages 18 to 25, 2002–2009.

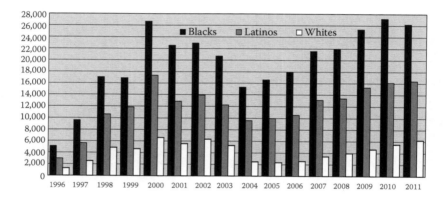

Figure 6.4 Marijuana arrests of Blacks, Latinos, and Whites in New York City, 1996–2011. (Use data are from U.S. Dept HHS, SAMHSA, Office of Applied Studies. Arrest date is from New York State Division of Criminal Justice Services, Albany, New York.)

of marijuana arrests. It also shows in which precincts the majority of residents are Blacks and Latinos, and those precincts where the majority of residents are mostly Whites plus some others, chiefly Asians. In all 15 precincts with the lowest marijuana arrest rates, the majority of residents are Whites and others.[13] In 13 of the 15 precincts with the highest rate of per capita marijuana arrests the majority of the residents are Blacks and Latins.

There are enormous differences in the rates of arrest for marijuana possession in the precincts with the highest and lowest arrest rates. The wealthy Upper East Side of Manhattan, where Mayor Bloomberg lived, has the lowest marijuana arrest rate in the city, despite its many schools serving teenagers from upper-middle class and wealthy families. The low-income and predominately Black and Latino precincts of Ocean Hill Brownsville and East

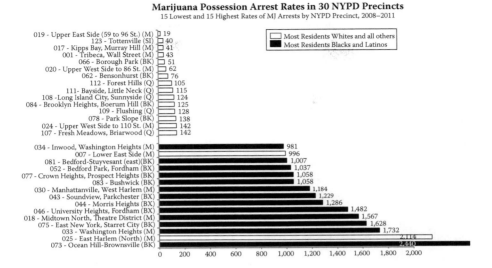

Figure 6.5 These tables show only the lowest level misdemeanor marijuana possession arrests and charges. 4-year average of rates, 2008–2011. (From the New York State Division of Criminal Justice Services, Computerized Criminal History System. Includes all fingerprintable misdemeanor arrests for NYS Penal Law Article 221.10 as the most serious charge in an arrest event. Ages 16 and older.)

Harlem, however, have marijuana possession arrest rates 125 times higher than where Bloomberg lives. See Figure 6.5.

How did it happen that the NYPD shifted from averaging about 3,000 lowest-level marijuana possession arrests for 20 years to averaging 35,000 marijuana arrests a year for the next 15 years? What changed?

First of all, the leadership changed. In the spring of 1996 Mayor Rudolph Giuliani fired William Bratton as police commissioner and appointed Howard Safir.[14] By the end of 1996, marijuana possession arrests jumped from 5,700 arrests in 1995 to the new high of 9,400. In 1997 under Safir, the arrests jumped again to 17,900, double the number of marijuana arrests during Bratton's two years as police commissioner combined.[15] In 1998, the number of lowest-level marijuana possession arrests climbed to 32,936, beginning an arrest crusade that New Yorkers are still experiencing.

Howard Safir did not come to this unprepared. He had spent 15 years working for the U.S. Drug Enforcement Administration (DEA) rising from narcotics agent to deputy commissioner. Safir and Giuliani had known each other since the early 1980s when they both worked in the anti-drug office of the Reagan administration during the creation of the "War on Drugs." There was a meeting of minds between Giuliani, who was always strongly anti-drugs, and his police commissioner about making many lowest-level marijuana possession arrests. Furthermore, by the last third of the 1990s the crack cocaine crisis had ebbed, but use of marijuana was as prevalent as ever and more prevalent than for any other drug. Marijuana was also popular among teenagers and young people in their 20s who are easy to find, intimidate, and arrest. Safir proudly reported that as police commissioner he "established thirty-nine major anti-drug initiatives." Almost certainly, one of them was the marijuana possession arrest crusade.[16]

Michael Bloomberg became Mayor in January 2002, shortly after the devastation and disruption caused by the bombing of the World Trade Center in September 2001. Bloomberg had campaigned as a moderate, a Republican of convenience, who famously admitted that he had smoked marijuana and "liked it." At the time, the huge numbers of marijuana possession arrests under Giuliani were poorly understood, even by close observers of the city, and their racial disparities were unknown. Even so, there was reason to believe that Bloomberg would soften many of the policing policies of the fiercely combative Giuliani. And Bloomberg appointed Raymond Kelly as police commissioner; Kelly had served as police commissioner under David Dinkins and had publicly criticized the kind of heavy-handed policing, especially of petty offenses, that had become Giuliani's trademark.

But Bloomberg and Kelly continued and expanded Giuliani's policing policies. In 2002 the number of marijuana arrests increased over Giuliani's last year. The number of marijuana arrests declined for two years, and then began a steady increase that soon outstripped even Giuliani. Under Giuliani's two terms from 1994–2001, the NYPD made a total of 196,000 of the lowest-level marijuana possession arrests, an extraordinarily large number of arrests for one minor offense (and for one that had been supposedly, and officially, decriminalized). Under Giuliani the NYPD averaged 25,000 arrests a year for eight years. Yet Bloomberg in his first two terms, from 2002–2009, made nearly 300,000 marijuana arrests, 50% more than under Giuliani, and an average of 38,000 marijuana possession arrests a year.

By the end of 2012, the NYPD under Bloomberg had made an astonishing 440,000 lowest-level marijuana possession arrests, and for many years this has been the single offense for which more people have been arrested and charged than any other. It is not an exaggeration to say that New York City has led the world in the number of marijuana arrests and that its overall rate of marijuana possession arrests has been among the highest anywhere.

6.3   Searching Pockets and Possessions for Marijuana

How did the NYPD accomplish the enormous growth in marijuana possession arrests from a few thousand a year to an average of 35,000 a year? Police did so by focusing great attention on the contents of people's pockets and possessions. Focusing on the contents of people's pockets and possessions was

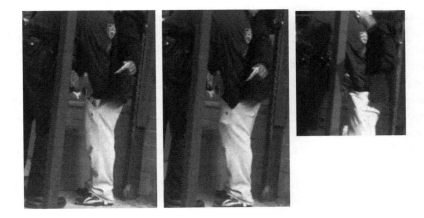

Figure 6.6 A NYPD uniformed officer reaching into the pockets of a man being frisked and searched in April 2011 in Brooklyn.

a form of policing that narcotics officers (antidrug police) had long used in apprehending people for possessing small amounts of "hard" drugs, almost entirely heroin and cocaine. In effect, Safir and Giuliani applied the street-level policing style of narcotics squads—where people are stopped, frisked, and searched—to the policing of possession of small amounts of marijuana. The technique, although financially costly and damaging to the lives of the young people arrested, has produced an amazing number of arrests for tiny amounts of marijuana (see Figure 6.6).

How do the police find a bit of marijuana, often a few grams, in a tiny plastic bag about the size of a silver dollar, or a thin marijuana cigarette, or even part of one? First of all, in the course of a pat-down or frisk an officer simply reaches into the person's pockets. When we began researching marijuana arrests, we interviewed many people who had been arrested who told us that police retrieved the marijuana by reaching into their pockets. Public defenders and other attorneys also told us that many of their clients reported that police had simply reached into their pockets and belongings, pulling out whatever they had. Sometimes police just ordered people to empty their pockets, or even tricked them into doing so.

Partly as a result of our research and the advocacy of others, beginning in 2011 experienced journalists first reported that people arrested for marijuana possession commonly described encounters in which police officers simply reached inside a suspect's pockets or belongings. For example, in February 2012 Jennifer Peltz of the Associated Press reported on the case of Stephen Glover who had been arrested for marijuana possession when he was standing outside a Bronx job-training center. Glover had been "sharing a box of mints with friends, when police came up to him, asked him whether he had anything in his pockets that could hurt them, and searched them [his pockets] without asking his permission. They found the remains of two marijuana cigarettes in his pockets, he said. 'They just take it upon themselves to search,' the 30-year-old Glover said." [17]

In 2011, writer Steve Wishnia published a long article quoting several attorneys describing common types of marijuana arrest cases. Sydney Peck, a Brooklyn public defender, said, "A police officer pulls marijuana out of someone's pocket, and all of a sudden, it's marijuana in public view." Wishnia quoted a staff attorney at the Brooklyn Defenders who said he had "seen a lot of 'dropsy' cases, in which police say they saw the defendant drop the marijuana on the ground." This attorney described a case of a man arrested for marijuana possession while in front of a small grocery store. The police officer's report said that the man was "in possession of a quantity of marijuana, which was open to public view," but the officer also reported that he "recovered [the marijuana] from defendant's pants pocket." The attorney, perplexed by how marijuana in a pocket could be open to public view, wondered if his client had worn "transparent pants." [18]

Most thorough of all was the DuPont Award-winning, two-part series by Ailsa Chang, the police and criminal justice reporter for WNYC, which first broke the story about illegal searches for marijuana by the NYPD. In April 2011 she reported a number of cases of police putting their hands inside people's pockets and searching their clothing. Wrote Chang:

WNYC tracked down more than a dozen men arrested after a stop and frisk for allegedly displaying marijuana in public view. Each person said the marijuana was hidden—in a pocket, in a sock, a shoe, or in underwear. There's no videotape to confirm their accounts, but they each said the police pulled the drugs out of his clothes before arresting him for having marijuana in public view. None of them had been buying their drugs outside. And none of them were carrying a weapon when they were stopped....

Antonio Rivera, 25, said he gets stopped by police up to five times a month. In January, he said he was stopped and frisked near the corner of E. 183rd Street and Creston Avenue in the Bronx. He was arrested for misdemeanor marijuana possession. Critics of the police say his case is an example of how officers may be conducting illegal searches when making marijuana arrests. Rivera said his marijuana was in his pants and that police pulled it out of his clothes after searching him without his consent. "So they checked my pockets, my coat pockets, and they patted my jean pockets," Rivera said, "and then once he felt the package I had in my crotch area, he went into my pants and he pulled it out."

Rivera had lodged a soft Ziploc bag of marijuana between his legs inside his pants while still in the room where he bought it. He said he never took the drugs out when he went outside, but the police officer who arrested him told prosecutors Rivera was openly displaying his drugs. In the criminal complaint against Rivera, the arresting officer stated that he "observed the defendant to have on his person, in his right hand 1 Ziploc bag containing a dried-green leafy substance with the distinctive odor alleged to be marijuana in public view"....

Leo Henning, an African-American, said he was walking with a Ziploc bag of marijuana in his sock—under his foot—when two officers stopped him in March on a street corner in East Harlem. He had just bought the marijuana inside a warehouse several blocks away and had tucked the bag in his sock before he stepped outside, he said. Henning said one of the officers who stopped him placed his hands on him almost immediately.... "He went into my front right pocket. Then he went into my front left pocket," Henning said. "Then he went into my right back pocket. Then he went into my left pocket." Finding nothing, Henning said the officer stuck his fingers down Henning's left sock. "And then he switched over to my right sock," Henning said. "He stuck his hands in. His fingers were going under my foot inside my sock. That's when he felt it, I gather." At that point, the officer allegedly pulled out the bag of marijuana and arrested Henning for displaying marijuana "open to public view." Henning spent the night in jail.[19,20]

It is illegal for police to reach inside someone's pockets without prior "probable cause," meaning evidence sufficient to justify an arrest. The U.S. Supreme Court established in *Terry v. Ohio* 392 U.S. 1 (1968) that police officers may formally, officially stop and detain someone only when they have "reasonable suspicion" that something illegal or dangerous is going on that warrants further investigation. But this is not sufficient to legally frisk someone. In order to conduct a legal pat-down—what the Supreme Court called "a limited search of the outer clothing for weapons," especially a gun—the officer must have "reasonable suspicion" to believe that the person is armed and dangerous, posing a threat to the officer or others. But even this frisk, this pat-down, this "limited search" is to be of only the "outer clothing." A full search, in which the person stopped is required to empty his pockets, or one that goes beyond the pat-down of outer clothing, requires "probable cause," that is, enough evidence to justify an arrest. Police have no legal justification for reaching into someone's pockets or possessions unless the officer feels a weapon, and guns are relatively easy to feel. As Ira Glasser has explained,

What *Terry* means, therefore, is that in the absence of probable cause—that is, in the absence of enough evidence to justify an arrest or a search warrant issued by a court—a police officer may frisk someone who has been legally and forcibly stopped only if the officer has good and specific reasons to suspect a concealed weapon. What the officer may not legally do is frisk someone because he "suspects" a crime other than the possession of a concealed weapon.[21]

Yet this is precisely what happened for 15 years in New York City's marijuana arrest crusade.

The second principal way that police officers retrieve marijuana is that some individuals take out their marijuana and hand it over. Few people do this without being asked or ordered. When we began our research on the marijuana arrests some years ago, we had many reports from public defender and legal aid attorneys, and from people who had been stopped and searched, that police, in effect, tricked people into emptying their pockets or taking out their marijuana.

In September of 2011, after numerous reports of the police searching people, and of police tricking and ordering people to empty their pockets revealing only a bit of marijuana, Police Commissioner Kelly broke his many years of silence about the marijuana arrests when he released a formal Operations Order concerning "Charging Standards for Possession of Marihuana in a Public Place Open to Public View." The order instructed that unless "the public display of marihuana" was "an activity undertaken of the subject's own volition," the charge must be a violation, not a misdemeanor.[22]

In his order, and in its voluminous press coverage, it became clear that police officers commonly, in Kelly's words, "recover marihuana pursuant to a search of the subject's person or upon direction of the subject to surrender the contents of his/her pockets or other closed container." Commissioner Kelly also referred to individuals who are "requested or compelled" by police officers to empty their pockets and reveal their marijuana. As Kelly's order acknowledged, police officers sometimes ask people to empty their pockets, but police also "direct" or "compel" people to do so.[23]

In June of 2012, Governor Cuomo broke his own long-standing silence about New York City's marijuana arrests in a press conference he held announcing he was going to introduce legislation to further decriminalize (or "re-decriminalize" as some put it) marijuana possession in all of New York State entirely because of the large number of marijuana arrests in New York City. Addressing the cameras and the press, the governor described the common occurrence of NYPD officers ordering people to turn out their pockets and the result:

> I understand the intent of the law in 1977, and ... that is not [the] current effect of the law. There is a blatant inconsistency. If you possess marijuana privately, it's a violation; if you show it in public, it's a crime. It's incongruous; it's inconsistent the way it has been enforced. There have been additional complications in relation to the stop-and-frisk policy where there are claims that young people can have a small amount of marijuana in their pocket; during the stop and frisk the police officer says "turn out your pockets" and marijuana is now in public view. [The offense] just went from a violation to a crime.

Numerous newspaper and other media stories have also reported cases where people were told (or directed, ordered, commanded, or instructed) to empty their pockets and turn their pockets inside out.[24]

6.4 Marijuana Possession Arrests as Response to Decline in Number of Serious Crimes

Why has the New York Police Department been making historic and unprecedented numbers of arrests, many of them blatantly illegal, for possession of small or even tiny amounts of marijuana? Why has it been doing so when state law has long decriminalized simple possession of marijuana? And why, despite the ever-growing opposition to these arrests from advocates, attorneys, elected officials, and prominent reporters and columnists, and despite a great many news stories documenting the (at best) devious ways the arrests are made and their harmful consequences, have the arrests continued unabated? Why did Mayor Bloomberg, Police Commissioner Kelly, and the top commanders of the NYPD continue to make ever more of these lowest-level possession arrests, year after year?

It is surprising that neither Mayor Bloomberg nor Police Commissioner Raymond Kelly has ever answered those questions directly. Some reporters have said that, off the record, top people in the Bloomberg administration say that the marijuana arrests "bring crime down." But the administration has never provided any evidence for that, or even made an extended argument to present and defend such a claim.[25] Strange as it seems, the marijuana arrest crusade has gone on, producing more than 600,000 arrests for marijuana possession by 2012 (at a cost of nearly a billion dollars) without a serious explanation of the policy for taxpayers, citizens, and the general public.[26]

In order to understand this process we have therefore relied upon the experiences and insights of veteran police officers and long-time observers and researchers of New York's criminal justice system, and on an ever-growing body of statistical and qualitative data about police activities, including about the NYPD's huge number of racially skewed stop and frisks.

Only one study, published in 2007 in *Criminology and Public Policy*, one of the two peer-reviewed journals of the American Society of Criminology, has examined whether New York City's marijuana possession arrests have reduced violent and serious crimes. And it strongly concluded that the marijuana arrests had not reduced serious crimes. University of Chicago professors Bernard Harcourt and Jens Ludwig used highly technical methods to analyze statistically the effects of the marijuana arrests on serious crimes including violent crimes, but they explained their key findings clearly. Referring to the marijuana possession arrests as MPV (marijuana in public view) arrests, they wrote:

> Whatever the conceptual underpinning of this marijuana policing strategy ... we find no good evidence that the MPV arrests are associated with reductions in serious violent or property crimes in the city. As a result New York City's marijuana policing strategy seems likely to simply divert scarce police

resources away from more effective approaches that research suggests is capable of reducing real crime. ...

[New York City's] experiment with misdemeanor MPV arrests—along with all the associated detentions, convictions, and additional incarcerations—represents a tremendously expensive policing intervention.... [The marijuana possession arrests have] had a significant disparate impact on African-American and Hispanic residents. Our study further shows that there is no good evidence that it contributed to combating serious crime in the city. If anything, it has had the reverse effect. As a result, the NYPD policy of misdemeanor MPV arrests represents an extremely poor trade-off of scarce law enforcement resources.[27]

Harcourt and Ludwig's study is in accord with the observations of patrol officers we interviewed in New York and other cities. These experienced police officers point out that when officers spend several hours arresting and booking teenagers and young adults simply for possessing marijuana, they are off the street and unable to engage in other police work. Likewise, narcotics squads searching for and arresting people possessing small amounts of marijuana are not available for other crime-fighting work. In describing these marijuana arrests, a number of police officers used exactly the same phrase, calling them "a waste of time."

The question remains: why make all these marijuana possession arrests?

Since the rise of professional policing, police departments have sought to measure officer productivity, with numbers of arrests and other enforcement activities serving as the primary quantitative measures of productivity. In the 1990s, the availability of computers and computerized databases gave police commanders access to much more information about crime patterns, and about policing patterns. A number of other technological developments, including the shift from foot patrols to patrol cars, the use of computer terminals in police vehicles, and the rise of cell phone use, have also allowed supervisors to more closely supervise officers on the street.

Fueled in part by these developments, two important phenomena overlapped in New York City beginning around 1990. First, a nationwide and international decline in the number of serious and violent crimes began in the late 1980s and continued and expanded in the 1990s.[28] Some observers conclude that the use of computers to track crime patterns, along with other economic and social shifts, including the availability of better locks and physical security, contributed to making the widespread reduction in serious crimes in the 1990s and continuing in the 2000s. To repeat: this decline in reported serious felonies occurred in many U.S. cities and states, and in a number of other countries.[29] As the two graphs show (Figures 6.7 and 6.8),

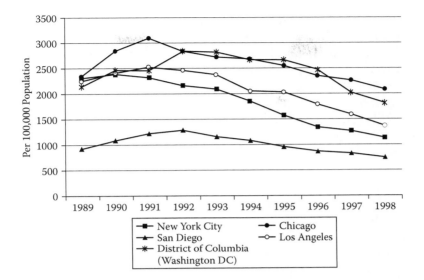

Figure 6.7 Reported rate of violent crime: Five U.S. cities, 1989–1998. (From Marshall, J., *Zero Tolerance Policing*, Australian Institute of Criminology, Australian Government, Australian Capital Territory, Australia, March 1999. Available at http://www.ocsar.sa.gov.au/docs/information_bulletins/IB9.pdf)

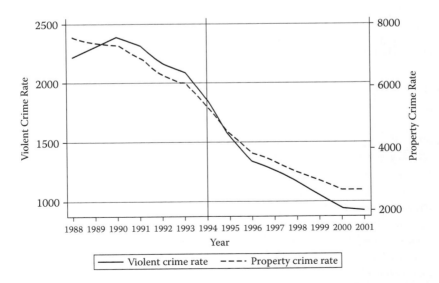

Figure 6.8 Violent and property crime rates, New York City, 1988–2011.

New York City first had fewer reports of serious crimes around 1990, when David Dinkins was mayor and Raymond Kelly was his police commisioner.

Second, beginning in 1994, with considerable fanfare, the NYPD under Mayor Giuliani and Police Commissioner Bratton shifted its patrol and crime-fighting focus to minor crimes and offenses, to misdemeanors and even civil infractions. This policy continued and expanded under Giuliani's next two police commissioners, and then under Mayor Bloomberg and Police Commissioner Kelly.

For U.S. police departments, the decline in the number of serious crimes presented an unusual but not entirely unanticipated question: what do managers of police departments experiencing a decline in serious crime do with the police officers who formerly spent much of their time responding to the serious felonies? In addition, a prominent initiative of President Bill Clinton funded 100,000 more police officers nationwide. As a result, in the 1990s the question of how to assign and supervise officers in an era of declining crime was a real one, and it did not go away in the 2000s.

Giuliani, Bratton, and their top law enforcement advisors had a number of motivations for focusing heavily on misdemeanors and other petty offenses (not all of them admitted).[30] But they certainly recognized that if serious crime continued to decline, they would have to assign police in new ways. And they also understood that officers freed from working on felonies could be deployed to focus on low-level offenses, on misdemeanors and even on infractions such as writing graffiti, urinating on the street, and having loud boom boxes. Assigning officers to police minor offenses kept them busy and also provided a valuable paper trail of their activities showing when and where they wrote summonses, filled out stop-and-frisk forms, and made misdemeanor arrests.[31]

Until the early or mid-1990s, half or more of all arrests in New York occurred when police officers investigated reported crimes, after someone reported a robbery, burglary, assault, rape, or other crime by calling the police or coming to a police station, or occasionally when a body turned up. Police officers then were assigned to investigate and if possible arrest a suspect. For many years, the NYPD made about equal numbers of arrests for felonies (serious crimes) and for misdemeanors, most of them in response to crimes that people reported. But with the decline in serious crimes, and with the increase in the number of police officers in the 1990s, the NYPD and some police departments shifted to a new kind of "proactive" policing focusing on petty offenses.

In order for this policy emphasis on petty offenses to go into effect, officers on the street had to cooperate. But people do not typically become police officers in order to write tickets and give warnings for minor offenses; people become police officers to catch bad guys and make arrests. Therefore, patrol police had to be given the authority to make more arrests for minor offenses. Indeed, they had to be encouraged to do so, in part through overtime pay. Nowhere was this emphasis on making arrests of people for minor offenses carried out more publicly and adamantly than in New York City, first under Rudolph Giuliani and then under Michael Bloomberg.

One veteran NYPD patrol officer who came on the force in 1984 explained how this transformation was effected for marijuana possession within the microcosm of the police station. During his first 10 years, he said, an officer who brought in a simple marijuana possession arrest might be teased or even ridiculed by the desk sergeant or other officers: "Hey, look at what Jones brought in: a really dangerous case of pot possession. Major criminal you've got there, Jonesy."

Beginning around 1996, after Bratton had left and Safir was in charge, the attitude within the department changed: marijuana possession arrests became not just acceptable but desirable and worthy of praise. Now the sergeant or commander would say: "I'd like to see the rest of you making those marijuana collars like Jones has been doing. You know they're out there. Go get some."

Another veteran officer told us that shortly after Giuliani appointed Bratton as his first police commissioner, Bratton addressed over 20,000 police officers at a huge police-only event at Madison Square Garden. Bratton told the troops that there was a new regime in town with a new policy: NYPD officers should make full-fledged arrests for many minor offenses, and they would get overtime pay for doing so. This was followed by 20,000 police officers standing up, stamping their feet, applauding, and cheering in a "deafening roar."

It took a number of years for this change to be fully implemented. But the shift in policing in New York (and in some other cities) has transformed what it is that police officers do. In 1980, the NYPD made 86,000 felony arrests and 65,000 misdemeanor arrests. As the graph in Figure 6.9 shows, in 1994, Giuliani's first year as mayor, that pattern began to change. By 2011, the NYPD reported 89,000 felony arrests but nearly 250,000 misdemeanor arrests.

Chief among the misdemeanors in 2011 were the more than 50,000 arrests for marijuana possession and the 32,000 arrests for possession of tiny or miniscule amounts of all other drugs. Since the late 1990s, lowest-level drug possession arrests have constituted about a third of all misdemeanor arrests in New York City, and about a quarter of all arrests of any kind.

In a relentless, 20-year public relations offensive, the NYPD and its mayors have claimed that the chief reason there were fewer reported crimes, especially serious felonies including murders, shootings, assaults, robberies, and rapes, was because the NYPD was making many more arrests for minor offenses. This policy has been promoted under a number of slogans or brands. In 1994 and 1995 under Giuliani and Bratton, this policy was first called "broken-windows policing." It has also been called "quality of

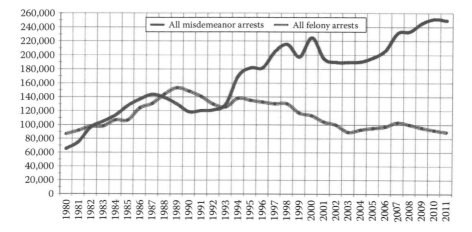

Figure 6.9 Felony arrests and misdemeanor arrests, New York City, 1980–2011.

life policing," "order maintenance policing," and "zero tolerance policing."[32] In all forms it has had the backing of important conservative Republicans, who in New York were centered at the Manhattan Institute, which became a major promoter of misdemeanor-focused policing.[33]

The number of serious crimes reported did drop in the years following Giuliani and Bratton's shift to focusing on petty offenses. But, as a substantial body of research has pointed out, and as even Bratton noted in 1994 when he became police commissioner, this drop in violent and serious crimes had also clearly been happening before Giuliani and Bratton came upon the scene, and it happened in many cities in the United States and in other countries that did not adopt this policy of focusing on petty offenses.[34,35] Indeed, recent scholarship on the striking international character of the crime drop (in Canada, England, Wales, the Netherlands, France, and other countries) makes very clear that no single policing strategy or set of conditions produced the widespread, international crime decline.[36]

In 2013, as this chapter is being finished, it is becoming easier to see that, at least after the first few years, the NYPD's focus on misdemeanor arrests, including the huge number of marijuana possession arrests, was in part, probably in large part, a response to the much broader decline in the number of serious crimes.[37] The numbers of marijuana arrests began to rise because Giuliani and Safir wanted officers to make these arrests, which were consistent with the policies of the war on drugs they both had helped create. But the marijuana arrests became so common and numerous, and have continued in 2013, because they were useful and beneficial to significant constituencies within the police department, including supervisors at all levels and many patrol and narcotics police.

6.5   Usefulness to Police of Marijuana Arrests

To the emphasis on low-level offenses and misdemeanor arrests, New York City added one more critical factor: hundreds of thousands of stop and frisks a year. By 2012, under Michael Bloomberg alone, the NYPD had made 3,300,000 recorded stop and frisks, and an unknown number of unrecorded and unreported ones, perhaps half again as many. By 2012, the stop and frisks had gained national notoriety and the attention of the U.S. Justice Department because of the hard work and advocacy of many civil rights and civil liberties advocates, researchers, journalists, editorial writers, elected officials, attorneys, public defenders, and a number of federal lawsuits.[38]

New York City's stop-and-frisk practices have been subjected to intense and frequent public debate among the groups just mentioned, including respected journalists for the *New York Times*, Associated Press, *New York Daily News*, and many other publications on one side, and Mayor Bloomberg, Police Commissioner Kelly, top commanders at the NYPD, and their defenders including the Manhattan Institute and the editorial pages of the *New York Daily News* and the *New York Post* on the other side.

One thing they all accept is the number of stop and frisks made each year as reported by the NYPD based on forms, called UF-250 forms, which were filled out by individual officers. Since 2004 the NYPD has filed an average of 500,000 UF-250 forms a year, and about half the time the stops led to frisks. In 2011, the huge volume of forms filed led to the mind-boggling fact, announced by the NYCLU, that more young Black men were stopped and searched by police that year than actually lived in New York City.[39]

By now (2013) it has become very clear that the marijuana arrests are a direct by-product of the stop and frisks.[40] Year after year, police officers have filled out forms indicating that they have stopped at least 500,000 people a year, 87% of them Blacks and Latinos, and 10% of them Whites, about the same percentages as are arrested for marijuana possession, and in about the same age groups. The two charts in Figure 6.10 show the stop and frisks and the marijuana arrests from 2004 through 2012. There are many more of the former, but the two lines follow an uncannily parallel trajectory. And both the stop and frisks and the marijuana possession arrests were down the same 22% in 2012.[41]

The New York Police Department is an avowedly top-down paramilitary organization. Individual officers and low-level commanders did not decide on their own to make millions of stop and frisks and hundreds of thousands of marijuana possession arrests. They were ordered to do so, sometimes indirectly, sometimes very directly. Patrol and narcotics police were pressured to make and record stop and frisks, and to make arrests for marijuana

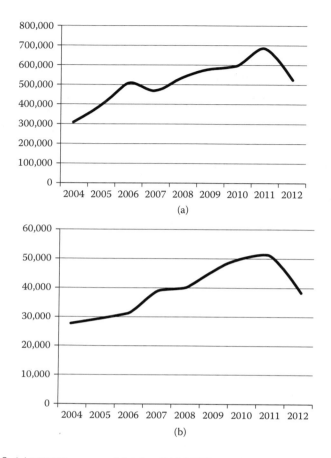

Figure 6.10 (a) NYPD stop and frisks; (b) NYPD marijuana possession arrests.

possession and other minor offenses. They were rewarded for doing so and punished for not doing them enough.

From our research and interviews, we identified several major incentives for narcotics and patrol officers, and for NYPD commanders and supervisors at all levels, to support the policy of making many marijuana arrests. As veteran officers explained, the marijuana possession arrests have served multiple needs and interests of NYPD commanders, and of significant numbers of patrol and narcotics officers.

Many reports[42] have documented that the NYPD uses quotas to achieve its high numbers of stop and frisks, of misdemeanor arrests for marijuana and other minor offenses, and of criminal court summonses (about 600,000 a year) for even lower-level offenses such as holding an unsealed alcohol container, riding a bike on the sidewalk (even slowly on an empty sidewalk in front of one's home), sitting quietly on a park bench in a housing project shortly after sundown, and similar minor offenses. Officers assigned to certain precincts (meaning neighborhoods where most residents are Blacks and Latinos, especially public housing developments and other low-income areas) have been heavily pressured to fill out five or more stop-and-frisk forms a month, issue 20 or so criminal court summonses for quality of life infractions, and make one, two, or three arrests. Officers do not like filling out the stop-and-frisk forms, and many object to needlessly burdening people, especially young and poor people, with criminal court summonses; many of the revelations that police officers have made about quotas have focused on the stop and frisks and the summonses. But unlike the other two duties the NYPD has imposed on officers, making arrests, in particular the marijuana arrests, has apparently not required as much pressure, especially among narcotics police who seem to have taken to the job with relish and gusto.

For narcotics police, for rookie officers who experience the most pressure to meet quotas, and for some patrol police, making the marijuana arrests is not an unpleasant part of the job. Police work can be dangerous. In our interviews, rank-and-file police officers reported that making marijuana arrests is safer and easier than many other forms of police work. Officers are unlikely to get shot or stabbed arresting someone for marijuana. People arrested for possessing marijuana tend to be nonviolent and easy to handle. Furthermore, as one veteran officer put it, marijuana arrestees are "clean," meaning physically clean, not smelly or dirty. This matters because the arresting officer is "married" to the arrestee throughout the booking process, sometimes for many hours. Unlike drunks or heroin junkies, people arrested for possessing marijuana are unlikely to throw up in the back of the squad car. Most people possessing a bit of marijuana, especially ordinary teenagers and young people, tend not to have AIDS, hepatitis, tuberculosis, or even body lice. In effect, making marijuana and other misdemeanor arrests has become a "quality of life" issue, *for the police*. According to some news reports, narcotics officers have resisted efforts to shift them to other duties or even to higher-level anti-drug work, which is often more dangerous and more tedious, and provides less opportunity for overtime.[43]

Marijuana arrests allow police officers to make much-desired overtime pay. Because NYPD pay scales have been at historically low levels, many officers naturally desire overtime work. The main way that patrol officers can generate overtime on their own is by hunting for suspects (especially teenagers and young adults) who may have some sort of "contraband" in their possession and then stopping, frisking, and searching them. The item that men and women of any race or class are most likely to have in their possession that can justify an arrest is a small amount of marijuana. A marijuana arrest (or other low-level misdemeanor arrest) near the end of a shift guarantees an officer several hours of relatively clean, easy overtime, at time-and-a-half pay. This is so much a part of life within the NYPD that, among themselves, officers refer to marijuana and other misdemeanor arrests, especially at the end of a shift, as "collars for dollars." Apparently every police officer in New York City knows the expression; many learn it from others in the first weeks of police academy. In recent years most officers can usually obtain at least 35 hours of overtime a month. Veteran police officers assured us that although this number is nowhere written down, many police and their commanding officers know it and live by it, with even greater overtime opportunities for special circumstances and projects. For many officers, making arrests toward the end of a shift is by far the most common way to obtain this much-desired overtime pay.

One technique that narcotics police use for generating many marijuana arrests of buyers we have termed "net fishing." This occurs when narcotics police stake out a storefront such as a small grocery which is selling five- and ten-dollar bags of marijuana. Instead of raiding the place and closing it down, a narcotics team puts an undercover officer close by to observe. When he sees people who may have bought marijuana coming out of the store, he radios or phones a description of them to fellow officers who have set up their operation a block away. When the suspects reach the next corner they are stopped and told that they have been observed coming out of a "known drug dealing establishment" and must be searched. When the just-purchased marijuana is discovered, the people arrested—usually young Blacks and Latinos—are locked in a van parked nearby, the operation continuing until the van is filled.

Like fishermen who put nets across a river to catch fish swimming downstream, the narcotics team may return a couple of times a week for many months, setting up their "nets" and making arrests. If they bring in a group of arrestees toward the end of a shift, the officers can accumulate substantial overtime. A surprising number of journalists' interviews with people arrested for marijuana possession were of people who had just purchased their marijuana and were stopped and arrested by police a block way. They had been caught in these net-fishing operations.

As with the 500,000 stop-and-frisk forms filled out a year and the 600,000 criminal court summonses the police write a year, the marijuana arrests allow officers to show productivity, which counts for promotions and more desirable assignments and schedules. The marijuana arrests also allow police supervisors to keep much better track of what their officers are doing.

Those of us researching the marijuana arrests have concluded that this police supervising and monitoring function of the stop and frisks, of the criminal court summonses, and of the seemingly pointless arrests for marijuana possession and other minor offenses is a major reason they have continued and why the top police commanders have resisted so fiercely any efforts to give them up or even reduce them. In short, police supervisors from the precinct level to the top commanders benefit from marijuana arrests. The arrests generate records, facilitate supervision of police activities, and allow police supervisors to show that they and their officers are productive.

Perhaps the number one concern of police supervisors at all levels is, "Where are my officers right now and what are they doing?" When officers make many arrests for marijuana possession and other misdemeanors (and make many stop and frisks and write many summonses), they keep busy. As a police lieutenant said, "You don't have to worry that they are goofing off or doing something else." At a time when serious and violent crimes (and therefore arrests) have declined significantly, officers who write up many stop and frisks, write many criminal court summonses, and make arrests for marijuana and other misdemeanors enable supervisors, from the precinct on up, to show that the officers they supervise are not sloughing off and are being productive. In addition, supervisors also accumulate overtime pay when the officers working directly under them do.

For NYPD commanders, police officers whose days are filled making stop and frisks, writing summonses, and making arrests for possession of small amounts of marijuana or other drugs provide much-desired staffing flexibility because these officers can be easily shifted elsewhere when needed. If something big happens—a fire, bombing, watermain break, subway accident, or other emergency, or when the president or other dignitary is in town—these officers can be shifted elsewhere without taking resources from more important patrols and operations. No ongoing investigation or anti-crime operation is affected by temporarily reducing marijuana possession arrests or stop and frisks. This flexibility is so central to ordinary NYPD functioning that, in at least some years, many of the 900 or so uniformed officers on duty during games at Yankee Stadium were plainclothes narcotics police temporarily assigned to uniformed patrol duties (and paid overtime to do so). In a sense, officers making marijuana and other misdemeanor arrests function as a kind of "reserve army" of police to be called upon when needed, which is quite useful for the top brass of the department.

For the NYPD, marijuana arrests provide an easy way to target and acquire information, to institutionalize and routinely surveil young people, particularly people of color. Along with national and other local police agencies, the NYPD seeks to have as many young people as possible "in the system," meaning having them fingerprinted, photographed, eye-scanned, and now increasingly DNA tested. Howard Safir, the police commissioner from 1996 to 2000, regarded collecting information as a critical police task and became one of the most prominent national advocates for collecting what he termed "DNA fingerprints." Similarly, Mayor Bloomberg and Police Commissioner Kelly have been enthusiastic supporters of expanding criminal databases to include many ordinary Americans.

Marijuana arrests are the best and easiest way currently available to acquire actual fingerprints, photos, and other data on young people, especially Black and Latino youth, who have not previously been entered into the criminal justice databases. There is nothing else the police can do to put as many new people "into the system," and to update information on those already entered, as the wide net of marijuana possession and other misdemeanor arrests.

A researcher who worked every day for nearly a year interviewing arrestees in the criminal court detention cells of one borough told us of one guard's daily talk to the people arrested for marijuana possession and other petty offenses. In a speech delivered every day for years, the guard dramatically told the tired, hungry, misdemeanor arrestees under his watch that everyone else had lied to them about why they were arrested, but that he would tell them the truth. The truth, he said, was they were arrested for their fingerprints and photos. We think that he correctly reported one source of support for the arrests among some commanders within the upper echelons of the NYPD, including Commissioners Safir and Kelly.

There is one other essential service that the marijuana arrests and the stop and frisks provide for NYPD commanders: training rookie officers. There is perhaps no occupation or profession where the gap between what new hires learn in their training programs and what they actually do on the job is greater than in police work. In the police academy the trainees learn what the laws and regulations are, ways to defend themselves, and other essential knowledge. In their months and years on the street they learn a whole different curriculum: how policing works in the real world. For police commanders, rookie police fresh out of the academy are a management nightmare. They are inexperienced, untested, and many come from suburban, exurban, and even rural areas with little or no previous contact with Blacks, Latinos, or big city life. Every big-city police department has to figure out how to manage that transition.

In New York City as in other American cities, police commanders have settled on a convenient solution: assign new officers mainly to foot patrols in low-income Black and Latino neighborhoods (also called "high-crime" areas), and assign them to write many summonses, do many stop and frisks, and make arrests for petty offenses, especially involving teenagers. This accomplishes several things at once. It gets the new officers out on the street, seeing what goes on, and stopping and talking to many young people their own age. Some officers first have to learn to understand the dialects, accents, and slang to even communicate. It also focuses the young officers' attention and efforts on teenagers and ordinary young people who are less likely to be dangerous or even physically threatening. This work further emphasizes communication skills and basic tasks such as filling out summonses or stop-and-frisk forms, or writing up arrest reports. In stopping people to question them, and in writing summonses and filling out stop-and-frisk forms, the

new police get used to routinely using their brains, words, and pens for policing, and not their guns.

If, in the course of frisking and searching people, the rookie officers
find some marijuana or, less commonly, some other contraband, they make
arrests, again usually of less dangerous, easily intimidated young people,
many of whom have never been arrested for anything. The officers gain valuable experience putting on handcuffs; bringing their arrestees back to the
police station; taking the fingerprints, photographs, and eye scans; writing up
the police reports; sending the records to be checked against the FBI's databases; and often accompanying the arrestees to the courthouse and sometimes even waiting until they appear in court. They also often have to speak
with commanders, prosecutors, and other criminal justice personnel. If an
officer screws up the paperwork or fingerprints in the course of making one
of these marijuana possession arrests, there is no harm done, because nobody
really cares about these marijuana arrests anyway. And even the rookies get
overtime pay so they have an incentive to make these misdemeanor arrests
and, ideally, not mess them up. If brand new officers do this kind of work
all day every day for six months or a year, by the end of the process they are
well on their way to becoming functioning police. Some will wash out in this
process, some will excel, and all will learn much that needs to be understood.

For the police department and the mayor this is, indeed, an effective way
to train young officers. Many police departments do this kind of thing quietly and in a limited way, but the NYPD proudly trumpets and promotes
this not as training (they never mention that) but instead promote it as a
genuine "crime-fighting" innovation under the slogan, "Operation Impact."
The Manhattan Institute even gave Police Commissioner Kelly an award for
Operation Impact. The only real downside to this, of course, is that this training program for new police subjects hundreds of thousands of young people
from low-income neighborhoods, primarily Black and Latino young men, to
the repeated indignity of the stop and frisks, and to the expensive and time-
consuming criminal court summonses they receive. And the really unfortunate young people whom the rookies capture and charge with marijuana
possession and other minor misdemeanors get to experience the traumatic
ordeal of a criminal arrest, a scary night in the dungeons of New York City,
and a life-time criminal record.

The NYPD, the mayor, and the great many middle-class New Yorkers
who have no idea this goes on benefit from having experienced, trained, and
professional police. The suburban police departments, which make many of
their hires from the NYPD, also gain. The cost of this on-the-street training
is borne by the people of the neighborhoods where Operation Impact and
similar policies are carried out, especially by the least powerful people in the
city, Black and Latino teenagers and young people, especially young men.[44]

6.6   What Happens Now?

When we first published a long report about the marijuana arrest crusade and the stop and frisks in 2008, we ended a section like the one above with a question: "Is this what the people of New York City want their police to be doing?" The answer only five years later from many New Yorkers has been a resounding "No!"

As this is being written in the summer of 2013, it is fair to say that a broad-based and unprecedented movement to reform the NYPD is growing and thriving. No single organization leads this movement; there are no celebrity or charismatic leaders, although a few members of the New York City Council have become strong advocates for the basic principles of openness, fairness, democracy, and an end to biased and discriminatory policies and practices. A loosely organized alliance of 26 member organizations, and 35 supporting organizations, has come together under the name Communities United For Police Reform (CPR). Its website describes it well:

> Communities United for Police Reform (CPR) is an unprecedented campaign to end discriminatory policing practices in New York, bringing together a movement of community members, lawyers, researchers and activists to work for change. The partners in this campaign come from all 5 boroughs, from all walks of life and represent many of those most unfairly targeted by the NYPD. This groundbreaking campaign is fighting for reforms that will promote community safety while ensuring that the NYPD protects and serves all New Yorkers. We are a movement that is here to stay—a Campaign that will be a visible, lasting presence on the streets of neighborhoods citywide. We will be in communities and on the streets, educating people about their rights; and in the courts and on the steps of City Hall and the state capitol, demanding change to the NYPD—until these policies end. For general information about the campaign, please sign-up for campaign news and updates. For press inquiries, please email press@changethenypd.org.[45]

Currently at least half a dozen lawsuits against the NYPD and New York City for its policing practices are working their way through the federal courts. Suits have been filed independently and sometimes in partnership by the Center for Constitutional Rights, the New York Civil Liberties Union, the Legal Aid Society Special Litigation Unit, the Bronx Defenders, the NAACP Legal Defense Fund, and some private attorneys. Pro bono attorneys and legal staff from some of the city's top private and corporate law firms have assisted in the work. The suits have targeted stop and frisks, marijuana arrests, trespassing arrests in public housing and private buildings, illegal searches, the criminal court summons system, the surveillance of Islamic student organizations, the NYPD's police training materials and programs, and more.

A series of bills to rein in the NYPD and change its policies, collectively entitled The Community Safety Act and drafted by Communities United for Police Reform, has been introduced in the New York City Council and two of the bills were passed by the Council on June 27, 2013. Although Mayor Bloomberg vowed to veto them, both passed by veto-proof majorities. One bans "bias-based" policing and gives victims a "private right of action" to vindicate their rights.[46] The other, entitled The NYPD Oversight Act, assigns responsibility for NYPD oversight to the commissioner of the department of investigation. (In New York City, the DOI currently oversees about 300 city agencies, including the Fire Department, Department of Education, and Human Resources Administration, but not the NYPD.)[47]

Governor Cuomo has committed himself to passing statewide marijuana reform legislation to stop the NYPD's marijuana arrests. It seems certain that in the next few years other police and criminal justice reform legislation will be introduced in both the state legislature and the city council. For example, recently the quite staid and respectable New York state senator from the upper east side of Manhattan, the wealthiest district in the city, announced her intention to recruit others in the legislature to join her in sponsoring a bill to flat out legalize marijuana possession and use in New York state. A news story about Senator Liz Krueger illustrates the kind of broad support for these reform efforts that are arising from diverse constituencies:

Why is Krueger carrying the standard for marijuana legalization, anyway? A White, 55-year-old woman representing an Upper East Side district in which arrests for marijuana aren't exactly a monumental issue, and who says she last smoked weed at a Cheech and Chong movie in 1977, would seem to be an odd champion for the case. But Krueger says those things are precisely what make her the right person to get it done, or to try....

"I have a very White, upper-middle-class district," she continued. "The kids of my constituents are not getting busted, and if they get busted, they have really good lawyers and they're not ending up with criminal records."

And yet, she said, "I saw the pain and suffering that our current laws were inflicting, disproportionately on young, poor people. I saw the amount of money we were spending in the criminal justice system unnecessarily. And I can come up with endless better ways to spend that money. I saw young people having their lives ruined before they ever got out of high school, because they ended up with the kind of criminal record that wouldn't let them get college tuition assistance, or scholarships, or be eligible to apply for certain kinds of jobs.

"If you have a marijuana bust, you can never go to work as a policeman, or fireman or a sanitation worker. Like, seriously?"[48]

Like this article about Liz Krueger, columnists, reporters, editorial pages, newspapers, magazines, video, television and radio news, and many, many websites have risen to the challenge and provided an extraordinarily rich array of writing, reporting, and images about the harm that the NYPD and New York's larger criminal justice system has been doing, especially to its most vulnerable people. A number of NYPD officers have come forward to tell what they know. Some uniformed officers have surreptitiously recorded their commanders ordering them to write more criminal court summonses, do more stop and frisks, and make more arrests. Reporters have transcribed these recordings and posted segments of the recordings on the website of the *Village Voice* and other publications.[49]

Two columnists for the *New York Times* have written brilliantly about marijuana arrests and other NYPD practices, and the *New York Times* editorial page has been alive with strong writing about stop and frisks, illegal searches, the failures of broken-windows policing, police unnecessarily harassing and arresting people in public housing developments and private buildings, the huge virtually unknown summons court system, and more.[50] Social science, public health, urban studies, social welfare, and law professors have written, spoken, and contributed research, which in turn has been picked up and reported by the increasingly knowledgeable and informed journalists in the news media and on the Web.[51]

In effect, many New Yorkers have been going through a remarkably smart, informed, detailed, public education program about their police department and criminal justice system. And things once learned are not forgotten but built upon. To repeat: this movement is growing and thriving.

And this is happening in New York City, the biggest city in America, a world city, and a world media center. So what happens in New York City definitely does not stay in New York City. There is even a sense among some advocates that New Yorkers have a special responsibility in police reform because this is where two mayors and a number of other prominent individuals played major roles in promoting and spreading the gospel of broken-windows policing and its intense focus on the policing of minor offenses, overwhelmingly among people from low-income families and neighborhoods, young people, and people from racial and ethnic minorities.

Although the problems and crises of policing in New York City are extreme, they are not unusual. Many cities in the United States engage in the same or similar practices with the same results: the targeting of only some people for stop and frisks, criminal court summonses, and arrests for minor offenses including marijuana possession. In our age of cable news, e-mail, podcasts, YouTube, social media, and the instant availability on the Internet of many recorded radio and television broadcasts, it is not difficult for people in other cities to also learn about policing and criminal justice reform from what is happening in New York.

This lesson has not been lost on the leadership of large, national civil rights and civil liberties organizations. Benjamin Jealous, the young, active executive director of the national NAACP, has spoken out repeatedly about the blatant racial bias in the NYPD's stop and frisks and steered the NAACP to issue a strong condemnation of the entire war on drugs. And on June 4, 2013, the American Civil Liberties Union released a 190-page report about the severe racial bias in marijuana arrests in every one of the 50 states and in hundreds of U.S. cities and counties. The ACLU's report, "The War on Marijuana in Black and White," explicitly drew from the data, arguments, and analysis exposing the NYPD's marijuana arrest crusade. The ACLU report also argues that the only real way to fix the scandalously disproportionate arrests of young Blacks throughout the United States is to completely legalize the possession, use, and sale of marijuana for adults 21 and older. This report has already generated much news and a number of proposals including a federal investigation of race and marijuana policing.[52]

Finally, it is important to note that in November of 2012 voters in Colorado and Washington State approved by significant margins ballot measures to legalize completely the possession, use, and sale of marijuana. Almost immediately police and prosecutors in both states stopped arresting and charging adults for marijuana possession offenses, and they even dismissed charges against people arrested before the election explaining that the voters had sent a clear message. In both states marijuana legalization passed with 55 to 45% of the vote, and in Colorado marijuana legalization received more votes than Barack Obama did for president. Although it was unclear for many months whether the federal government would allow the legal production and sale provisions of both measures to go into effect, it seems increasingly likely that both states will indeed be allowed to create systems for legal production and sale of marijuana products. It is difficult to express fully what a profound and history-making change Colorado's and Washington's ballot measures have introduced and begun.

The main opposition to marijuana reform thus far, and likely in the coming years, is law enforcement: police, sheriffs, and prosecutors. But in the long run they are going to lose. And as has happened in New York City since 2008, when people in many states, cities, and counties learn how the police and prosecutors across America have been manufacturing 700,000 racially biased marijuana possession arrests a year, they will also learn lessons about more general police and prosecutor practices.

Marijuana possession arrests and marijuana policing policy make a uniquely effective cutting-edge issue for police reform for a number of reasons. But one of the most important reasons is that marijuana use is the one "crime" for which there is very good, reliable, and long-standing data about who has been breaking the law by committing this crime. Many years of government studies have found that adult Whites and Blacks of all ages use marijuana at about equal rates, and that White teenagers and young adults age 18 to 25 use marijuana at higher rates than do young Blacks and Latinos. But as the new ACLU study has documented in stunning detail, Blacks everywhere are arrested for marijuana possession at much higher rates than Whites. And this severe racial disparity is not the result of some prejudiced officers, or "bad apples," or a lack of training. Rather, it is the result of where and how police commanders routinely deploy their officers.

It is not hard for many people to understand that this racist pattern of policing is not unique to marijuana arrests. Rather, more and more people find it easy to see that the marijuana arrests are so racially skewed because so much other policing is racially skewed or biased. And as events in New York and elsewhere show, a movement to change that—a new kind of civil rights and civil liberties movement focused on the criminal justice system—is being born all around us.

Endnotes

1. According to New York State Penal Laws 221.05 and 221.10, possession of a small amount of marijuana is not a crime, not a misdemeanor, as long as the marijuana is not "burning or open to public view." Beginning in 1996 and 1997, the NYPD began to make these arrests by claiming that the marijuana they extracted from someone's pockets or belongings was "in public view." Numerous news stories (some cited in this chapter) and a study by the Bronx Defenders have documented that, during a police stop, marijuana in a pocket has frequently turned into an arrest and prosecution for "marijuana in public view."

   Police Commissioner Raymond Kelly implicitly acknowledged in his Operations Order in September 2011 that police officers "direct" or "compel" suspects to empty their pockets and then charge them with marijuana in public view. Governor Cuomo has also described this process in his press conference in June 2012 and in his State of the State address and report in January 2013. A pdf copy of Kelly's order is at http://marijuana-arrests.com/docs/NYPD-ORDER-RE-MARIJUANA-ARRESTS-SEPT-19-2011.pdf. For news stories about Kelly's order and marijuana arrests immediately following the news about his order, see http://marijuana-arrests.com/breaking-news.html. For Cuomo's address remarks and written State of the State text linking the stop and frisks with the "out of the pocket" marijuana arrests see http://marijuana-arrests.com/docs/Gov-Cuomo-on-marijuana-arrests-Jan-9-2012.pdf

   No day in court: Marijuana possession cases and the failure of the Bronx criminal courts, The Bronx Defenders, New York, April 2013. http://www.bronxdefenders.org/wp-content/uploads/2013/05/No-Day-in-Court-A-Report-by-The-Bronx-Defenders-May-2013.pdf

   In addition to much press coverage, New York City's marijuana arrests have generated at least one law journal article about the entrapment issues raised by the arrests. See Ari Rosmarin, The phantom defense: The unavailability of the entrapment defense in New York City "plain view" marijuana arrests, *Journal of Law & Policy*, 21, 1, October 2012.

2. The enforcement, penalties, and collateral or "embedded" consequences of decriminalized marijuana possession are no bed of roses, but they *can be* substantially less harmful than the full-on, heavy-handed form of punitive criminalized enforcement that New York City has adopted. However, failure to appear in court at the required time in response to a violation summons (an innocuous looking "pink ticket") automatically results in an arrest warrant, and then a full handcuffs-and-criminal-record arrest when a routine police stop, including a traffic stop, reveals the outstanding warrant. In New York (and other cities) these arrest warrants for summonses never expire and can lead to an arrest years or even a decade later.

3. About 30% of everyone arrested for marijuana possession had never been arrested before for anything; another 40% had never been convicted or pled guilty to anything, not even a misdemeanor. In other words, 70% of everyone arrested had never been convicted of any crime whatsoever. Another 11% of those arrested for marijuana possession had a previous conviction for a misdemeanor. Only 19% of the people arrested for marijuana possession had been previously convicted of a felony, mostly a low-level felony for nonviolent drug offenses such as selling small amounts of marijuana. All data are from the New York State Division of Criminal Justice Services.

4. See the excellent report from Human Rights Watch, *A red herring: Marijuana arrestees do not become violent felons*, New York, November 2012.

[According to Human Rights Watch] people who enter the criminal justice system with an arrest for public possession of marijuana rarely commit violent crimes in the future. Over the last 15 years, NYC police have arrested more than 500,000 people, most of them young Blacks or Hispanics, on misdemeanor charges of possessing small amounts of marijuana in public view. Although Mayor Michael Bloomberg and the police have said the arrests have helped reduce violent crime, they have never specified how.

"Our findings support those of other researchers who question the public safety gains from massive marijuana arrests," said Jamie Fellner, senior adviser to the U.S. Program at Human Rights Watch and coauthor of the report. "Public officials need to explain exactly how placing thousands of people in cuffs each year for possessing pot reduces violent crime."

Using data provided by the New York Department of Criminal Justice Services, Human Rights Watch tracked until mid-2011 the subsequent criminal records of nearly 30,000 people who had no prior convictions when they were arrested for marijuana possession in public view in 2003 and 2004. Of the group 90% had no subsequent felony convictions. Only 3.1% were subsequently convicted of one violent felony offense. An additional 0.4% had two or more violent felony convictions. See http://www.hrw.org/news/2012/11/23/usnew-york-few-arrested-pot-become-violent-criminals

5. See Figure 6.4 showing the marijuana use rates of young Whites, Blacks, and Latinos; it is also at http://marijuana-arrests.com/graph9-use.html

6. The racial disparities in New York City's marijuana arrests have been the focus of our work. For various reports, graphs, tables, and other material showing the racial disparities over many years see http://marijuana-arrests.com/

7. The initial work on this marijuana arrest research project was by Harry G. Levine and Deborah Peterson Small, a civil rights attorney and advocate. Since 2009 the project has been directed by Harry Levine and Loren Siegel, an attorney who for many years was director of public education for the American Civil Liberties Union. It has also been helped immeasurably by Troy Duster, Ira Glasser, Craig Reinarman, Jesse Levine, and staff at the Drug Policy Alliance, especially Gabriel Sayegh and Tony Newman, and at the NYCLU, especially Donna Lieberman and Robert Perry.

8. Excerpts, full information, and links to newspapers, magazines, Associated Press, and other news sources can be found at marijuana-arrests.com at http://marijuana-arrests.com/NYC-pot-arrests-journalism.html

9. As this chapter was being finished in the summer of 2013, the second attempt at changing slightly New York State law in order to stop or reduce the NYPD's marijuana possession arrests failed, despite the support of the governor, the state assembly, and many others including the editorial boards of the *New York Times* and the *New York Daily News*.

10. We have described and documented our findings in a series of reports and testimony, which have then been reported in news articles and editorials. See *Marijuana Arrest Crusade: Racial Bias and Police Policy in New York City*, by Harry G. Levine and Deborah Small, New York: New York Civil Liberties Union, 2008 and number of other reports available at http://marijuana-arrests.com/nyc-pot-arrest-docs.html

In this chapter we have not tried to describe the serious, harmful collateral and embedded consequences of the arrests and criminal records for marijuana possession and other minor offenses, but that has been an important part of almost everything else we have written about the marijuana arrests. See our various reports and testimony on our website given in the last note above. Also see the specific web page with excerpts from and links to articles about the collateral consequences of misdemeanor arrests at http://marijuana-arrests.com/consequences-of-arrest.html. For the essential scholarly discussion of the harmful consequences of the Giuliani and Bloomberg–era focus on the heavy policing of minor offenses see K. Babe Howell, Broken lives from broken windows: The hidden costs of aggressive order-maintenance policing," *New York University Review of Law & Social Change*, 33, p. 271, 2009.

11. All data about the marijuana possession arrests in New York City are from the New York State Division of Criminal Justice Services, Albany, New York. Sources for the marijuana use data are

U.S. Dept HHS, SAMHSA, Office of Applied Studies, National Survey on Drug Use and Health, 2002–2010.

2003–2005: Table 1.80B Marijuana Use in Lifetime, Past Year, and Past Month among Persons Aged 18 to 25, by Racial/Ethnic Subgroups Annual Averages Based on 2002–2003 and 2004–2005. http://www.oas.samhsa.gov/NSDUH/2k5NSDUH/tabs/Sect1peTabs67to132.htm#Tab1.80B

2006–2010: Table 1.26B—Marijuana Use in Lifetime, Past Year, & Past Month among Persons Aged 18 to 25,

2006–2007: http://www.oas.samhsa.gov/NSDUH/2k7NSDUH/tabs/Sect1peTabs1to46.htm#Tab1.26B

2008–2009: http://www.oas.samhsa.gov/NSDUH/2k9NSDUH/tabs/ Sect1peTabs1to46.htm#Tab1.26B

2009–2010: http://www.samhsa.gov/data/nsduh/2k10NSDUH/tabs/ Sect1peTabs1to46.htm#Tab1.26B

12. Jim Dwyer, Whites smoke pot, but Blacks are arrested. *New York Times*, Dec. 22, 2009.

13. Asians and "all others" (meaning not Whites, Latinos, or Blacks) constitute about 3% of the NYPD's marijuana arrests. See the table at http://marijuana-arrests.com/graph8.html

14. Giuliani fired Bratton after two years as police commissioner, not because Bratton failed, but, as is widely acknowledged, because he received too much public and media attention. See, for example, The NYPD chief who did his job too well, by Michael Duffy and Massimo Calabresi, *Time Magazine*, Nov. 15, 2007; Analyzing Rudy's Bratton behavior, by Leonard Levitt, *NYPD Confidential*, October 2000, http://nypdconfidential.com/columns/2000/001002.html

15. Although Bill Bratton is the police chief and commissioner most identified with broken-windows policing, he did not emphasize making marijuana arrests in New York, nor in his seven years as police chief in Los Angeles from 2002 through 2009. Furthermore, academic and think tank explanations and defenses of broken-windows policing have not emphasized marijuana possession arrests, especially not those as in New York City where police are commonly finding the bit of marijuana buried deep in someone's clothes or possessions.

16. For information about Howard Safir see, for example, The commish bites back: Howard Safir explains his life to his critics, by Josh Benson, *New York Observer*, May 17, 1999; Safir plans to add 400 detectives to narcotics units, *New York Times*, August 7, 1997; He still gets no respect, by Leonard Levitt and Howard Safir, *NYPD Confidential*, December 10, 2007; Minority men: We are frisk targets. *News* poll finds 81 of 100 have been stopped by cops, by Leslie Casimir, Austin Fenner, and Patrice O'Shaughnessy, *New York Daily News*, March 26, 1999. The numbers of narcotics officers each year from 1980 to the present is not available. However, veteran police officers who were on the force in the 1990s and early 2000s have said that under Safir the number of narcotics officers increased substantially.

17. Jennifer Peltz, Pot arrests top 50K in 2011 despite NYPD order, *Associated Press*, Feb 1, 2012 (over a hundred papers across the United States carried this AP story), http://news.yahoo.com/pot-arrests-top-50k-2011-despite-nypd-order-182052393.html

18. Steven Wishnia, Hypocritical NYPD continues racist pot arrest crusade, *Alternet*, Dec 30, 2011, http://www.alternet.org/module/printversion/153617

19. Ailsa Chang, Alleged illegal searches by NYPD may be increasing marijuana arrests, *WNYC*, April 26, 2011 (excellent 10-minute radio show plus text), http://www.wnyc.org/articles/wnyc-news/2011/apr/26/marijuana-arrests/ Also Ailsa Chang, Alleged illegal searches by NYPD rarely challenged in marijuana cases, *WNYC*, April 27, 2011 (excellent 8-minute radio show plus text), http://www.wnyc.org/articles/wnyc-news/2011/apr/27/alleged-illegal-searches/

20. Also see Kristen Gwynne, How "stop and frisk" is too often a sexual assault by cops on teenagers in targeted NYC neighborhoods, *Alternet*, January 21, 2013, http://www.alternet.org/print/civil-liberties/how-stop-and-frisk-too-often-sexual-assault-cops-teenagers-targeted-nyc. Gwynne writes:

> I've reported on stop and frisk for two years, and in that time I've talked to young men who have experienced stop and frisk, and the stories they tell are harrowing. A Black teenager in Bedford-Stuyvesant described how embarrassed he was to have "old ladies" watch as his pants landed around his ankles while police searched him. A 17-year-old in the Bronx explained that police, "They go in my pants. You're not supposed to go in my pants." Being touched by a female police officer can be especially upsetting for adolescent males. "It's annoying because it doesn't matter what kind of cop it is, female or male, they're gonna frisk you. If you say something to the female about it, the female says something to you like 'What? I can do what I want.' And they still frisk you. You can't say sexual harassment, nothing," 18-year-old South Bronx resident Garnell told me last year, adding, "And they go hard, grabbing stuff they're not supposed to."
>
> A New York attorney told me last year he has video of a cop saying he just "credit card-swiped" a man's ass—without gloves, naturally. What kind of gun can fit between two butt cheeks? And why are cops touching penises, anyway? The answer is simple: They're not looking for guns, but hoping to make arrests. While stop and frisk is only legally allowed for the purpose of uncovering weapons, it has been linked to far more low-level summonses and pot busts than guns. As 18-year-old Lower East Side resident "Twin" recently told me, "They run their hands down your ass crack because they think you're hiding drugs there." In the public housing on Baruch Street, he says police hang out until they see someone "suspicious" enough to grope.
>
> One of our marijuana arrest research project researchers witnessed a conversation between a Latino teenager who had been arrested for marijuana possession and his attorney. The young man explained that he handed over his bit of marijuana when the police officer started to reach inside his pants. The young man got upset and visibly angry just telling what happened; he said he did not want the cop grabbing his genitals.

21. Ira Glasser, Executive Director of the American Civil Liberties Union for 23 years, is the author of numerous works on the Constitution including *Visions of Liberty: The Bill of Rights for All Americans* (New York, 1991). The quotes are from a pamphlet written in direct response to the NYPD stop and frisks and marijuana arrests: *Stop, Question and Frisk: What the Law Says About Your Rights* (Drug Policy Alliance, 2011), http://www.drugpolicy.org/resource/stop-question-and-frisk-what-law-says-about-your-rights

22. New York Police Department Operations Order: Charging Standards for Possession of Marihuana in a Public Place Open to Public View by Direction of the Police Commissioner, September 19, 2011. A pdf copy of Kelly's order is at http://marijuana-arrests.com/docs/NYPD-ORDER-RE-MARIJUANA-ARRESTS-SEPT-19-2011.pdf. For news stories about Kelly's order and marijuana arrests immediately following the news about his order, see http://marijuana-arrests.com/breaking-news.html

23. For a critical but neglected source of rich descriptions about how NYPD narcotics police routinely made illegal searches and arrests in the 1980s and early 1990s, see Chapter 4, "Perjury and falsifying documents," *The City of New York Commission to Investigate Allegations of Police Corruption and the Anti-Corruption Procedures of the Police Department, Commission Report,* July 1994 (pp. 36–43). This is the report of the "Mollen Commission," appointed by Mayor Dinkins to investigate police corruption. Although much of the report focuses on gangs of police who robbed drug dealers, one chapter focuses on the most common and routine form of corruption which the Commission termed "perjury and falsifying." We have excerpted and posted on our website parts of that chapter describing the routine illegality that occurred when narcotics police sought to make drug arrests on the street. For those unfamiliar with its findings, or who wish to understand what narcotics policing has historically meant in New York City, it is an eye-opening work, available at http://marijuana-arrests.com/docs/Mollen-Excerpts-Falsification.pdf

24. There is a type of narcotics squad, based in police precincts, that may make many of the marijuana possession arrests. The squads are called Street Narcotics Enforcement Units, or SNEU (pronounced Snew). A SNEU team officer was responsible for the shooting death of Ramarley Graham in the Bronx in February 2012. Police believed the teenager had a gun, but he had only a bit of marijuana. According to the *New York Times*, about half of the police precincts in the city have SNEU teams. The *Times* reporter was unable to obtain from the police or the DA's office a list of the police precincts, but we hypothesize that they are likely many or most of the precincts that have high levels of marijuana arrests. In nearly all of these precincts the majority of the population is Black and Latino. For maps showing the 75 neighborhood police precincts by race and by marijuana arrests see http://marijuana-arrests.com/maps-NYC-pot-arrests-race.html

25. In 2012, *New York Times* columnist Jim Dwyer listed the three on-the-record quotes he was able to obtain from Bloomberg administration representatives defending the marijuana arrests by asserting they reduced crime. Each defense was one sentence or shorter. Wrote Dwyer:

> In 2008, a police spokesman, Paul J. Browne … accused the New York Civil Liberties Union, which had issued a report on the subject [of marijuana arrests], of smearing the department while acting as a front for a marijuana-legalization group. Taking care of little crimes, including pot possession, "helped drive crime down," Mr. Browne said.
>
> In 2009, John Feinblatt, a mayoral aide, said, "This continued focus on low-level offending has been part of the city's effective crime-reduction strategy, which has resulted in a 35 percent decrease in crime since 2001."
>
> Last year, another aide, Frank Barry, said, "Marijuana arrests can be an effective tool for suppressing the expansion of street-level drug markets and the corresponding violence."

That is all they have said. No evidence, no research, no studies, just one sentence claims, kind of like the advertising claims of health products. See Jim Dwyer, Altering a law the police use prolifically, *New York Times*, June 5, 2012.

26. The cost of the marijuana arrests is discussed in $75 Million a Year: The Cost of New York City's Marijuana Possession Arrests, by Harry G. Levine and Loren Siegel, New York: Drug Policy Alliance, March 2011. http://marijuana-arrests. com/docs/75-Million-A-Year.pdf. Also see One Million Police Hours: Making 440,000 Marijuana Possession Arrests in New York City, 2002–2012, by Harry Levine, Loren Siegel, and Gabriel Sayegh, New York: Marijuana Arrest Research Project and Drug Policy Alliance, March 2013. http://www.drugpolicy.org/ sites/default/files/One_Million_Police_Hours.pdf

27. Bernard E. Harcourt and Jens Ludwig, Reefer madness: Broken windows policing and misdemeanor marijuana arrests in New York City, 1989–2000, Criminology and Public Policy, 6:1, pp. 165–182, 2007. Available at http://papers. ssrn.com/sol3/papers.cfm?abstract_id=948753

28. The comprehensive work on the crime decline is Alfred Blumstein and Joel Wallman, The Crime Drop in America, revised edition, New York: Cambridge University Press, 2006. Also see Jeremy Travis and Michelle Waul, Reflections on the Crime Decline: Lessons for the Future? Washington, DC: Urban Institute Justice Policy Center, August 2002; Franklin E. Zimring, The Great American Crime Decline, New York: Oxford University Press, 2007; Leonard A. Marowitz, Why Did the Crime Rate Decrease Through 1999? (And Why Might It Decrease or Increase in 2000 and Beyond?) A Literature Review and Critical Analysis, California Department of Justice, Division of Criminal Justice Information Services, December 2000; Claude Fischer, A Crime Puzzle: Violent Crime Declines in America, Berkeley Blog, UC Berkeley, June 2010. http://blogs.berkeley. edu/2010/06/16/a-crime-puzzle-violent-crime-declines-in-america/

In September 2011, John Jay College, CUNY, hosted a two-day conference on the crime decline. Among the papers presented and distributed was one by Eric Baumer and Kevin T. Wolff which presented numerous graphs comparing rates for a range of crimes for 76 large U.S. cities from 1980 to 2010. There was a widespread drop in property and violent crimes beginning in the early to mid-1990s and continuing until 2007. Baumer and Wolff's paper is at http://www.jjay.cuny. edu/Baumer_Wolff.pdf. All the conference papers and many video presentations are at http://www.jjay.cuny.edu/academics/4893.php. For an examination of the crime decline internationally, see note 36 below.

29. Some NYPD insiders and deeply knowledgeable students of the department have also produced strong evidence showing that the drop in serious crimes, especially in the 2000s, has been partly manufactured by what the HBO series The Wire called "juking the stats." The enormous pressure to keep the "crime numbers down" has led precinct commanders and others to the wholesale downgrading of felonies to misdemeanors, recording robberies as "lost property," making it difficult for crime victims to file crime reports, and other methods of keeping serious crimes off the books. See John A. Eterno and Eli B. Silverman, The Crime Numbers Game: Management by Manipulation, Boca Raton, FL: CRC Press, 2012; Eli B. Silverman, John A. Eterno, and Jesse Levine, Manufacturing low crime rates at the NYPD: Reputation versus safety under Bloomberg and Kelly, Huffington Post, August 13, 2012; John A. Eterno, Policing by the numbers, New York Times Op-ed, June 17, 2012.

Some of Eterno and Silverman's findings have been confirmed in a special report to the NYPD released in July 2013. See Thomas Tracy, Crime review finds NYPD downgrades hundreds of felonies: The Crime Reporting Review Committee found that the NYPD downgraded hundreds of felony robberies, assaults and grand larcenies to misdemeanors each year, *New York Daily News*, July 3, 2013; Joseph Goldstein, Audit of city crime statistics finds mistakes by police, *New York Times*, July 2, 2013; Christopher Robbins, Here's why the NYPD changes your stolen property to "lost property," *Gothamist*, July 3, 2013.

30. A number of things that Giuliani and Bratton did were just clever or even brilliant public relations moves. The very public war on "squeegee men," for example, which Giuliani had promised in 2003 in his campaign for mayor, was not about reducing crime. But the squeegee men, who appeared at busy intersections, especially those entering and exiting bridges and tunnels, deeply irritated middle-class commuters and drivers. And getting rid of them produced a visible and much appreciated sign of change. If *that* is what broken windows policing meant, then many middle-class New Yorkers and commuters from the suburbs in New Jersey, Long Island, Westchester, and Connecticut were for it. For contrasting views of Giuliani and his "style," see Wayne Barrett, Giuliani's legacy: Taking credit for things he didn't do, *Gotham Gazette*, 2008, http://www.gothamgazette.com/commentary/91.barrett.shtml; John Tierney, Giuliani's legacy: A change in the way New Yorkers think about crime, welfare, quality of life, squeegee men, *Gotham Gazette*, 2008, http://www.gothamgazette.com/commentary/91.tierney.shtml

31. The rise in misdemeanor arrests is much greater than the decline in felony arrests. This is partly or even largely because felony arrests usually involve an investigation to find a perpetrator and are often labor intensive and time consuming. Misdemeanor arrests, however, are quick: the perpetrator is caught in the act of panhandling, possessing marijuana in a pocket, not paying the subway fare, or being somehow "disorderly."

32. The rivalry and feud between Bratton and Kelly dates back to at least 1990 to 1992, when Kelly was police commissioner under Mayor Dinkins and Bratton was chief of the transit police, and continues to this day. Bratton and his colleagues and supporters strongly dislike the term "zero tolerance policing" and argue that is what Safir, Kerik, and Kelly have done. The Brattonists say that only they did "true" broken-windows policing. Nonetheless, the term has been commonly used to describe the policies under all three NYPD police commissioners and both mayors. See, for example, Bratton's chapter "Crime is down in New York City: Blame the police," in Norman Dennis (Ed.), *Zero Tolerance: Policing a Free Society*, enlarged and revised second edition, London: IEA Health and Welfare Unit, 1997.

33. Not surprisingly, the very powerful real estate interests in New York City have strongly backed Giuliani and Bloomberg's policing focus on misdemeanor arrests and petty offenses. There is no doubt that this policy has made life significantly more difficult and shaky for low-income people, made it harder for people to get and keep apartments and jobs, stay in school, or even in public housing. This had had the effect of "churning" the residents of low-income

neighborhoods, and allowing developers to renovate and build in convenient low-income neighborhoods abutting more middle-class or even wealthy areas. Significant swathes in Manhattan, Brooklyn, and now the Bronx have become "developed" in this way. It may be that part of the "crime decline" in New York is that some especially troublesome and troubled people and families moved away, becoming the problems of Newark, Yonkers, Bridgeport, and dozens of other cities, including even Southern cities. *New York Times* "Numbers" columnist Charles Blow suggests this in Escape from New York, *New York Times*, March 18, 2011.

34. In January 1994, at the time of his swearing-in as police commissioner, Bratton noted that the crime rate in New York City had been going down for years. As the *New York Times* reported: "Mr. Bratton acknowledged that crime had dropped during the tenure of his predecessor, Raymond W. Kelly," in George James, Bratton urges a shared covenant of reverence for law, *New York Times*, January 12, 1994.

35. A large and still growing literature has reviewed and debunked various claims of the NYPD and of broken-windows policing with its heavy emphasis on misdemeanors and other minor offenses. Some of the most thorough and impressive work has been by University of Chicago Professor Bernard Harcourt. See *Illusion of Order: The False Promise of Broken Windows Policing*, Cambridge, MA: Harvard University Press, 2001; Bernard Harcourt, Policing disorder. *Boston Review*, May 2002, http://new.bostonreview.net/BR27.2/harcourt.html; Bernard E. Harcourt and Jens Ludwig, Broken windows: New evidence from New York City and a five-city social experiment, *University of Chicago Law Review*, 73, 2006, http://ssrn.com/abstract=743284; Bernard Harcourt, Bratton's "broken windows." *Los Angeles Times*, April 20, 2006, http://articles.latimes.com/2006/apr/20/opinion/oe-harcourt20; Harcourt writes:

> Everybody agrees that police matter. The question is how to allocate scarce police dollars. Should cops be arresting, processing and clogging the courts with minor-disorder offenders or focusing on violence, as well as gang and gun crimes, with the help of increased computerized crime tracking? The evidence, in my view, is clear: Focusing on minor misdemeanors is a waste.
>
> I recently concluded a study with my colleague, Jens Ludwig, of 1990s New York crime data. We found no evidence for the proposition that disorder causes crime or that broken-windows policing reduces serious crime. Rather, the pattern of crime reduction across New York precincts during the 1990s, when Bratton was first experimenting with broken-windows policing, is entirely consistent with what statisticians call "mean reversion." Those precincts that experienced the largest drops in crime in the 1990s were the ones that experienced the largest increases in crime during the city's crack epidemic of the mid- to late-1980s. What goes up must come down—and it would have come down even if New York had not embarked on its quality-of-life initiative.

Also see Emily Badger, The study that could upend everything we thought we knew about declining urban crime, *Atlantic Cities*, Feb 07, 2013, http://www.theatlanticcities.com/politics/2013/02/was-nypd-really-responsible-new-yorks-famous-drop-crime/4616/; David F. Greenberg, Studying New York City's crime decline: Methodological issues, *Justice Quarterly*, 2013,

http://stopandfriskinfo.org/content/uploads/2013/05/Greenberg-2013.pdf.
Greenberg, an extremely accomplished quantitative criminologist, finds "no
evidence that misdemeanor arrests reduced levels of homicide, robbery, or
aggravated assaults. Felony arrests reduced robberies, but only to a modest
degree. Most of the decline in these three felonies had other causes."

For an independent analysis by an Australian government researcher, see Jane
Marshall, Zero tolerance policing, Australian Government, Australian Institute
of Criminology, March 1999, http://www.ocsar.sa.gov.au/docs/information_
bulletins/IB9.pdf

William Bratton is probably the best exponent and defender of his vision of
policing. See his chapter "Crime is down in New York City: Blame the police,"
in Norman Dennis (Ed.), *Zero Tolerance: Policing a Free Society*, enlarged and
revised second edition, London: IEA Health and Welfare Unit, 1997. Much of
the book is a defense of Bratton's style of policing. Also see William J. Bratton,
The Turnaround: How America's Top Cop Reversed the Crime Epidemic, New
York: Random House, 1998.

36. On the international decline in crime see

Jan van Dijk, Andromachi Tseloni, and Graham Farrell, *The International
Crime Drop: New Directions in Research*, London: Palgrave Macmillan, 2012.
The authors write: "Our conclusion is that since 1995 volume crime has
dropped significantly across Europe." And, they say, "Improved security against
volume crime has initiated a prolonged recession on criminal markets in the
West, a downturn that appears largely independent from criminal policies of
individual governments." Professor Jan van Dijk, the lead author, was the 2012
winner of the Stockholm Prize in Criminology. See http://files.m17.mailplus.
nl/user317000013/12983/leafletJvD.pdf

Paul Knepper, An international crime decline: Lessons for social welfare
crime policy? *Social Policy & Administration, Special Issue: Crime and Social
Policy*, 46, 4, 359–376, August 2012. The author writes: "During the past two
decades, crime rates have declined in Europe and North America.... The discussion here includes the possibility of a convergence across social welfare
improvements, the danger of misreading the U.S.A. as a trend-setter, [and] the
potential of the Scandinavian way in situational crime prevention."

Graham Farrell, Andromachi Tseloni, Jen Mailley, Nick Tilley, and Jill Dando,
The crime drop and the security hypothesis, *Journal of Research in Crime and
Delinquency*, 48, 2, 147–175, May 2011. The authors write: "Major crime drops
were experienced in the United States and most other industrialized countries
for a decade from the early to mid-1990s. Yet there is little agreement over
explanation or lessons for policy. Here it is proposed that change in the quantity
and quality of security was a key driver of the crime drop. From evidence relating to vehicle theft in two countries, it is concluded that electronic immobilizers
and central locking were particularly effective. It is suggested that reduced car
theft may have induced drops in other crime including violence."

Andromachi Tseloni, Jen Mailley, Graham Farrell, and Nick Tilley, Exploring
the international decline in crime rates, *European Journal of Criminology*, 7,
5, September 2010. The authors write: "This paper examines aggregate crime
trends and variation around them from 1988 to 2004 for 26 countries and five
main crime types using data from the International Crime Victims Survey...."

The study results suggest that, with the exception of burglary, all examined crime types fell by roughly the same rate across countries. The sample's small number of countries in Latin America, Africa and Asia experienced even steeper reductions in burglary than occurred in Europe, North America and Australia."

Richard Rosenfeld and Steven F. Messner, The crime drop in comparative perspective: The impact of the economy and imprisonment on American and European burglary rates, *The British Journal of Sociology*, 60, 3, 445–471, September 2009.

Alan Travis, Fall in UK crime rate baffles experts: The classic theory that property crime rises faster in times of economic strife no longer seems to apply, latest figures show, *Guardian*, January 24, 2013; Marc Sandeep Mishra and Martin Lalumie, Is the crime drop of the 1990s in Canada and the U.S.A. associated with a general decline in risky and health-related behavior? *Social Science and Medicine*, 68, 39–48, 2009.

Marc Ouimet, Explaining the American and Canadian crime drop in the 1990's, *Canadian Journal of Criminology*, 44, 1, January 2002. The author writes: "Although Canada's crime trends are similar to those found in the U.S., there has been little or no change in policing practices or incarceration trends. This paper suggests that the causes of the decline in crime rates lie elsewhere, namely, in demographic shifts, improved employment opportunities and changes in collective values."

Why has crime fallen around the world? Parliament, UK, Briefing Papers, January 2013, http://ukbriefingpapers.co.uk/briefingpaper/SN06567. The authors write: "In the U.S.A. the reduction in crime that began around 1990 has been the subject of much academic debate. There has been less discussion surrounding European crime levels, which reached a plateau around 1995 and then steadily declined over the subsequent decade."

37. To be clear, we are not at all suggesting that the NYPD played no role in the decline in violent and other serious crimes in the 1990s and since. Computerized tracking of crimes, better and more complete computerization of crime reports, closer supervision of at least some officers, some improvements in morale (especially under Bratton), and other factors helped bring down the number of serious crimes. One recent study suggested that drug felonies declined in part because the NYPD ceased to prioritize them (even as the NYPD did prioritize misdemeanor marijuana arrests). See James Austin and Michael Jacobson, *How New York City Reduced Mass Incarceration: A Model for Change?* (with a Foreword by Inimai Chettiar), New York: Brennan Center for Justice at New York University School of Law, January 2013, http://www.brennancenter.org/publication/how-new-york-city-reduced-mass-incarceration-model-change

William Bratton, by all accounts, was an energetic, inspiring, and charismatic police commissioner in New York City. In his two years as chief of the New York Transit Police (1990–1992) and as NYPD commissioner (1994–1996), he did many things to boost the morale of ordinary officers, made small improvements in their lives, and sought to empower and energize them. Bratton redesigned police uniforms and belts, gave police new cars, different guns and more bullets, and sought to improve policing across the board. He believed that changing small things for police—and in policing—could produce large changes in reducing serious crimes and public fear, and raise public confidence in the police. And at Transit and at the NYPD he had an extraordinary assistant in Jack Maple. But Bratton and Maple (and a number of others) were gone in 1996 after two years, and that was over 17 years ago. Much changed quite quickly under Police Commissioner Safir, and then since. The policing focus on petty offenses and misdemeanor arrests was begun for many reasons, but it has continued and expanded, we have suggested, in part because it was so useful and beneficial to both NYPD commanders and to many patrol and narcotics officers.

38. So much has been written about the stop and frisks that it now constitutes a small library of reports, academic studies, video interviews, graphs, pie charts, tables, spreadsheet files, court testimony, legal briefs, and more. For links to organizations focusing work on the stop and frisks, see http://marijuana-arrests. com/NY-stop&frisk-info.html; also see http://ccrjustice.org/racial-disparity-nypd-stops-and-frisks; http://www.nyclu.org/issues/racial-justice/stop-and-frisk-; http://stopandfriskinfo.org/; http://www.policereformorganizingproject.org/

39. See, for example, in 2011, NYPD made more stops of young Black men than the total number of young Black men in New York by Ali Gharib, *Think Progress*, May 10, 2012, http://thinkprogress.org/justice/2012/05/10/481589/nypd-stop-and-frisk-young-black-men/

    See also NYPD targets minorities in stop and frisk, by Rocco Parascandola, *New York Daily News*, May 9, 2012, http://www.nydailynews.com/news/crime/nypd-targets-minorities-stop-frisk-report-article-1.1075037; Injustices of stop and frisk, *New York Times* Editorial, May 13, 2012, http://www.nytimes.com/2012/05/14/opinion/injustices-of-stop-and-frisk.html

40. One hypothesis about the NYPD's apparent reluctance to give up making marijuana arrests suggests that the overtime pay officers earn by booking marijuana arrests would be hard to make up in other ways (at least under current priorities and policies). Bloomberg and Kelly believe strongly in the importance of making large numbers of stop and frisks. But, as news stories about quotas have made clear, it can be difficult to get ordinary patrol officers to do the stop and frisks. In this context, the marijuana arrests provide an incentive for officers to make the stop and frisks. For each 10 or 15 stop and frisks, officers can usually find one or two young people with a bit of marijuana, allowing the officers to make arrests and collect overtime pay. This is partly the explanation for why marijuana possession has been the number one criminal arrest and charge in New York City for many years. In effect, the marijuana arrests function as a kind of "Crackerjack prize" for officers doing the stop and frisks. Kelly, Bloomberg, and their top advisors may fear that if they take away the prize of overtime pay, the number of stop and frisks will drop.

41. The mayor and the police department do not explain why the numbers of stop and frisks and marijuana arrests were down in 2012, and certainly not why they are down the same percentage (22%). But this pullback by the police department appears to be an effort to show some response to the extraordinary public outcry about the stop and frisks and the marijuana arrests, to proposed legislation to install a monitor over the police, to the much-publicized federal lawsuits about the stop and frisks and the marijuana arrests, and to the news that the U.S. Attorney General is considering installing a federal monitor over the

NYPD. It is worth noting that in 2012 former Mayor Ed Koch, who was quite conservative on policing matters, denounced the marijuana arrests as racially biased and called on the city's district attorneys to stop prosecuting any of them.

42. The NYPD's use of quotas for arrests, criminal court summonses, and stop and frisks has been documented by hundreds of news stories over the years. Some of them have been collected and excerpted at http://marijuana-arrests.com/quotas-arrest-quotas.html. *Village Voice* reporter Graham Rayman has documented a number of the more recent revelations in his series called "The NYPD Tapes." In one report he quotes a veteran NYPD officer:

> Marquez Claxton spent 20 years as a police officer and a detective in the NYPD, most recently in Williamsburg's 90th Precinct. He retired as a detective second grade. He worked in narcotics as an undercover, in vice, in domestic violence, and was involved in the investigation of thousands of cases.
>
> "Quotas have always been a part of the Police Department for as long as I was a member.... What makes it worse is now there are quotas on everything." The CompStat model means numbers alone gauge the success of crime fighting. "It's like factory work," he says. "The difficulty is that you can't quantify prevention. There is no number which says I stopped seven burglaries today. People have made careers out of summonses and arrests, but that's not even the main component of police work. "A lot of cops come on the job to have relationships with the community, to be public servants," he says. "But in today's PD, the officers are ostracized unless they have their numbers. You're punishing officers who say their job is not to be the hammer." Graham Rayman, Quotas and victim intimidation? Of course, says another NYPD veteran. (*Village Voice*, May 7, 2010)

Also see Robert Gearty and Bill Hutchinson, Second NYPD whistleblower testifies he was called a "rat" for protesting stop-and-frisk quotas: Officer Pedro Serrano said he was ostracized for protesting the stop-and-frisk quotas that were demanded at the 40th Precinct where he worked in the South Bronx, saying he was told "you can't fight a losing battle." *New York Daily News*, March 20, 2013; Ross Tuttle, New York's police union worked with the NYPD to set arrest and summons quotas, *The Nation*, March 19, 2013, http://www.thenation.com/article/173397/audio-new-yorks-police-union-worked-nypd-set-arrest-and-summons-quotas?rel=emailNation; Ben Muessigm, Cop: NYPD quota is 20 summonses, 1 arrest per month, *Gothamist*, March 3, 2010, http://gothamist.com/2010/03/03/cop_claims_nypd_quota_is_20_summons.php

43. See Rocco Parascandola, Narcotics cops told: Think big, sources say the new strategy of limiting misdemeanor busts puzzles and angers some drug officers, *New York Newsday*, June 23, 2005.

44. Recently Bratton explicitly criticized Kelly over the Operation Impact patrols in an address to the Manhattan Institute, the conservative think tank that has promoted broken windows policing in both Bratton and Kelly eras. Jonathan Lemire and Rocco Parascandola, Ex-cop William Bratton slaps Kelly on police frisks; Two spar over operation impact, *New York Daily News*, June 15, 2013.

45. Communities United for Police Reform website is http://changethenypd.org/. Its mission statement and list of members and organizational supporters are at http://changethenypd.org/campaign/intro-members

46. The new law establishes a strong and enforceable ban on profiling and discrimination by the New York City Police Department. It:

Expands the categories of individuals protected from discrimination to also include age, gender, gender identity or expression, sexual orientation, immigration status, disability, and housing status.

Creates a meaningful "private right of action" for individuals who believe they have been unjustly profiled by the NYPD.

Enables New Yorkers to challenge NYPD policies and practices based on intentional discrimination and disparate impact (meaning that even if a policy is not intentionally discriminatory, if it has the effect of discrimination, then a lawsuit may be brought to change the city policy that led to the effect of discrimination). See http://changethenypd.org/intro-1080-summary-changes

47. See http://changethenypd.org/about-community-safety-act. Two other Community Safety Act bills are still pending:

Protecting New Yorkers against unlawful searches (Intro. 799): Ends the practice of the NYPD deceiving New Yorkers into consenting to unnecessary searches; requires officers to explain that a person has the right to refuse a search when there is no warrant or probable cause; and requires officers to obtain proof of consent to a search.

Requiring officers to identify and explain themselves to the public (Intro. 801): Requires officers to provide the specific reason for their law enforcement activity, such as a stop and frisk, and requires officers to provide documents to the person with the officer's name and information on how to file a complaint at the end of each police encounter.

See http://changethenypd.org/about-community-safety-act

48. Dana Rubinstein, Albany's unlikely marijuana legalization champion, *Capital New York*, May 24, 2013, http://www.capitalnewyork.com/article/politics/2013/05/8530368/albanys-unlikely-marijuana-legalization-champion-sees-interest-no-m

49. Some of the coverage of the NYPD's activities and policies has been excerpted and linked to at http://marijuana-arrests.com/

For coverage of the NYPD marijuana arrests, see http://marijuana-arrests.com/NYC-pot-arrests-journalism.html

For coverage of the stop and frisks, see http://marijuana-arrests.com/stop&frisk-NY.html

For coverage of a variety of NYPD scandals see http://marijuana-arrests.com/scandals-nypd.html

For coverage of the case of Adrian Schoolcraft and other NYPD officers who have come forward to talk about the quotas and pressures to make stop and frisks, write criminal court summonses, and make misdemeanor arrests including for marijuana, see http://marijuana-arrests.com/adrian-schoolcraft.html

50. On the marijuana possession arrests see, for example:

Jim Dwyer, Whites smoke pot, but Blacks are arrested, *New York Times*, Dec 22, 2009

Jim Dwyer, A smell of pot and privilege in the city, *New York Times*, July 21, 2010

Jim Dwyer, A call to shift policy on marijuana, *New York Times*, June 14, 2011

Jim Dwyer, Side effects of arrests for marijuana, *New York Times*, June 16, 2011

Jim Dwyer, Out of one gram of marijuana, a "manufactured misdemeanor," *New York Times*, March 21, 2013

Charles M. Blow, Smoke and horrors, *New York Times*, Oct 22, 2010

Charles M. Blow, Drug bust, *New York Times*, June 10, 2011

Charles M. Blow, Escape from New York, *New York Times*, March 18, 2011

Colleen Long, A little pot is trouble in NYC: 50k busts a year, *Associated Press*, November 5, 2011 (over a hundred papers across the United States carried this AP story)

New York Times Editorial, Trouble with marijuana arrests, September 26, 2011

New York Times Editorial, Police powers in New York, March 17, 2012

New York Times Editorial, Examining marijuana arrests, April 2, 2012

New York Times Editorial, No crime, real punishment, June 4, 2012

New York Times Editorial, What's missing from this picture? June 22, 2012

New York Times Editorial, An ineffective way to fight crime, November 22, 2012

Brent Staples, The human cost of zero tolerance, *New York Times* Editorial, April 18, 2012

Kristen Gwynne, Tale of two cities: NYPD's racist arrests create class war, *AlterNet*, May 13, 2012

Alexander Zaitchik, The whole system relies on these arrests: The NYPD's racist marijuana arrest crusade and its national implications, *AlterNet* and *American Independent News Network*, May 15, 2012

Thomas Kaplan, Cuomo seeks cut in frisk arrests, *New York Times*, June 3, 2012

Bill Hammond, Cuomo's pitch: Yes, we cannabis: Weeding out the worst of stop-and-frisk, column, *New York Daily News*, June 5, 2012

James King, New Yorkers are systematically screwed by "public view" marijuana law. These are their stories, *Village Voice*, June 13, 2012

Drug Policy Alliance, Marijuana arrests (brief video interviews with 13 New Yorkers, 2012, http://www.youtube.com/playlist?list=PL1C39C63C08181217&feature=plcp

Natasha Lennard, Why marijuana decriminalization won't kill NYPD discrimination, *Alternet*, June 16, 2012

Wendy Ruderman and Joseph Goldstein, Lawsuit accuses police of ignoring directive on marijuana arrests, *New York Times*, June 22, 2012

Ed Koch, Stop-and-frisk and the marijuana misdemeanor arrests outrage, *Huffington Post*, June 26, 2012

51. On the summons court system see Brent Staples, Inside the warped world of summons court, *New York Times* [editorial], June 16, 2012; Joseph Goldstein, Sniff test does not prove public drinking, a judge rules, *New York Times*, June 14, 2012; Joseph Goldstein, Stop-and-frisk trial turns to claim of arrest quotas, *New York Times*, March 20, 2013; Graham Rayman, Federal judge lets [summons] quota lawsuit go forward, *Village Voice*, April 24, 2012; Rocco Parascandola, Law enforcement or reaching quotas? Stats show NYPD focusing on pot possession, boozing in public, *New York Daily News*, July 23, 2010; Harry Levine and Loren Siegel, Summonses issued by the NYPD, Marijuana-Arrests.com, April 2012. On the beginnings of the emphasis on summonses and the warrants they produce see Norimitsu Onishi, Police announce crackdown on quality-of-life offenses, *New York Times*, March 13, 1994. About the many warrants open on

these summonses see Shane Dixon Kavanaugh, 1 million outstanding warrants in New York City: From open alcohol containers to littering, one-eighth of the city's population face arrest for unresolved summonses, *New York Daily News*, February 23, 2013.

52. The war on marijuana in Black and White, American Civil Liberties Union, Criminal Law Project, New York, June 2013, http://www.aclu.org/criminal-law-reform/war-marijuana-black-and-white

The Rise of Command and Control Protest Policing in New York

7

ALEX S. VITALE

Contents

The NYPD received a raft of negative publicity for their handling of the Occupy Wall Street (OWS) protests of 2011. Videos of police pepper spraying demonstrators, mass arrests, and constant harassment undermined the reputation of the agency. A Quinnipiac Poll showed that almost half of New Yorkers disapproved of the NYPD's handling of the protests and more than half disapproved of Mayor Bloomberg's handling of OWS (Taintor, 2011). Although Bloomberg's decision to evict the encampment at Zuccotti Park was central to undermining the movement, the day-to-day policing by the NYPD created a climate of fear and hostility that hindered the movement's growth and opened the police department to charges of stifling dissent. OWS was subjected to extensive restrictions and a variety of invasive and aggressive police tactics including pervasive surveillance, zero tolerance enforcement of minor legal violations, mass arrests, and excessive force, leading some to claim that a new militarized form of protest policing was emerging in New York City (Badish, 2011; Chiroux, 2011; Stamper, 2011; Turse, 2011). Others claimed that the NYPD was actively protecting the interests of Wall Street and the financial industry through the use of unusually repressive tactics. In reality, none of these tactics was new to the NYPD (Elliot, 2011; Wolf, 2011). Over the last 20 years the NYPD has undertaken a broad and consistent practice of restricting, micromanaging, and even pre-emptively disrupting protest.

7.1   Styles of Protest Policing

Policing throughout the United States suffered a major crisis of legitimacy in the wake of the urban unrest of the 1960s and 1970s. In response many cities looked to more community-oriented models of policing that relied on improved communication, flexibility, and in the best cases an attempt to co-produce safety along with community partners. This trend could be seen very clearly in the area of protest policing. Although the 1960s and '70s were characterized as a period of police confrontation with protestors, along with a high level of force being used, the 1980s saw the emergence of a new form of protest policing, referred to as "negotiated management" that relies on good communication with demonstrators before and after protests in an effort to reduce tensions and coordinate protest tactics and police responses, flexibility toward permits and minor violations of the law in order to maintain the peaceful character of demonstrations, and respect for the First Amendment rights of demonstrators (McCarthy & McPhail, 1998; McPhail, Schweingruber, & McCarthy, 1998). This chapter is a story about how the NYPD abandoned negotiated management in the 1990s in favor of a new more intensive and invasive command and control form of protest policing, characterized by the micromanagement of all aspects of demonstrations, an intolerance of disorder, and the willingness to use force in response to even minor violations of the law (Vitale, 2005, 2007).

This new style of policing has become the dominant form of protest policing in New York City and affects both large and small demonstrations. Its most visible characteristics are the use of protest pens to contain and often subdivide demonstrations, the deployment of huge numbers of officers to maintain this system of controlled access, and a zero tolerance approach toward any activities that the police believe fall outside the parameters of a lawful and orderly demonstration. In addition, this system relies on tight restrictions on the issuance of permits, relegating many rallies and marches to marginal locations, or denying them access to the city's public spaces altogether. The effect has been to isolate, disempower, and even criminalize political protest. I have argued previously (Vitale, 2005) that this new regime of protest policing is tied to the department's overall rejection of community policing approaches in favor of a "broken windows" based form of policing that emphasizes the control of disorder through both legal and extralegal means to retake control of the streets and reduce crime (Vitale, 2008). The broken-windows theory argues that crime emerges when disorderly behavior such as aggressive panhandling, public drinking, street-level prostitution, and graffiti go unchallenged. This supposedly creates a climate of moral deregulation in which latent predatory tendencies are unleashed. What is needed to restore safety, they say, is for the police to intervene as agents of civility by tightly regulating every aspect of public life that threatens the "quality of life" of the city. This requires a form of policing that manages public behavior and invades the privacy of all those who reside in high crime areas, threaten the civility of public spaces, or "fit the description."

This has resulted in an intensive and invasive street policing in the form of stop, question, and frisk, the suppression of street-level drug dealing, and zero tolerance policies targeting young people of color, the homeless, and the socially marginalized. In the same way, command and control protest policing has resulted in the intensive and invasive regulation of protests. The NYPD attempts to monitor and control all aspects of demonstrations. They limit when and where they can occur and make people submit to pervasive surveillance and even warrantless inspections of bags. They microregulate the points of access and the ability to move about demonstration areas, even when permits are granted. They aggressively enforce every minor law and permit requirement, even when that causes an escalation of conflict, producing otherwise unnecessary arrests and injuries. Just as the right to move about freely without police harassment and illegal searches has been lost for young people of color in New York, the right to free assembly has been greatly abridged as well.

The contours of command and control policing are troubling enough; however, in some cases the NYPD goes further. Beginning around the time of the Republican National Convention in 2004, some groups such as Critical Mass and at times Occupy Wall Street have been subjected to an even more aggressive form of protest policing that relies on pre-emption and disruption rather than just restriction and regulation. This new form of protest policing is a response by many police departments to the failures of policing at the World Trade Organization (WTO) meeting in Seattle in 1999, in which demonstrators successfully blockaded delegates attempting to get to the meeting, forcing significant delays, and contributing to the overall failure of the meetings to reach agreement on most important issues. In 2002, the city of Miami hosted a meeting to coordinate a new Free Trade Area of the Americas (FTAA). Fearing what had happened in Seattle they undertook a massive program of militarizing their policing though the purchase and use of numerous less lethal weapons, armored vehicles, and body-armored police, and the pre-emptive disruption of the protests through permit restriction, surveillance and infiltration, negative advance publicity from named and unnamed police sources, the arrest and use of force against nonviolent demonstrators, and the use of extended detention, high bails, and excessive criminal charges to keep demonstrators off the streets. This new approach has become known as the Miami Model and has become the primary form of policing in the United States at large summit protests (Vitale, 2007).

7.1.1 From Negotiated Management to Command and Control

In 1982 an estimated one million people marched through midtown Manhattan to a rally in Central Park calling for an end to the nuclear arms race. The city went to great lengths to facilitate what would turn out to be the largest protest in American history. Essentially all of Manhattan from the United Nations on 42nd Street to Central Park was shut down for the protest. Simultaneous marches proceeded up most of the city's avenues, and the entire southern half of the park became a giant rally point. The primary job of the police was to redirect traffic and provide service to demonstrators with medical problems, give directions, and protect people from possible criminal activity. Officers were rarely seen and had a relaxed posture and even interacted with demonstrators. Mayor Koch welcomed demonstrators to the city and even saw it as an opportunity to encourage tourism as hundreds of thousands of out-of-town demonstrators stayed in local hotels and ate out in the city's restaurants (Soffer, 2012). There were no arrests, no confrontations, and the event generated tremendous good will between the demonstrators, police, and the Koch administration.

This stands in stark contrast to the events of February 15, 2003 in which several hundred thousand people attempted to demonstrate against the impending war in Iraq as part of the largest weekend of coordinated international protest in history (Walgrave, 2009). On that day the NYPD prevented hundreds of thousands of people from reaching a permitted rally, attacked peaceful crowds with horses and pepper spray, and virtually imprisoned people in thousands of inflexible interlocking metal barriers surrounded by thousands of police officers (New York Civil Liberties Union, 2003). Even before the event began the police and Mayor Michael Bloomberg struck an inflexible tone by denying demonstration organizers a march permit and forcing them into a stationary rally on the far east side, several blocks away from their intended target of the United Nations. Relying on the security concerns following 9/11 the city argued that they were incapable of both securing the city from terror attacks and facilitating a large permitted demonstration. Despite the profound First Amendment implications, a federal judge upheld the city's reasoning (New York Civil Liberties Union, 2003).

When the first demonstrators arrived on First Avenue, they were met with a complex set of access points leading to individual block-long protest pens surrounded by dozens of officers. People were allowed to enter only the southernmost pen that wasn't already filled. As pens filled they were completely enclosed, with some people even being refused exit. As the pens closed, people reaching the rally were diverted up Second Avenue to the constantly changing single entry point. Very quickly, crowds attempting to access the demonstration ran into a never-ending barrage of checkpoints and diversions that caused thousands to spill out into surrounding streets. These crowds were then ordered to disperse because they were blocking traffic. Confused, angry, and in many cases unaware of police orders, these crowds were then subjected to horse charges, baton blows, arrest, and pepper spray.

The NYPD and the Bloomberg administration showed a dramatic hostility toward dissent and a fundamental intolerance of the most minor "disorderly behavior" which primarily took the form of disrupting traffic in an attempt to attend a legally permitted and nonviolent demonstration. City Council hearings were called to review the actions of the police at which dozens of people testified about their mistreatment at the hands of the police and their inability to participate in a lawful demonstration because of police actions. The New York Civil Liberties Union received hundreds of complaints about the policing of the event and issued a major report based on hundreds of letters, hours of videotape, and their staff's direct observation of the demonstration. The report "Arresting Protest" provided extensive evidence of excessive use of force and a basic denial of people's right to protest (New York Civil Liberties Union, 2003). Civil tort claims stemming from these events are ongoing. However, in 1994 a federal judge ruled that the intensive control of access to and from protest pens and the overall demonstration area was unconstitutional and issued an injunction against such practices in the future.

7.1.2   Giuliani and Command and Control

This basic orientation toward demonstrations was not new. Its basic elements could be seen in three separate protest actions in 1998 under then-Mayor Rudolph Giuliani. These three events, the Million Youth March, the Matthew Shepard emergency march, and the October 22nd march, all contained central elements of the new more restrictive command and control model.

The Million Youth March (MYM) took place in Harlem on September 5th, 1998. This event was organized by a variety of Black nationalist organizations and modeled after the Million Man March in Washington, DC, organized by the Nation of Islam. The demonstration was intended to be the focal point of youth organizing in communities of color.

Mayor Giuliani was strongly opposed to the politics of these organizations and was opposed to allowing them to march (Waldman, 1998). As a result, the police department denied them a permit to either march or rally. The event organizers, however, successfully sued the city in federal court and won a permit to hold a rally but not a march. The permit set a specific start and end time, and the police let it be known that they would strictly enforce them. They also stated that no one would be allowed to march or demonstrate outside the approved rally area.

To demarcate the rally area, the police established a complex set of interlocking barricades, which divided the crowd up into one-block segments, restricting movement from one pen to another. The NYPD also used barricades to create a limited number of entry points to the demonstration area. As a result, people wishing to attend the event had to circle around up to several blocks to find an entry point and then pass through a phalanx of officers visually inspecting everyone who entered. Three thousand police were deployed to maintain this complicated system of restricted access and movement. Just before 4 p.m. police officers in riot gear assembled off to the side of the stage. At a few minutes after 4, as the last speaker was ending the event and urging participants to return to their homes and families, the police charged the stage, while a police helicopter hovered low over the crowd. The police were met with some thrown bottles and chairs and some pushing and shoving. After this brief confrontation, the police took control of the stage and dispersed the crowd. During the scuffle several arrests were made and a few police and demonstrators were slightly injured (Texiera, 1998).

On October 19th an emergency march was held following the death of Matthew Shepard, who was killed in an anti-gay bias attack in Wyoming. Because the event was called as an emergency demonstration, there was no possibility of going through the normal police permitting process, which generally takes weeks and sometimes months. In response, the police made it clear that they would not allow a march in the street under any circumstances. Police and demonstrators expected about 500 people to attend the event near Fifth Avenue and 59th Street. Instead, closer to 5,000 people showed up, overwhelming police plans to keep the group confined to the sidewalk. The result was a major confrontation in which 84 people were arrested and several police and demonstrators were injured.

As the demonstrators gathered, there was a hurried negotiating session with the police on the scene. The protest organizers requested that a lane of traffic be made available for a march, given the swelling ranks of demonstrators. The police refused any concession and told protest leaders that anyone stepping into the street would be immediately arrested. The organizers decided that they would attempt to defy the police by using their large numbers to go into the street anyway. As the sidewalk march began over 100 people at the front of the march moved into the street (along with media and legal observers) in an attempt to overwhelm the police. The police responded by arresting the leaders of the march and many of the legal observers. The now leaderless march entered the street further down Fifth Avenue while the police were busy arresting the first group. In response, the police called for a citywide emergency mobilization that brought approximately 1,000 officers to the area. After an hour of demonstrators moving in and out of the street depending on their numbers relative to the arriving police units, the police set up a cordon of several hundred officers and mounted units at 23rd Street to stop the march.

During the event the police utilized batons, motorized scooters, and horses to try to stop demonstrators from entering the street. Several people were injured including three who were seriously hurt by police horses. All three later sued the NYPD and received a combined $548,000 in damages (Weiser, 2001). Gay and lesbian leaders including future city council speaker Christine Quinn claimed that this zero tolerance approach cost the city hundreds of thousands of dollars in litigation costs and police overtime, denied police coverage to other parts of the city, caused numerous serious injuries, and seriously strained relations between the gay and lesbian community and the NYPD (Graves, 1998).

On September 14, 1998, the October 22nd Coalition Against Police Brutality requested a permit from the NYPD to conduct a march from Union Square, down Broadway, to City Hall in one lane of traffic. The NYPD refused to respond to the permit request for a month before denying it just days before the scheduled rally, citing concerns about traffic disruption. An appeal to the Federal Court was successful despite the strong objections and additional appeals by the city. Mayor Giuliani criticized the Federal Courts as "imperial," and claimed that only the mayor and local police were in a position to judge the potential hazards of allowing such a march. Federal Judge John S. Martin reacted strongly in his ruling, stating that the city was abridging the group's First Amendment rights based on the political content of their anti-police brutality march (Roane, 1998).

In response to the court order, the march of about 2,000 people was allowed to proceed in one lane of traffic. The entire march route was lined with interlocking steel barriers, with gaps at the intersections. The system of barriers was staffed by hundreds of officers, many in riot gear. In addition, dozens of motorized scooters and officers on foot walked between the marchers and traffic as an additional barrier. There were no arrests and no reports of injuries.

During the course of 1998 the police were also criticized for their handling of a large labor demonstration in which 30–40,000 union members clashed with police after the police attempted to contain them in a complex set of barricades resulting in dozens of arrests and injuries, despite the presence of a permit (Risen, 1998). Earlier in the year the mayor moved to prevent demonstrations of cab drivers, with the mayor threatening their licenses for participating in the protests (Allen, 1998; Sengupta, 1998). Also, the mayor banned large press conferences and rallies from the steps of City Hall, a historic center of protest activity. All of these developments indicated a strong aversion to protest by Giuliani as well as the development of a set of techniques, including the denial of permits, intensive control of access to protest areas, the penning in of demonstrators at both rallies and marches, heavy police presence, and a willingness to use high levels of force to enforce these restrictions.

7.1.3 Bloomberg

The command and control approach to protest policing continued under the Bloomberg administration (2001–2013). Although Bloomberg expressed more support for some First Amendment activities involving the right to free speech than had Giuliani, protest policing under his administration became even more restrictive. It was the NYPD under Bloomberg that developed the extensive restrictions of the 2003 anti-Iraq war demonstration. It was also during the Bloomberg administration that the NYPD requested the lifting of the Handshu consent decree that restricted political intelligence gathering by the NYPD (New York Civil Liberties Union, 2013). The City argued that following 9/11 the police needed greater latitude to engage in surveillance of individuals and groups that might be linked to terrorism. Although this change did lead to increased surveillance of Muslims, leading to a lawsuit charging violations of the consent decree (Neumeister & Sullivan, 2013), it was also used extensively against nonviolent demonstrators. The NYPD now routinely videotapes demonstrations even when there is no unlawful activity. In addition they undertook extensive international surveillance of political activists prior to the 2004 Republican National Convention (see below).

The NYPD under Bloomberg also orchestrated an extremely restrictive plan for managing a protest against the World Economic Forum the summer following the 9/11 attack. The NYPD indicated early on that they were going to treat this as a major policing challenge. Nearly 4,000 officers were assigned to secure the convention site and police the demonstrations (Marzulli, 2004). The main demonstration was called for February 2nd. Organizers planned a march from Central Park to the meeting location in the nearby Waldorf-Astoria Hotel. Police agreed to the march but insisted that it not come within three blocks of the hotel. They lined the entire march route with barricades, restricting the march to one lane of traffic. In addition, they took an aggressive posture toward anyone thinking of breaking the law or violating the permit in any way. People attempting to arrive at the march as a group were told that if they walked on the street or blocked pedestrians on the sidewalk they would be arrested. They also announced that they would strictly enforce a local ordinance passed in 1845 that prohibits groups from wearing masks in public. This was motivated by fears of bandana-wearing youths with radical politics, referred to as either anarchists or the "black block" for their choice of all black clothing. Joseph Esposito, the highest ranking uniformed officer of the NYPD and the officer in charge on February 15th, told the press that "if three or more people are marching with masks on, they are violating the law, and that will not be tolerated" (Marzulli, 2002).

This is in fact what happened. Near the rear of the march, as it left the park, dozens of riot police waded into the march to arrest a handful of people with bandanas on. This led to a scuffle in which several protestors and police suffered minor injuries. This caused march organizers to stop the march in an attempt to negotiate with the police to prevent further intrusions into the line of march. The police response was that if the march did not continue, they would start arresting people. Overall, there was a massive show of police force with a police-to-demonstrator ratio again close to 1 to 2 (Hays, 2002). In addition, the police deployed horses and used barricades to control access to the rally area and to subdivide the crowd. Finally, the police took a zero tolerance approach to any violations of the law, even if it resulted in confrontations and injuries.

7.1.4   Bloomberg and the Miami Model

Beginning in 2004, the NYPD started to use even more troubling tactics. Rather than just trying to highly regulate and restrict protest activity, the NYPD actively began to disrupt and even pre-emptively quash some protests. This process could be seen most clearly in the policing of the Critical Mass bike rides before and during the Republican National Convention (RNC) in the summer of 2004. This is a regular event held on the last Friday of the month in hundreds of cities around the world to promote bicycling as a form of transportation.* During the previous year attendance had peaked at about 2,000 participants, who ride together without police permits for about two hours on a route determined as the ride proceeds. In the previous year there had been only a few citations issued to cyclists for traffic infractions. As the rides grew in size police officials became increasingly concerned about the disruption to automobile traffic caused by the ride. They were also troubled by the apparently disorganized nature of the rides (Moore, 2004). No permits were requested, no organization or individual was in charge, and decision making was diffuse and impossible to monitor. Riders made limited efforts to communicate with the police, asserting their right to use the city streets with the same freedom as drivers.

On August 27th, just before the opening of the RNC, approximately 5,000 cyclists and several hundred police showed up for the regularly scheduled Critical Mass ride (Wald, 2004). The police initially made threats that they would try to prevent the ride from occurring, giving out leaflets stating that those violating traffic laws would be arrested and their bikes confiscated. So many cyclists showed up, however, that the police were not adequately equipped to stop the event from taking place. Therefore, the ride was able to commence. After about an hour of riding through midtown, and just as the ride neared the area of the convention, which would not begin for another three days, the police began to make arrests in three different ways. In some

---

* See http://www.critical-mass.org.

cases large phalanxes of officers were used to stop the flow of the ride, encircle parts of it with orange mesh flexi-barriers, and make mass arrests of all those enclosed. Undercover officers riding on unmarked Vespa scooters also made a smaller number of arrests. These officers rode into cyclists forcing them to stop and then arresting them. Finally, some cyclists were pulled off their moving bikes by high-ranking officers, seemingly at random.

Altogether, over 250 people were arrested, several of whom were not participants in the event but merely running errands or commuting from work (Okie, 2004). Those who were arrested were transported to an unused bus depot on a nearby pier on the Hudson River, which had been converted into a temporary holding and processing facility. The conditions at the facility were a source of numerous complaints from both protestors and the police forced to work there (New York Civil Liberties Union, 2005, p. 36).* All of the participants were brought before a judge within 24 hours after being arrested primarily for traffic infractions, which would normally result in a summons rather than processing. The bicycles of arrested protestors were held as evidence, meaning that most of them could not be retrieved until weeks after the convention ended, despite that fact that almost all of the charges were eventually dropped by the city, or resulted in acquittals.

The police showed some flexibility in the beginning, but that came to a quick end as arrests were ordered without warning or negotiation for minor traffic violations (Dobnik, 2004; New York Civil Liberties Union, 2005, p. 28). There was significant use of force in the arrest process with officers pulling people off moving bicycles and scooters being used to knock over riders (New York Civil Liberties Union, 2005, p. 43). There was evidence of surveillance of event organizers prior to the event, and there were police taking videos during the event. Special weapons in the form of mesh netting and undercover scooters were heavily used (Okie, 2004).

Following the RNC police took even stronger pre-emptive action at future rides. In October the city attempted to get an injunction in federal court to stop the ride altogether, arguing that the failure to apply for a permit made the event illegal. The court, however, refused the city's request pointing out that the city had managed to allow the ride for years without incident and that it represented a form of protected political speech (Anderson, 2004). It left open, however, some question regarding the interpretation of state law, which prompted the city to attempt an injunction in state court. This also failed (Siegel, 2006). Even without an injunction the NYPD undertook aggressive efforts to disrupt the ride. In some cases riders were allowed to exit the gathering location only to be surrounded and arrested en masse a block away

---

* After the convention week ended, 40 police officers filed medical reports claiming that they had gotten ill while working there as a result of exposure to toxic chemicals embedded in the uncovered concrete floors (Dwyer, 2007b).

in a more controllable location. Riders would proceed down a long block only to find the front end blocked by police, who would then enclose the rear end of the block arresting all those on the block in a type of "kettling" action. In some cases police also sawed off the locks and confiscated dozens of bicycles they believed had been used on the rides, prompting a series of lawsuits from participants in the rides (Times Up, 2009).

In 2005 a judge overturned the arrests of the Critical Mass riders claiming that the city's parade permit laws were too vague. In response, in 2007 the city introduced new permit rules, that more tightly restricted protest action on city streets. The new law, upheld by the federal courts in 2010, requires that any group of 50 or more using the roads in any organized way as part of a race, procession, or parade have a permit. These new rules were vigorously enforced, resulting in hundreds of arrests. These actions by the police succeeded in discouraging all but a handful of highly committed activists from continuing the rides.

There were also other instances of pre-emptive policing during the RNC. NYPD detectives were sent around the world to collect intelligence on individuals and groups who might be organizing to participate in the RNC protests (Dwyer, 2007a). This involved police working undercover, rather than just attending open meetings and monitoring open source material. In many cases those targeted for this infiltration had no history of violence or even unlawful protests including street theater groups, musicians, and peace groups. Three New York City elected officials also appear in the reports made by police. This information was also shared with local police. The NYPD claimed that the intelligence did not violate the new expanded Handschu guidelines, despite the fact that almost none of the reports indicate any intent to commit criminal acts.

During the actual convention, the NYPD also took steps to pre-emptively disrupt protests. A diffuse collation of radical activist groups under the heading of A31 (for the date of the action, August 31st) called for a large decentralized disruptive action. The event was organized by an ad hoc coalition of individuals and organizations, many oriented toward anarchist politics and direct action tactics. The group did not request any permits, and details of the exact nature, timing, and location of the actions were not made public. The goal of the event was to disrupt the convention and daily life in Manhattan as much as possible through a variety of "decentralized street actions targeting corporate fetes for delegates as well as the headquarters of 'war-profiteers' like the Carlyle Group and Hummer of Manhattan, followed by a mass convergence to 'reclaim the streets' outside Madison Square Garden with sound systems, marching bands and free food" (Ferguson, 2004). The police, however, had engaged in extensive intelligence gathering and were present in force wherever demonstrators gathered that day. There were over 1,100 arrests made including large groups near including the World Trade Center site, Union Square, Herald Square, and the main Public Library (Cardwell, 2004; New York Civil Liberties Union, 2005, p. 21). Orange netting was used in many of these instances to corral large groups (New York Civil Liberties Union, 2005, p. 12). Arrestees were held an average of 32.7 hours before seeing a judge at arraignment (Dwyer, 2007b).

Police were organized into mobile teams that were positioned as deemed necessary based on police intelligence. There was extensive surveillance of groups and individuals planning on taking part in the A31 day of action through infiltration of groups and open meetings in New York and around the country. In addition, the NYPD shared information and worked cooperatively with a number of other local and national law enforcement agencies (Dwyer, 2007b; New York Civil Liberties Union, 2005, p. 16; *New York Times*, 2004). Both named and unnamed police sources made reference to the possibility of violence at the demonstrations in the media on several occasions (Friedman, 2004; Meek, 2004; O'Shaughnessy, 2004; Parascandola, 2004). There were also extensive use of orange mesh netting to effect mass arrests and undercover officers as forms of special weapons and tactics. All of the arrestees were held in excess of the legal maximum of 24 hours at Pier 57 (New York Civil Liberties Union, 2005, p. 14).

Other demonstrations during the RNC received more of the command and control approach. Events such as the March for Our Lives and a massive anti-war protest by United For Peace and Justice were allowed to proceed, but in both cases there were extensive delays in receiving permits, restrictions on access to the demonstration, extensive use of barricades, heavy police presence, and intolerance and inflexibility by police that led to escalations of tensions during otherwise lawful and peaceful demonstrations (New York Civil Liberties Union, 2004).

7.1.5   Occupy Wall Street

The Occupy Wall Street movement received a similarly bifurcated treatment by the NYPD. OWS was an ad hoc collection of activists, with very little institutional backing and strong orientation toward direct action and noncompliance with the police. The group did not apply for permits for its demonstrations and made clear its intention to disrupt Manhattan's financial district. OWS did, however, have some strong supporters in the form of labor unions and some progressive community-based organizations. What emerged was a two-sided strategy of managing OWS. The police attempted to apply the command and control model toward the actual OWS encampment at Zuccotti Park and at demonstrations organized largely by OWS supporters. On the other hand, the NYPD acted pre-emptively during numerous smaller demonstrations organized and carried out primarily by OWS, creating the same kind of "good demonstrator/bad demonstrator" dichotomy seen at the RNC.

The initial OWS protest was intended to be an attempt to physically occupy the streets and sidewalks around the New York Stock Exchange on Wall Street. In response, police took steps to completely seal off the streets directly adjacent to the Exchange, including several blocks of Wall Street, effectively creating a no-protest zone, based on practices developed in the wake of 9/11 to create a flexible frozen area around the Exchange. Some areas around the actual entrances have become permanently closed, and adjacent areas are open or closed as warranted by police assessment of potential threats. This kind of pre-emptive risk-based form of crowd control is consistent with the Miami Model and the broader trend of strategic incapacitation (Gillham, Edwards, & Noaks, 2012; Gillham & Noaks, 2011).

Anticipating these police tactics, organizers had identified the quasi-public space at Zuccotti Park as a potential fallback location. A so-called "bonus plaza," the park is a private plaza that must remain open to the public as part of a larger land use deal, allowing the developers of a major office tower across the street to exceed normal zoning regulations. Because the status of the space allowed for 24-hour access to the public, police were unable to evict the protestors legally. Instead they undertook a program of zero tolerance enforcement of a variety of minor infractions to arrest demonstrators, including the use of amplified sound, disorderly conduct, obstructing governmental administration, blocking the sidewalk, and even writing with chalk on the sidewalk. This kept tension between the police and demonstrators high and created a climate of confrontation, animosity, and distrust, which undermined later efforts to reduce conflict.

At the end of the first week of occupation, a group of occupiers and their supporters marched to Union Square to participate in a racial justice march in support of death row inmate, Troy Davis, who was subsequently executed. As marchers spilled out into the street on Washington Avenue police attempted to corral them back onto the sidewalks through the use of police scooters, skirmish lines, and orange mesh netting. In response to sporadic resistance, police became more aggressive, making arrests, using force, and in a now infamous incident, using pepper spray by a high-ranking officer against several women on the sidewalk surrounded by orange netting, and several others nearby. This escalation in force was consistent with the command and control model in that it represented a zero tolerance approach toward the unpermitted march. The NYPD's systematic intolerance is indicated by the fact that the force was used, not by an individual patrol officer, but the highest-ranking commander on the scene, with extensive protest experience. Similar incidents occurred at later events as other white-shirted commanding officers used batons, punches, and pepper spray against demonstrators in skirmishes over marching in the street without a permit.

The next week, however, the NYPD escalated their tactics in an effort to pre-emptively end the now rapidly growing movement. On September 30th, OWS marchers proceeded toward the Brooklyn Bridge. Initially the bulk of marchers entered the pedestrian walkway. However, another large group gathered near the roadway entrance. Normally, when a large demonstration is slated to go near the entrance to the bridge, large numbers of officers, including mounted units and barricades, are assigned to prevent a march across the roadway. The NYPD are very experienced in preventing unauthorized marches on the roadway and have repelled numerous attempts to occupy the bridge. In this case a large group, with a history of direct action, signaled in advance that they were marching to the bridge. Top NYPD command staff, including the chief of department, the highest-ranking uniformed officer in the department, were on hand. Despite this, there was almost no effort to defend the bridge. Instead of mounted units and tactical police in riot gear, demonstrators were met by a few community affairs officers in soft uniforms and a single bullhorn ordering people not to march on the roadway. As the demonstrators first gathered and then proceeded toward the roadway in an effort to "take the bridge," no reinforcements were called and police on the scene made no effort to block them physically. Instead, they turned around and began walking on the roadway ahead of the demonstrators, creating the impression of consent.

About a thousand people walked onto the roadway, many of whom never heard the initial police warnings. Halfway across the bridge, police blocked the march at both ends and arrested over 700 people. Later it was learned that police had prepositioned numerous prisoner transport vehicles nearby. All of this indicates that the police were hoping to entice a large group onto the bridge in hopes of arresting them and bottling them up in the criminal justice system as a form of harassment, intimidation, and deterrence from participating in future protests.

In response, a large coalition of labor unions and community groups organized a major march in support of OWS from Foley Square to Zuccotti Park on October 5th. Unlike OWS, this group met with police to negotiate a permit. Although a permit was granted, the entire length of the march was surrounded by metal barricades that kept the march to one lane of traffic. When the march ended at the park, protestors were forced into the adjacent street, where they found only limited points of exit, surrounded by hundreds of police. In essence there was a massive barrier between the protestors and the public. After the march many people attempted to march on the sidewalk to Wall Street. Once again the entire Wall Street area was closed off to vehicular and pedestrian traffic by metal barriers and large numbers of officers in riot gear. At one point a small group of demonstrators attempted to climb over the fences at Wall and Broadway. They were met with baton blows, pepper spray, and arrests.

On November 14–15, under orders from Mayor Bloomberg, the NYPD undertook an eviction of the encampment. At approximately midnight, police informed people that they must leave. In addition, the police closed off air space above the demonstration, keeping out news helicopters, and informed reporters who had been stationed across the street from the park, that they were in a "frozen zone" and must leave, leading to the arrest of seven journalists (Committee to Protect Journalists, 2011; Harlow, 2011). Over the next few hours police removed the remaining protestors making it possible for sanitation crews to remove the physical encampment. During this time the police aggressively dispersed those trying to witness and protest the eviction. In the process several were arrested and injured including a member of the City Council (Massey, 2011).

In response to the eviction, another large coalition protest was called. And once again a large permitted march was allowed under the condition that it be completely enclosed in steel barriers with a massive police presence. A small staged civil disobedience action was also arranged near the entrance to the Brooklyn Bridge, in which several dozen labor and community leaders were arrested for blocking traffic. The march then proceeded across the pedestrian walkway of the bridge. This event went smoothly, with no unplanned arrests, but the experience was very disempowering for many. The march was essentially completely isolated from the public. There was an extremely small number of points where people could enter or exit the march. In the area around City Hall and leading to the bridge, control was especially tight. At one point a large group refused to march until barricades were loosened. Nearby, another group opened up barricades on their own to allow easier exit from the march for those who did not want to go over the bridge. This was command and control policing in its fully realized form. The police attempted to micromanage every movement of the group, not through the use of force, but through controlling the parameters of the event with permit restrictions, total control of the movement of people, and a massive police presence.

This is in contrast to the tactics used on smaller unpermitted sidewalk marches that occurred frequently during OWS. On an almost daily basis people would undertake unpermitted sidewalk processions targeting a variety of political and financial targets. In some cases the loose, unpermitted, and almost spontaneous nature of these marches allowed for a greater feeling of freedom because police were unable to utilize extensive systems of barriers, protest pens, and large deployments of officers. However, when the events were announced in advance and police had more time to plan, the policing was often aggressive and at times invasive and pre-emptive. In the area around Wall Street, police pre-positioned large numbers of barriers and officers on a regular basis to allow them to corral demonstrators quickly by creating ad hoc "frozen zones" and protest barriers. The system became so regular and extensive that local businesses and residents began to complain about access to shops and restaurants, prompting an official protest from the local state assembly member (Horan, 2011).

In several instances there were reports that police targeted individuals for arrest that they believed were playing a leadership role. In many of these cases only one or two individuals would be singled out for arrest for disorderly conduct or blocking the sidewalk, when the whole group was engaged in the same activity. There were also two incidents of invasive police harassment and intelligence gathering in 2012. Prior to a major march on May Day five activists reported being visited by police at their homes and questioned about their plans for the event (Chen, 2012). And before the first anniversary of OWS on September 17th, Occupy organizers claimed that several well-known activists had been pre-emptively arrested by police (Walker, 2012).

The overall effect of these police practices was to instill a climate of fear among movement participants and the general public. OWS became associated in the minds of the public with confrontation with the police and arrest, despite the fact that OWS almost never targeted the police for protest, maintaining their focus on financial elites and political leaders. Although the NYPD's tactics were invasive, aggressive, and at times pre-emptive, they cannot generally be described as militarized. Officers were often deployed without riot control equipment of any kind, and body armor and shields were only used during the eviction of Zuccotti Park. There were some notable incidents in which individual officers used pepper spray, but large-scale use of pepper spray, tear gas, or other "less lethal" weapons did not occur. This stands in stark contrast to the handling of Occupy Oakland protests in which tear gas and projectile weapons were used as well as more recent protests in Turkey and Brazil in which water cannons, tear gas, and rubber bullets were regularly utilized.

The NYPD has extensive expertise in protest policing. They regularly manage large crowds without having to rely on violence or even mass arrests. This has been accomplished, however, by dramatically shrinking the allowable space and permissible actions at demonstrations through a massive and costly system of micromanaging demonstrators that has undermined the true meaning of freedom of assembly. When these systems of regulation break down, they are quick to either lash out in violence situationally or develop plans for proactive interventions that in some cases result in pre-emptive interference with the right to protest. Although this basic intolerance of disorder comports well with the institution's internal commitment to order maintenance policing based on the broken-windows theory, it has also meshed with the aversion to protest shared by Mayors Giuliani and Bloomberg. The latter has had a better record on allowing freedom of speech; however, both have had a very narrow interpretation of the freedom of assembly, seeing it as a tangential adjunct to speech, which they are free to substantially limit. As inequality and political discord grow globally and domestically, this restricted view of the right to assemble may come under increasing pressure. Mayor de Blasio may face a greater challenge in maintaining strict order and in politically justifying any attempts to do so.

References

Allen, M. (1998, May 15). Giuliani threatens action if cabbies fail to cancel a protest. *New York Times.*

Anderson, L. (2004, December 29–January 4). Critical Mass gets 'ride of way;' Injunction denied. *The Villager.* 74, 34.

Badish, D. (2011, November 15). Occupy Wall Street: NYPD military assault, raid, evict Zucotti protestors. *The New Civil Rights Movement.* http://thenewcivilrightsmovement.com/occupy-wall-street-nypd-military-assault-raid-evict-zucotti-protestors/news/2011/11/15/30214

Cardwell, D. (2004, September 1). At least 900 arrested in city as protesters clash with police. *New York Times.*

Chen, A. (2012, April 30). NYPD raids activists' homes before May Day protests. *Gawker.* http://gawker.com/5906500/nypd-raids-activists-homes-before-tomorrows-occupy-wall-street-protests.

Chiroux, M. (2011, November 17). NYPD using army "snatch and grab" techniques against OWS protesters. *Huffington Post.* http://www.huffingtonpost.com/matthis-chiroux/occupy-wall-street-nypd_b_1100209.html

Committee to Protect Journalists. (2011, November 15). *Journalists obstructed from covering OWS protests.* Committee to Protect Journalists. http://www.cpj.org/2011/11/journalists-obstructed-from-covering-ows-protests.php

Dobnik V. (2004, August 27). Police arrest 250 in mass bicycle protest. *Associated Press.*

Dwyer, J. (2007a, March 25). City police spied broadly before G.O.P. convention. *New York Times,* pg. A1.

Dwyer, J. (2007b, February 8). Records show scrutiny of detainees in '04 protests. *New York Times, pg.* B3.

Elliot, J. (2011, October 7). The NYPD, now sponsored by Wall Street. *Salon.com.* http://www.salon.com/2011/10/07/the_nypd_now_sponsored_by_wall_street/

Ferguson, S. (2004, August 27). Dispatch from New York: Whose streets? *Mother Jones.*

Friedman, S.C. (2004, August 23). Radicals plot bad weather. *New York Post.*

Gillham P.F., Edwards, B., & Noaks, J. (2012). Strategic incapacitation and the policing of Occupy Wall Street protests in New York City, 2011. *Policing and Society.* 23, 1, 81–102.

Gillham P.F., & Noaks, J. (2011). Securitizing America: Strategic incapacitation and the policing of protest since the 11 September 2001 terrorist attacks. *Sociology Compass.* 7, 636–652.

Graves, N. (1998, October 21). Pols rip cops in gay riot, but Rudy defends them. *New York Post.*

Harlow, S. (2011). Journalists arrested during "media blackout" as police evict Occupy Wall Street protesters from New York City park. *Journalism in the Blog.* https://knightcenter.utexas.edu/blog/journalists-arrested-during-media-blackout-police-evict-occupy-wall-street-protesters-new-york

Hays, T. (2002, February 4). Protestors say police presence hindered their efforts. *Associated Press.*

Horan, K. (2011, November 2). Fewer barricades occupying Wall Street. *WNYC,* http://www.wnyc.org/articles/wnyc-news/2011/nov/02/less-barricades-occupying-wall-street/

Marzulli, J. (2002, January 29). Steer clear of Econ Forum: Major traffic gridlock expected near Waldorf till Sunday. *Daily News,* p. 22.

Massey, D. (2011, November 16). Councilman charges cops with roughing him up. *Crain's New York Business.*

McCarthy, J.D., & McPhail, C. (1998). The institutionalization of protest in the United States. In D.S. Meyer & S. Tarrow (Eds.), *The Social Movement Society.* Boulder, CO: Rowman and Littlefield, pp. 83–110.

McPhail, C., Schweingruber, D., & McCarthy, J.D. (1998). Protest policing in the United States, 1960–1995. In Donna della Porta & Herbert Reiter (Eds.), *Policing Protest: The Control of Mass Demonstrations in Western Democracies.* Minneapolis: Minnesota University Press.

Meek, J.G. (2004, August 19). Violence at RNC feared: Protests may turn bloody, feds warn. *Daily News,* p. 8.

Moore, M.T. (2004, November 15). Big pack of bikes piques police. *USA Today.*

Neumeister, L., & Sullivan, E. (2013, February 4). NYPD Muslim spying program violates Handschu Rules, say civil rights lawyers. *Huffington Post.*

New York Civil Liberties Union. (2003). Arresting protest. New York Civil Liberties Union.

New York Civil Liberties Union. (2005). Rights and wrongs at the Republican National Convention. New York Civil Liberties Union.

New York Civil Liberties Union. (2013). *Handschu v. Special Services Division (Challenging NYPD surveillance practices targeting political groups).* New York Civil Liberties Union, http://www.nyclu.org/case/handschu-v-special-services-division-challenging-nypd-surveillance-practices-targeting-politica

New York Times. (2004). Police surveillance and the 2004 Republican National Convention. *New York Times,* Document File, www.nytimes.com/ref/nyregion/RNC_intel_digests.html

Okie, B. (2004). What's scarier than 6000 bicyclists? *Portland Independent Media Center,* http://portland.indymedia.org/en/2004/09/296942.shtml

O'Shaughnessy, P. (2004, August 26). Anarchists hot for mayhem. *Daily News.*

Parascandola, R. (2004, August 13).What to expect when you're...; expecting the worst; Cops' manual on dealing with demonstrators at the GOP convention tells them to watch out for dirty tricks and ignore verbal abuse. *Newsday,* p. A3.

Risen, J. (1998, July 1). Police concede they were caught off guard by size of the protest. *New York Times.*

Roane, K. (1998, October 22). Judge rules for police brutality rally. *New York Times.*

Sengupta, S. (1998, May 20). After pressure from Giuliani, taxi group cancels a protest. *New York Times.*

Siegel, J. (2006, February 22–28). Another judge denies injunction on Critical Mass. *The Villager.* 75: 40.

Soffer, J. (2012). *Ed Koch and the Rebuilding of New York City.* New York: Columbia University Press.

Stamper, N. (2011, November 28). Paramilitary policing from Seattle to Occupy Wall Street. *The Nation.*

Taintor, D. (2011, December 12). Poll: Majority of New Yorkers disapprove of Bloomberg on Occupy Wall Street. *TPM,* http://tpmdc.talkingpointsmemo. com/2011/12/poll-majority-of-new-yorkers-disapprove-of-bloomberg-on-occupy-wall-street.php

Texiera, E. (1998, September 6). Peaceful Harlem rally ends in skirmish with police "Million Youth March" draws perhaps 6,000, *Baltimore Sun.*

Times Up. (2009). *Excerpt from Critical Mass lawsuit claimant,* http://www.times-up. org/2009-releases/excerpt-critical-mass-lawsuit-claimant-0

Turse, N. (2011). New York becoming a police state? Occupy Wall Street meets the "ring of steel" at Liberty Square. *AlterNet.* October 13. http://www.alternet.org/ story/152729/occupy_wall_street%3A_people_power_vs._the_police_state.

Vitale, A.S. (2005). From negotiated management to command and control: How the NYPD polices protests. *Policing and Society.* 15, 283–304.

Vitale, A.S. (2007). The command and control and Miami models at the 2004 Republican National Convention: New forms of policing protests, *Mobilization.* 12, 4.

Vitale, A.S. (2008). *City of Disorder: How the Quality of Life Campaign Transformed New York Politics.* New York: NYU Press.

Wald, J. (2004, August 28). 264 arrested in NYC bicycle protest. *CNN,* CNN.com

Waldman, A. (1998, August 6). Giuliani assails organizers of youth march. *New York Times.*

Walgrave, S. (2009). Government stance and internal diversity of protest: A comparative study of protest against the war in Iraq in eight countries. *Social Forces.* 87, 3, 1355–1387.

Walker, H. (2012, September 19). Occupy organizers say NYPD targeted and arrested key leaders before anniversary protest. *Politicker,* http://politicker.com/2012/09/ occupy-organizers-say-nypd-targeted-and-arrested-the-movements-leaders-before-anniversary-protest/

Weiser, B. (2001, 11 January). Three trampled by horses reach settlement with city. *New York Times,* p. B 6.

Wolf, N. (2011, December 17). NYPD for hire: How uniformed New York Police moonlight for banks. *The Guardian.*

Impact of Technology on Crime Strategies
Case Study of the New York Police Department

8

JOSEPH E. PASCARELLA

Contents

8.1 Introduction

Policing in the United States has endured rapid strategic organizational changes over the last three decades that have redefined the role of the police organization and raised the expectations of the police function in the United States. This most recent historical transformation of the police began slowly in the 1970s, gained traction in the 1980s, and then increased in momentum in the 1990s as seemingly intractable violent crime began to decline significantly. Most of these changes and rising successes of policing (in terms of eradicating violent crime) were based on technology and the focus and use of technology in policing. Technology had always evolved and was integrated slowly into policing; however, the 1990s realized rapid technological changes in policing that have redefined organizational strategies in policing.

As crime continued to decline throughout the 1990s, new policing management techniques and strategies began to emerge and develop including decentralized management accountability and the use of state-of-the-art information technology systems such as automated complaint recording systems and geographic information systems (GIS). These policing innovations were largely credited as the reasons for the crime decreases. Additionally, a renewed interest in the timeliness of raw community information and criminal intelligence became a significant part of crime reduction strategies. These new strategies, techniques, and the utilization of advanced information technology became the focus of attention in both the professional business community and the world of academe. The policing profession as a whole gained pre-eminence in that police management strategies and techniques and uses of technology became the agents of change and reform as opposed to a policing profession that historically required change and reform.

Much of this change in large urban police departments such as the New York Police Department (NYPD) was focused on technology and integrating technology into organizational strategies. As technology became more user-friendly, less expensive, and readily available, it became more pervasive throughout the NYPD, and the accumulated successes of the crime declines and uses of technology led to a changing perspective in role of technology in the NYPD. Historically, large police organizations such as the NYPD were reluctant and slow to integrate technology given the sizeable initial investment costs in equipment and training and lack of return on investment through quality and measurable outcomes in the short term.

The policing organizational strategic paradigm during this period of transformation in policing from roughly the 1960s through the 1990s shifted from confronting crime and disorder as an omnipresent rapid response force tactically geared toward preventive patrol to community and problem-solving strategies. The contemporary police agency that has evolved from the community and problem-solving agency is one focused on the efficient utilization of information technology, organizational accountability, and community responsiveness. The police organization today is drastically different from recent yesteryear. Police organizations still confront perennial challenges such as crime and disorder; however, the contemporary police agency uses new methods and strategies to utilize valuable police resources efficiently to confront enduring problems. Most of the improvements in policing efficiency (driven by an increased level of accountability and public expectations) are focused on technology.

In 1988, George L. Kelling and Mark H. Moore outlined the strategies of police organizations from the perspective that police organizations are beholden to both current and preceding historical events. According to Kelling and Moore (1988), the police organization is continuously dynamic and evolves based upon the organization's perception of historical events. However, interpreting these events and their relevance to policing strategies are both subjective and potentially problematic. Kelling and Moore foresaw in 1988 that the police organizations must manage community information successfully to maintain fruitful strategies, crime reduction, and community interaction.

As public expectations increased consistent with police successes in reducing crime throughout the 1990s, contemporary policing became more complex given the increase in responsibilities, the changing crime trends, and the threats of terrorism. The contemporary police must sustain the violent crime rate reduction strategies that have significantly reduced crime and disorder while evolving to address new emergent crimes of information, access the community to solve quality-of-life problems and issues collaboratively, implement homeland security and counterterrorism initiatives, and coordinate all public safety functions regarding planning and preparedness for emergency management (the "all-hazards" approach). These four strategic organizational objectives of contemporary policing have extended the original police functions and propelled the police as the prime government agency in maintaining the everwidening public safety function.

The first two strategic objectives, crime reduction and evolution strategies, and community relations are enduring challenges in policing that must be addressed by the police organization with new and innovative methods such as "information-driven" and "data-driven" policing strategies and an organizationally led renewed commitment to the problem-solving components of community policing.

The third and fourth strategic objectives, counterterrorism initiatives to ensure homeland security and coordination of public safety functions ("all-hazards" policing) were never fully embraced as a policing strategy nor was it as necessary or critical prior to September 11, 2001. The military was mandated with thwarting attacks against the United States, and homeland defense readiness and preparedness ebbed and waned cyclically as the United States' involvement in military conflicts heightened, intensified, and then de-escalated throughout the 20th century. Historically, the police played a minimal role in homeland defense and homeland security prior to September 11, 2001. The local police were expected to prepare for reactive measures such as first response in the event of such attacks, and proactive measures by local, state, and federal police agencies were usually limited to detecting and apprehending subversive threats to government infiltration (Faber, 1949).

In addition, part of the complacency of local police organizations regarding counterterrorism was an overreliance on federal law enforcement for counterterrorism. The post–September 11, 2001 world has blurred this distinction between homeland defense and homeland security, and a dispute born out of issues of primary responsibility (Norwitz, 2002) has muddled the nascence of practical homeland security initiatives. The complex responsibility sharing and distinction between the police and the military functions has still not been completely reconciled and partitioned (Brandl, 2003), nor is it clear when or if it ever will be.

Concurrently, the focus on the primary objectives of policing became increasingly centered on crime reduction, strategic crime evolution, and using community information as a major component of crime reduction strategy (Kelling & Moore, 1988) as public expectations of police organizational effectiveness increased. Kelling noted in 1988 the pre-eminence of community information in policing strategies; however, the advances in information technology and uses of information technology realized their projections to a near full transformation in policing strategies.

8.2   Technology and Policing in the NYPD

8.2.1   CompStat and GIS

CompStat was an organizational strategy implemented by the New York Police Department in 1994 that revolutionized policing strategies and accountability. Essentially, local police commanders were accountable for crime reduction and disorder strategies and the driving force behind successful CompStat principles were accountability and the use of technology. CompStat has been described as a "paradigm" shift (Kapia, 2004) in policing. The use of CompStat quickly spread to other large urban departments, but the original strategic principles intended for CompStat may not be prevelant in many urban police agencies. However, the original implementation of CompStat as a strategy was CompStat's reliance on information technology and organizational accountability to reduce crime and disorder. The dissemination and display of crime information on a weekly basis was intended to allocate resources efficiently and rapidly to address specific crime and disorder issues.

A major component to the early success of CompStat's strategy is the reliance on geographical analysis of crime and crime mapping. Geographical analysis has emerged as a leading crime analysis technique as an outgrowth of the general historical evolution of crime analysis that has become increasingly sophisticated and specialized. Early geographical crime analysis focused on "pin maps" that consisted of analyzing past crimes that were plotted on an underlying map of a specific geography using pins to display the geographic location of the criminal events. Vintage crime analyses using pin maps (Harries, 1999) to visualize crime locations along with advances in information technology and policing organizational changes thrust geographic analyses to the forefront of police and law enforcement agencies' crime control strategies. User-friendly mapping software combined with the need for sophisticated investigative techniques and the timely deployment of police and law enforcement resources increased the prevalence and primacy placed on geographical analyses of crime. Central to the much heralded CompStat crime reduction strategic and management accountability program established by the New York Police Department was the use of crime-mapping (Henry, 2002; Ratcliff, 2004; Silverman, 1999).

Essentially, police and law enforcement commanders could better visualize crime-prone locations and general problem areas on a map dotted with serious crime and then use that map as part of a cohesive crime reduction strategy. The quicker crime maps could be created, the faster the response with policing and enforcement-related resources. This "cops on the dots" crime reduction strategy can be considered the "first generation of hot spot policing and crime analysis." Police and law enforcement agencies recognized the need for geographic analysis of crime based on the success and emulation of the CompStat organizational program (and use of geographical analyses); however, geographic analyses go beyond computerized pin mapping to examine the crime dynamic spatially and temporally with the objective of identifying crime travel patterns of victims and offenders. One of the negative aspects of CompStat was the pressure of accountability placed on local commanders and specific focus on crime reduction strategies that ignored other very important components of urban policing (Eterno & Silverman, 2006).

8.2.2 Fusion Centers

Fusion centers are an evolving method to use crime information and technology in urban policing. Fusion centers existed prior to September 11, 2001, with the origins of fusion centers dating to military command centers as a centralized area to discuss strategies and tactics. Fusion centers became prevalent in the 1980s in policing in the form of high-intensity drug trafficking areas (Department of Justice, 2013). High-intensity drug trafficking areas (HIDTA) were designed to force collaboration and sharing criminal information and drug trafficking intelligence among the numerous and fractured law enforcement agencies involved in suppressing the illegal drug trade.

After September 11, 2001, fusion centers (based on the HIDTA model) became prevalent in policing given the need for cooperation among federal, state, and local law enforcement and the need for rapid dissemination of intelligence information that might assist in counterterrorism initiatives. The NYPD, on the forefront of the information- and technology-driven fusion center model, participates in external fusion centers (Johnson & Dorn, 2013) and also operates several fusion centers within the organization to address both crime and counterterrorism strategies, the Lower Manhattan Security Initiative (LMSI) and the Real Time Crime Center (RTCC). Both the LMSI and RTCC are designed with a major technology component. Officers' and analysts' primary tools in the LMSI and RTCC are information and technology and their primary objective is to obtain as much information as possible and then disseminate this information as rapidly as possible. The primary tool of policing in the RTCC and LMSI is technology and information, consistent with the prognostication of Kelling and Moore in 1988, however, not nearly at the scope and enormity that Kelling could have predicted.

8.2.2.1   *Lower Manhattan Security Initiative*

The Lower Manhattan Security Initiation is an information- and technology-driven fusion center (Coordination Center Operations Center) located in lower Manhattan that endeavors proactively to detect potential terror attacks by using surveillance and analysis technology on persons and vehicles entering lower Manhattan (NYPD, 2013a). Essentially, a network of cameras captures digitized information that is then analyzed by officers and analysts located in the Coordination Center Operations Center. Essentially, officers and analysts are proactively endeavoring to disrupt a terror attack by determining if any person or vehicle entering lower Manhattan has a connection to a terror group or cell.

8.2.2.2   *Real Time Crime Center*

The Real Time Crime Center is located in the NYPD and the primary function of the RTCC is to provide information support for police officers and detectives investigating crime throughout the patrol and detective units in the NYPD (2013b). The RTCC provides field officers and detectives with the most updated and timely information about a geographic location, person, and any other relevant information needed to support an investigation.

8.3   Conclusion

The role and continued use of information technology in large urban police agencies is continually evolving, but the effectiveness of using technology is not a guarantee for policing success. Garicano and Heaton (2010) studied the role of information technology and data in nearly 20,000 police agencies and found no correlation between increases in the use of information technology and a reduction of crime. However, there are many construct validity issues involved given the actual uses of information technology and variance in police agencies in the United States.

The New York Police Department is now on the forefront of using (and relying on) technology for community interaction, crime reduction, and counterterrorism initiatives, the current "big three" of contemporary urban police agencies. There are several individual rights concerns that will be a major issue and will need future discussion. The primary issue is that there are very few guidelines in maintaining data and information from the emergent information technology structures built, managed, and maintained by the New York Police Department. Technology and policing are now evolving analogously, as opposed to the perennial game of "catch up" in previous eras. The changing crime trends and threat of terrorism require a proactive use of technology by large agencies such as the New York Police Department;

however, the guidelines for the data obtained by using this technology must evolve also to preserve individual rights.

References

Brandl, S. G. (2003). Back to the future: The implications of September 11, 2001 on law enforcement practice and policy. Ohio State University Journal of criminal Law, 1, 133–154.

Eterno, J.A., & Silverman, E.B. (2006). The New York City Police Department's Compstat: Dream or nightmare? International Journal of Police Science and Management, 8, 3, 218–231.

Faber, H. (1949, 17 January). 400 Police on Duty as 12 Communists Go on Trial Today. New York Times, p. 1.

Fickes, M. (2004, June). The Juncture of Design and Technology. Government Security, p. 31, 32. New York: Penton Media.

Garicano, L., & Heaton, P. (2010). Information technology, organization, and productivity in the public sector: Evidence from police departments. Journal of Labor Economics, 28, 1, 167–201.

Goldstein, H. (1990). Problem-Oriented Policing. Philadelphia, PA: Temple University Press.

Harries, K. (1999). Mapping crime: Principle and practice (No. NCJ 178919).

Henry, V.E. (2002). The Compstat Paradigm. Flushing, NY: Looseleaf Law.

Johnson, B., & Dorn, S. (2013). Fusion centers: New York State intelligence strategy unifies law enforcement. The Police Chief. Retrieved: http://www.policechiefmagazine.org/magazine/index.cfm?article_id=1419&fuseaction=display&issue_id=22008

Kapia, R.E. (2004). A brief history of a venerable paradigm in policing. Journal of Contemporary Criminal Justice, 20, 1, 80–83. doi:10.1177/1043986203262311

Kelling, G., & Moore, M. (1988). The Evolving Strategy of Policing. Perspectives on Policing. Washington, DC: National Institute of Justice.

Lyons, W. (2002). Partnerships, information and public safety: Community policing in a time of terror. Policing: An International Journal of Police Strategies & Management, 25, 3, 530–542.

Monahan, T. (2010). The future of security? Surveillance operations at homeland security fusion centers. Social Justice, 37, 2/3, 84–98.

New York Police Department. (2013a). Counter terrorism units. Retrieved from http://www.nyc.gov/html/nypd/html/administration/counterterrorism_units.shtml

New York Police Department. (2013b). New York Police Department, Real Time Center Podcast (July 14, 2006). Available at http://www.nyc.gov/html/nypd/html/pr/podcasts.shtml

Norwitz, J. (2002, November 6). Combating terrorism: With a helmet or badge. Journal of Homeland Security. Anser Institute.

Office of National Drug Control Policy. (2004). High intensity drug trafficking areas. Available at http://www.whitehouse.gov/ondcp/high-intensity-drug-trafficking-areas-program.

Rengert, G. (1980). Spatial aspects of criminal behavior. In Daniel E. Georges-Abeyie and Keith D. Harries (Eds.), *Crime: A Spatial Perspective* (pp. 47–57). New York: Columbia University Press.

Sherman, L.W., Gartin, P.R., & Buerger, M.E. (1989). Hot spots of predatory crime: Routine activities and the criminology of place. *Criminology* 27, 1, 27–55.

Silverman, E. (1999). *NYPD Battles Crime: Innovative Strategies in Policing.* Boston: Northeastern University Press.

Walsh, W.F. (2001). Compstat: An analysis of an emerging police managerial paradigm. *Policing: An International Journal of Police Strategies & Management,* 24, 3, 347–362.

Walsh, W.F., & Vito, G.F. (2004). The meaning of Compstat: Analysis and response. *Journal of Contemporary Criminal Justice,* 20, 51–69.

Wiegler, L. (2008). Big brother in the big apple [national security—video surveillance]. *Engineering & Technology (17509637),* 3, 9, 24–27. doi:10.1049/et:20080902

A Grassroots Movement to Change the NYPD*

9

ROBERT GANGI

Contents

9.1 In the Beginning

I have lived in New York City (NYC) all my life—for 70 years and counting—and have had many encounters with the police as a citizen of the city going about my business and as a professional carrying out my duties. Most, though not all, encounters were decidedly negative. They involved officers

---

* This chapter is dedicated to Rosa Squillacote, the Police Reform Organizing Project's (PROP) policy advocate nonpareil. Rosa's talent, energy, savvy, good humor, and dedication—in short, her excellent personal and professional qualities—have been mainstays of PROP's efforts for over two years. Her good works have contributed significantly to the progress that New York's police reform movement has made toward achieving a fairer, livable, and inclusive city for all its residents.

191

who were rude, irresponsible, or physically aggressive. Four incidents stand out, all part of my professional experiences over time.

9.1.1 Charlie

For my first full-time job, I worked for an NYC agency that sent young men into low-income communities to intervene constructively in the lives of boys troubled and in trouble, and to divert them from addiction, crime, and violence. The city assigned me to work at the community center of the Church of St. Matthew and St. Timothy on West 84th Street in Manhattan. It was 1966, and I was 22 years old.

The most volatile community center member was Charlie Wilson, 17, African-American, energetic, charismatic, and at times, explosively dangerous. His hatred of cops was so impassioned that I found it almost admirable even while recognizing it as reckless and crazy.

Community center staff often took neighborhood boys and girls on trips to places of interest in and outside the city. This time we traveled to a Yankees game, 10 boys and I in a long row of seats at the old stadium in the Bronx.

In a mistake of mine, Charlie sat far from me, and empty soda cups shortly began flying from around his seat onto the people below. Before I could try to stop his antics, a man from a lower seat stood up yelling and challenged Charlie to a match in the aisle alongside the row where we sat. As I scrambled over the boys between the aisle and me, I noted two relevant things: Charlie was, unsurprisingly, delighted by the prospect of a fight and the man, luckily, was not. We were able to settle matters quickly with Charlie grinning and the man grumbling while they returned to their seats. I stood in the aisle for a minute to make sure that there was not another flare-up.

Stadium cops rushed up, some of whom, I learned later, were off-duty New York City Police Department (NYPD) officers. While explaining that their services were not needed, peace had been restored, I saw that they were wired for action. When George Lopez, one of the Center's well-behaved and respectful boys, held up his hand and said, "Be cool," a cop jumped across me and began pummeling George. In seconds, another officer pushed past me, I thought, to grab hold of his lunatic colleague. He too started beating on George. A mini police-instigated brawl took place with me in the middle pulling officers off the boys I often referred to as "my kids."

As the immediate follow-up to this incident, I was displeased to learn later that night that we missed seeing Mickey Mantle hit a three-run home run in the bottom of the eighth inning to win the game. On the other hand, I was pleasantly surprised that the Yankees community relations staff to whom I complained believed my police riot account and provided a dozen free, right behind home plate, tickets to another ballgame.

Later that summer the center took another trip, this time to Bear Mountain Park in upstate New York. Charlie participated. It was a hot, sweaty day, temperature in the 90s. Charlie, his shirt off and wrapped around his waist, and I, by his side by design, were walking across one of the park's large empty fields. A park cop approached us and I tensed up, ready to intervene in the hostile interaction that seemed likely. The officer spoke to Charlie: "I hate to have to tell you this. I know it's a miserably hot day, but we have a rule against walking around bare-chested, so would you please put your shirt on?" The man walked away as Charlie put his shirt on. "Now there's a cop I could respect," he said to me.

Coming at the beginning of my working life, the experience was soul-shaping. It showed me that treating individuals, even someone as volatile as Charlie, civilly and calmly, as you would like to be treated, almost always elicited a human and sought-after response.

9.1.2 Freddie and the Triboro Bridge

My next police encounter came several years later when I was a lead organizer for a citywide coalition of community day care programs. The Lindsay administration had threatened to cut off government funding for the centers. The coalition decided to protest by blocking traffic on the Triboro Bridge connecting Manhattan and Queens during morning rush hour. I had locked arms with a colleague in front of a car another colleague had stopped on the bridge. An officer approached and asked if the car belonged to me. When I said "No," he grabbed me by my upper arm and tried to toss me aside. My visceral response to his putting his hands on me in this way—it may be a cliché, but I felt violated—was to swing back at him. Very quickly five or six other officers came at me and a fight ensued between them and me. After about five minutes or so, they threw me to the ground and held me down, just in time, to avoid a swinging billy club aimed at my head by an officer who had apparently decided that the best way to subdue me was to bash my skull.

After spending the rest of the day in several crowded holding cells and pleading guilty to a disorderly conduct charge, I returned home. At 11:30 PM, having seen local news coverage of the protest on TV, my brother Freddie—half Sicilian-American like me—called to explain his feelings about my activity on the bridge. He first expressed praise and pride in my physical prowess and then his concern:

> "But Rob, did you consider what position you put me in?"
> "What do you mean?" I asked.
> "If that cop had clubbed you, I would've had to kill him."

9.2   The Correctional Association

Jump cut to about 15 years later. I'm the director of the Correctional Association of New York (CA), a nonprofit prison reform organization, a position I held for nearly 30 years.

A key CA activity involved monitoring conditions of confinement in New York City's court pens that hold recently arrested people just before they are arraigned, or officially charged with an offense, by a sitting judge. When we began these monitoring visits in February 1989, we observed abominable conditions, the most inhumane we saw during my tenure at the CA: extreme crowding; waits of two or more days; dark, filthy cells, often vermin-infested; inoperable toilets and sinks; no access to phones or medical services; and no ability to wash, change clothes, or brush one's teeth before appearing in court.

At least partly due to the CA's persistent and strategic efforts, supported by allies in and outside government, conditions improved dramatically over time: clean, well-lit cells; working phones, toilets, and sinks; reduced arrest-to-arraignment times; and access to medical services.

One thing did not change over time, the racial composition of the people locked up in these facilities. If CA representatives toured the Manhattan, Bronx, or Brooklyn pens on a Thursday morning and saw 250 people who had been arrested since Tuesday night, 248 would be people of color. Cell after cell of black and brown faces, sometimes we would not see one White person confined. We felt like we were visiting a South African jail at the height of apartheid, not the holding pens operated by the government of America's great progressive city.

Other harsh truths were known to us: that most detainees were not charged with serious offenses; turnstile jumping, trespassing, begging on the subway, selling umbrellas or flowers on the street, marijuana possession, and driving without a license were common charges. We also knew that the stark racial disparity—not merely disproportionate but virtually exclusive—was not an accident, but a function of the policies and practices of the NYPD. At the CA, through our visits to the court pens, we came face to face with law enforcement's deep dark heart, namely the unapologetic racial bias and stark shameless injustices that mark our criminal justice and policing practices.

In the letter announcing my 2011 resignation to the CA's members, I noted that a mixture of sadness and excitement marked my departure:

> The excitement comes from my new freedom of opportunity to focus on other justice-related issues, issues that for reasons of organizational resource constraints and/or mission scope we have been unable to take on at the CA, issues that go to the very heart of the kind of society we want to live in and the kind of criminal justice system we want to operate. Issues like the deployment of law-enforcement personnel that result in the starkly disproportionate arrest

and confinement of poor people of color and the often harsh treatment by the police of our most vulnerable and marginalized people such as the homeless, LGBT youth, and exploited girls and boys caught up in the sex trade.

9.3 Police Reform Organizing Project

Fortunately for me and my planned work, Doug Lasdon, the visionary executive director of the Urban Justice Center, invited me to join the organization and gave me the freedom to initiate a project of my choosing under its rubric. And so, the Police Reform Organizing Project (PROP) was born in the spring of 2011.

9.3.1 Fundamental Organizing/Advocacy Tenets

The name Police Reform Organizing Project reflects my effort to adhere to a time-honored organizing principle, that is, to choose names or slogans to represent your work and mission that are catchy and easy to remember and understand. In fact, much of what follows represents my colleagues' and my continuing efforts to follow time-honored organizing/advocacy principles as we advanced PROP's policy agenda.

9.3.1.1 Core Principles

A basic tenet in policy advocacy is that the effort should reflect first or core principles that inspire people, speak to people's basic value system, and reinforce society's fundamental moral compass. A significant factor that drew me to PROP's central mission to correct abusive police practices was that it was informed by two powerful core principles.

PROP's first guiding belief is that practices and policies of our police department and criminal justice system reflect the central values and priorities of our society and government. It is the truth that Winston Churchill (1910) presented when he said, "The mood and temper of the public in regard to the treatment of crime and criminals is the most unfailing test of any civilization." PROP's work is important and is enduring because it gets at the heart of things, at the heart of who we are as a people and who we wish to be as a people.

Another fundamental operating principle for PROP is the strong belief in the inherent dignity of all human beings. One way to think about our efforts is that when we see an unjust NYPD practice that violates that principle such as suspicionless stops of low-income Black and brown young men or the targeting and harassment of street vendors and sex workers, we take action. We plan and adopt strategies to address these problems.

9.3.1.2 Winability

It was e:sy to see that the issue of abusive policing was morally compelling to the many people in our city who care about racial and social justice, and that, therefore, inspiring core principles apply to the efforts to address it. The next consideration for whether to focus a campaign on a particular concern was a much trickier proposition. Was it a winnable issue? This was a very important question because it is impossible to organize people who do not have hope that their efforts can bear fruit, that their endeavor can bring about constructive change.

Taking on the NYPD was undoubtedly a daunting task. In my nearly 50 years of advocacy/organizing work, I had rarely seen a mainstream political or civic figure aggressively criticize policing in New York City except in response to an egregious and highly publicized brutal act such as the broomstick sodomizing of Abner Louima and the killing of the unarmed Amadou Diallo. Even then the outcry and organizing were focused on a single incident, not part of a sustained effort to achieve systemic changes.

Moreover, in the past decade, the department's political standing had grown due to several factors: the urban myth that the NYPD had been solely responsible for the dramatic drop in crime in New York, the terrible death toll of over 150 officers on September 11th, 2001, and the iconic status of the square-jawed police commissioner Ray Kelly, a law enforcement leader who could have been drawn from the imagination of Hollywood's top casting directors.

Still, my colleagues and I determined that the answer to the winability question was a solid and credible "Yes." The NYPD's harsh and sometimes brutal treatment of the Occupy Wall Street protestors, who, albeit scruffy, were mainly peaceful; the manhandling of an outspoken Black city councilperson at the Caribbean Day parade; the trial of narcotics officers revealing fabricated drug felony charges against innocent people; and the data about the ever-growing number of stop and frisks that were widely reported, and that revealed an undeniable racial bias in the use of the tactic, all these and related factors combined to pound at the NYPD's protected and inviolate status within the city politic. There was now a black eye on the face of the statue that had been constructed; the statue began to wobble on the pedestal where Bloomberg and Kelly had placed it. It was not about to topple, but it was no longer above the fray of a contentious public debate.

9.3.1.3 Hope, Its Central Importance

At the same time, and as a consequence, a hope that positive reforms were within reach began to grow in the hearts and minds of the people most concerned about these issues: criminal justice professionals and individuals in the larger society, mostly persons identified as liberals and progressives, who care deeply about social and racial justice; policy advocates and service providers: clergy, human rights lawyers, and organizers who work with discriminated-against groups; and most important, the members of our city's vulnerable groups: particularly low-income, young Black and brown men and their families, LGBTQ persons, especially homeless LGBTQ youth, sex workers, street vendors, people with mental illness, and the homeless.

While at the CA I helped organize the *Drop the Rock* campaign aimed at repealing the harsh mandatory Rockefeller drug laws. Sometimes at our coalition meetings, which many people of color attended, the discussion would wander off the agenda to focus on policing problems. Everybody at the table had a story, often multiple stories, about bad police encounters; everybody in attendance expressed fear and anger, and also a resignation, sad and defeated, to the reality of having to endure those encounters, because there was no hope that these long-standing policing practices could change. In contrast, the people there believed that they could support, join, and lead activities that would bring about true drug law reform. That hope was instrumental to, and a critical factor in, the eventual success of the *Drop the Rock* effort.

Helping to drive this palpable sense of hope and possibility was the looming reality of a mayoral election just two years away. The common wisdom shared by us at PROP was that no significant policing reforms could occur as long as Michael Bloomberg reigned as the head of city government. But shortly, New York City would have a new leader, and depending on his or her frame of mind and depending on the political climate regarding policing issues when he or she took power in January 2014, New Yorkers could very possibly see and experience sweeping reforms in NYPD practices.

The challenge for us at PROP now was how to best mount an organizing/advocacy campaign to harness this newly arrived on the scene hope and possibility in ways that would dramatically shift public attitudes to produce a positive electoral outcome in November 2013.

9.3.1.4 *Framing the Issue*

Our first step was to frame the issue, to present PROP's analysis of policing problems in language easy for people to understand, in language that was persuasive, making a case based on statistics, research, and practical experience, in language that suited our interest and pointed to new directions that New York's policy makers should take.

In my second month at PROP, after speaking to a number of knowledgeable people and reading several pieces of relevant literature, I felt grounded enough in the issue, sufficiently informed, to prepare a six-page analysis or white paper. The document doubled as a lengthy op-ed published by *AlterNet*, a politically minded online newsletter, and PROP's basic policy paper and main reference point for people who wanted to understand our positions on objectionable NYPD practices and the specifics of PROP's sweeping reform agenda.

Backed up by relevant data and analysis, the paper (Gangi 2013) made the case that the NYPD's practices were illegal, wasteful, ineffective, unjust, homophobic, transphobic, and marked by a stark racial bias. The main remedies proposed to address these problems were to abolish abusive and misguided practices such as stop and frisk and the quota system; to create a strong, independent, entity that monitors and assesses police priorities and policies and that effectively investigates and punishes misconduct; and to establish and implement community-oriented, problem-solving measures that strengthen neighborhoods while reducing crime.

9.3.1.5 Building a Diverse Coalition

Our next step at PROP, and from the standpoint of an effective overall political strategy, probably the most important, was to form a citywide coalition of like-minded groups and individuals. The flyer promoting the coalition's first gathering led with the heading, "New Yorkers for Police Reform have an important ally—YOU." We decided, unsurprisingly, to call the coalition *New Yorkers for Police Reform*. The central purpose of this effort, and of virtually all well-thought-out coalitions, was to expand our base of support by including allies who perceived that their interests were served by helping us achieve our objectives and who, by virtue of their numbers, their resources, and their status, enhanced our and their cause.

Early in developing PROP's stated mission and in building a broad coalition, we decided to focus our efforts not just on stop and frisk, the most infamous abusive NYPD tactic, but on the various perverse forms of bad police practices. PROP works as a discrete project under the nonprofit roof of the Urban Justice Center which houses other projects involved in doing advocacy for, and providing services to, many of the city's vulnerable groups: the homeless, people with mental illness, street vendors, sex workers, and LGBT youth. Partly because of our conversations with the leaders of these projects, we came to understand that although stop and frisk was a deservedly notorious practice, it did not represent the whole terrible story of bad policing in NYC. It was all too true that stop and frisk targeted young Black and brown men. Also too true was that NYPD officers, driven by an aggressively enforced quota system for evaluating their performance, regularly harassed and mistreated, needlessly ticketed, and falsely arrested members of all the city's marginalized communities. Here's a common way PROP presented the full disturbing picture, whether it be at private meetings, public forums, or letters to the editor:

... Black and brown young men arrested for trespass while standing in front of their apartment buildings; people in psychiatric crisis, disoriented and confused, thrown to the ground, hand-cuffed, and locked up; LBGT persons called derogatory names and inappropriately touched as they enter a local community center; sex workers arrested for simply carrying condoms, or coerced into providing sex in return for their release; street vendors fined and arrested for violating arbitrarily enforced minor rules; homeless people roughed up and apprehended for begging on the subway or sleeping on a park bench. (Police Reform Organizing Project, 2013)

Building on this analysis, we invited representatives of victimized groups to attend our meetings, support our activities, and join the movement for police reform. We pursued this outreach strategy because it was right and because it was effective: 60 to 70 people came to the early PROP meetings, people of all ages, colors, genders, sexual preferences, and neighborhoods in the city. The discussions were lively, informed, structured—we set and followed a strict, agreed-upon agenda—and productive. By each gathering's end, we had made certain to set aside sufficient time for discussing and deciding future PROP activities.

9.3.1.6 Emphasizing Action

At the first several monthly meetings of New Yorkers for Police Reform, we reached a consensus that PROP should move forward with a series of activities with the general purpose of establishing our presence in the policymaking arena and with the specific objectives of shifting the political landscape in the city so dramatically that even the mainstream mayoral candidates in the upcoming campaign would feel the public pressure to support meaningful changes in NYPD practices. The decision was our way of following two organizing/advocacy principles: first, to be as active as possible (in other words "to keep doing things") to draw attention and people to your cause and, second, to be as thoughtful and strategic (in other words, smart) as possible to increase the likelihood that your actions will have a constructive impact on your policy goals.

We at PROP chose essentially to carry out an old-fashioned, aggressive organizing/advocacy campaign aimed at exposing and correcting abusive policing practices and using as its tools time-honored tactics such as a citywide petition drive and new available technologies such as a YouTube channel on the PROP website.

Here are some of the activities/strategies we initiated as a result of the discussions and decisions made at those first gatherings of New Yorkers for Police Reform.

9.3.1.7   Educating Voters and Pressuring Policy Makers

As a nonprofit, nonpartisan effort, PROP cannot publicly endorse or oppose electoral candidates. We can, and planned to, prepare a voter's guide (see PROP 2013) consisting of a series of questions relevant to the issue of harsh police practices and to submit those questions to the campaigns of candidates seeking office in 2013. Through our citywide, community-based networks and extensive media contacts including editorial writers and columnists, we intended to distribute politicians' responses to a broad segment of New York City's population, thereby publicizing the issue, injecting our concerns into the on-going political debate, and placing pressure on elected officials to take stances favorable to our agenda.

By way of presenting a fuller picture of the nature and purpose of the guide, here is an excerpt from the cover page of the document that we completed and distributed to candidates in the spring and summer of 2013:

> PROP has prepared the following questions to gather information from candidates running for public office in New York City regarding the merits and effectiveness of NYPD policies and practices. Our intention is to provide each candidate with a chance to express his or her positions on issues such as stop and frisk, marijuana policy reform, and law enforcement tactics regarding the mentally ill and the homeless. Because vital civil liberties and criminal justice matters are at stake, it is crucial that New Yorkers go to the polls knowing where the candidates stand on these issues. PROP welcomes candidates to answer at whatever length and with whatever specificity that they and their campaigns choose. The more complete and detailed a candidate's position is, the clearer of an idea the voters will have about whom to support on election day. Educated voters make educated decisions, and PROP's goal is to create an informed voting public on issues central to the well-being of our city. (PROP questionnaire, 2013)

9.3.1.8   Preparing Interesting, Informative Literature

Critical to the success of a public education/policy advocacy effort, especially a campaign involving a highly controversial issue, is the production of well-written, well-reasoned, readable literature of various forms to serve different related purposes and to appeal to diverse audiences. PROP had already prepared its policy paper with its pointed critique of harsh police tactics, a fact sheet featuring dramatic information about the NYPD, and a petition highlighting the most salient negatives about police practice.

Our future plans included an *In Their Own Words* series of reports, the first containing quotes and statements of current and retired police officers, and the second, the words and testimonies of New Yorkers victimized by bad police practices. Both documents would provide dramatic evidence of a departmentwide toxic culture and an aggressively enforced quota system that directly and indirectly contributed to the day-to-day objectionable practices of NYPD officers.

Here are compelling and representative excerpts from each report (PROP 2013a):

In Their Own Words, "They Got Bandanas On, Arrest Them": How Productivity Goals Drive Harsh and Unjust Policing, 2012

Superior Officers' Directions

"Everybody goes. I don't care. You're on 120 Chauncey and they're popping champagne? Yoke 'em. Put them through the system. They got bandanas on, arrest them. Everybody goes tonight. They're underage? Fuck it."

"If they're on a corner, make 'em move. If they don't want to move, lock 'em up. Done deal. You can always articulate [a charge] later."

"Your goal is five in each of these categories [seat belt, cell phone, double-parking, bus stop violations], not a difficult task to accomplish on Monday … if it's not accomplished by Monday, you've got to follow-up with it on Tuesday…."

Officers' Objections

"I'm not going to keep arresting innocent people, I'm not going to keep searching people for no reason, I'm not going to keep writing people up for no reason, I'm tired of this…."

Officer Adhyl Polanco

"We are stopping kids walking upstairs to their house, stopping kids going to the store, young adults. In order to keep the quota…."

Officer Adhyl Polanco's response to a question

"We've talked about it …. Nobody feels this is right, asking us to write summonses just to meet a quota."

One of many officers from the 79th Precinct in Bedford-Stuyvesant who was considering a day-long summons boycott

"Quotas are bad for the community because they take away an officer's discretion, which is important to building a relationship with the neighborhood they patrol…."

Patrick Lynch, President of the Patrolmen's Benevolent Association (PBA)

In Their Own Words, "The Biggest Gang Here In New York City"

From Serve and Protect to Patrol and Control

"I can't count the number of times I've watched police throw my son and his friends up against a wall. Anywhere my son goes—the lobby, the courtyard, the stairwell—he can be stopped and harassed by the NYPD. A trip to the store can result in a weekend in jail for him."

Faun Bracy, Bronx Mother

"I told the DA that I didn't spit, so they said, "So, you have a choice. You're gonna pay this fine or you're gonna go to trial." I said, "I'm not gonna pay a fine for something I didn't do, so let's go to trial." So I'm actually going to trial for spitting, and I think that's the most absurd thing I ever heard of in my life."

Andrew, South Bronx resident, who was falsely accused of spitting by the NYPD

"When you're a street vendor in New York, every single day it's a different fight. Vendors like us, we start out with nothing and work hard for our families. We are committing no crime. We don't think it's a crime to work in New York."

Alberto Loera, who sued the city for excessive ticketing of his food truck

"We all feel the same way—degraded, harassed, violated and criminalized because we're Black or Latino."

Nicholas Peart, 23, on repeated stop and frisks

"The police department has become the biggest gang here in New York City."

Rev. Bernard Walker, Bronx father of Jateik Reed, who was beaten by NYPD officers

"They're supposed to serve and protect, but all they do is patrol and control. Walking down the street doesn't make you a criminal."

Eric Togar, Brooklyn resident

"This is what Harlem has turned into—an open air prison. You can get stopped for anything."

Joseph "Jazz" Hayden, who documents police–civilian encounters

Also in our plans was a second policy paper that would bring together in a single report a presentation of abusive policing regarding all the city's vulnerable populations and a set of remedies to be enacted by each level of government to correct those abuses. PROP produced such a document in early

2013, *Criminalizing Communities* (Clifford, Garnett, Najeeb, & Nudd, 2013), that was written mainly by students at the Leitner Human Rights Clinic at Fordham Law School and that covered the concerns of low-income Black and brown young men, street vendors, Muslim-Americans, sex workers, the homeless, and people with mental illness.

9.3.1.9 Working the Media

Because PROP did not and would not have the resources to place advertising on television, on the radio, or in newspapers as a visible way to promote our positions, our ability to garner media attention via our own outreach would be critical to the success of our public education efforts. PROP planned to and did develop a strategic communication plan, focused on ensuring a consistent presence and messaging of PROP's mission and activities, showcasing the organization as a leading and influential voice in the media on harsh police practices, and as a credible resource for topical coverage on these issues.

Our plans and follow-through efforts include maintaining and growing our relationships with media contacts such as reporters, columnists, editors, and editorial writers. We will regularly be in touch with them individually through phone conversations about our current work and relevant newsworthy issues as they arose, and through a steady stream of e-mails. We will send newsletters via e-mail that included our recently published materials such as a new expanded version of our policy paper, a PROP "In Their Own Words" report, or an announcement of our upcoming activities such as a public forum.

In addition to our focus on day-to-day news coverage, we have paid particular attention to generating interest on the editorial pages of New York's main newspapers and to placing our pieces on the op-ed space of print and online news outlets. We already had relationships with editorial writers at the *New York Times, New York Daily News,* and *Newsday,* and with editors of the op-ed pages and online outlets such as the *Huffington Post* and *AlterNet.* We have contacted these media professionals regularly, lobbying them to adopt favorable positions on our proposals to remedy the NYPD's unjust practices and submitting to them opinion pieces with our analysis and recommendations regarding objectionable police tactics. Here are some titles of PROP op-eds that have been published by the *New York Times, AlterNet,* and *El Diario:*

> Time for NYC to Stop Criminalizing Communities
> When Police Are Encouraged to Abuse, Not Protect
> Focused on Numbers, but Not the Ones That Count
> Harmful Practices by the New York Police Department
> Ray Kelly—The Wrong Choice
> Tyranny in NYC: The NYPD's Wasteful, Ineffective, Illegal, and Unjust
>   Targeting of Blacks and Latinos

All these efforts to generate media coverage are aimed at bolstering PROP's standing, credibility, and visibility, thereby enhancing our effectiveness in New York's policymaking arena.

9.3.1.10 Organizing and Promoting Public Forums

A tried and true tool of public education campaigns, organizing relevant public forums was a main focus of PROP's early plans. These events have had several specific purposes: connecting the topic clearly to the principal themes of PROP's advocacy agenda and having the speakers/panelists not only present noteworthy information, but also stress the need for people to engage in actions organized by PROP and other police reform groups.

From December 2011 through June 2013, PROP held six public forums, all at iconic Manhattan locations well known for their association with racial and social justice causes. All were promoted in old-fashioned ways—the distribution of flyers and colorful postcards—as well as through the aggressive use of the relatively new technologies of e-mail, Facebook, and Twitter. Attendance ranged from about 50–150 to over 250.

Here is a sample of PROP public forums in chronological order, the topics presented, and blurbs/write-ups we used to advertise the events:

Problems with Policing and Proposals for Reform
   The public forum will engage professors, policymakers, the press, and eventually the audience in a conversation about current abusive police practices and how all of us organizing together can address and correct them.

From Behind the Blue Wall of Silence
   A public forum featuring current and former NYPD officers speaking about their experiences on the job and presenting their critique of current NYPD policies and tactics.

The Conscience of the City
   Faith leaders speak out against abusive police practices in honor of Martin Luther King, Jr. Day.

Prosecutors: Serving the Police or Serving the Public?
   Part of our campaign to pressure the city's district attorneys to repudiate the NYPD's illegal and sometimes concocted arrests, the forum will present panelists with first-hand knowledge of these practices, how central they are to New York's criminal justice process and legal culture, and how they damage and compromise the lives of our city's most vulnerable citizens.

9.3.1.11 Reaching Out to the Community

From the beginning, we determined that PROP staff, interns, and volunteers would engage in an aggressive outreach effort, including the concentrated use of social media technology, to community groups throughout the city. We have placed a particular emphasis on connecting with and enrolling the constituencies most directly affected by harsh police practices, namely inner-city communities of color and groups that represent or provide services to New York City's most marginalized individuals.

In our outreach, we have informed the nonprofit public interest world generally and made direct contact with appropriate groups and agencies specifically to inform them that PROP representatives are ready, willing, and able to make brief or lengthy presentations on the NYPD's harsh practices and the remedies available to address the abuses.

We have appeared before high school, college, and graduate school classes; church groups; service providers; union meetings; re-entry programs; youth groups; conference workshops; and so on. Our commitment to take advantage of all opportunities to spread the word was captured in this expressed attitude, "If asked, we'll talk to six-year-olds working at a corner lemonade stand."

At these presentations, we seek to enroll people in various aspects of PROP's campaign, such as having them sign and distribute our petitions, inviting them to participate in the monthly meetings of New Yorkers for Police Reform, attend a PROP public forum, or support strategic events organized by PROP allies such as rallies or press conferences.

A main PROP outreach effort has been our citywide drive to gather signatures on a petition urging the city's policy makers to enact sweeping reforms of NYPD practices such as ending stop and frisk and abolishing the quota system. We have organized seven outreach petition days since 2011 where we dispatch PROP volunteers to well-trafficked sites in neighborhoods throughout the city to interact directly with New Yorkers, provide them with relevant information, and encourage them to sign the PROP petition. I've participated in all our petition drive days, and although some people ignore my colleagues and me, many others stop and want to express what they have seen or experienced at the NYPD's hands:

"They beat that boy on the stairs for no good reason."

"They stop me and everybody around here all the time."

"Our friend [a fellow skateboarder] asked them not to hurt him and they beat him so badly he had to go to the hospital."

From a Latino man who flashed his badge: "I'm a cop, but this stop and frisk is very bad business."

"A cop gave me a summons the other day for walking between cars on a stopped subway. Said he was sorry, but that it was the 26th of the month and he had to hit his number."

In addition, and also from the beginning, PROP has concentrated on building an active and vibrant social media presence. Although much of PROP's thinking about and approach to advocacy/organizing is old school in spirit and substance, even an old-timer like me realized the importance of using the new technologies to conduct outreach to the world at large, and to young people in particular. We have a website where we post all things PROP-related: reports on recent activities and announcements on what is upcoming, fact sheets, literature about and by PROP, and a YouTube channel presenting videos of individuals describing their first-hand encounters with bad police practices. We also have a Facebook and Twitter page where we post daily entries, usually either updates about PROP activities or news articles on policing issues, which we post to generate traffic to our site and spread the word about PROP's plans and purposes.

9.3.1.12 *Highlighting the Human Impact*

An important strategic goal of any advocacy effort is to put a human face on the issue. We at PROP knew that especially over the past two years, many informed and interested New Yorkers had become familiar with the undeniable statistical evidence of the NYPD's misguided and racially biased tactics: nearly 90% of the hundreds of thousands of people stopped each year are Black or Latino and nearly 90% of the persons arrested for marijuana possession each year are Black or Latino, this despite the research showing that the majority of people who smoke marijuana are White.

As advocates seeking to reach and teach a broad spectrum of the public effectively about the rightness of our cause, we also knew that we had to put flesh and blood on the bones of the available numbers, to present the terrible human consequences of stop and frisk and other objectionable NYPD practices. More people in the larger society understood that some, perhaps many, NYPD actions were illegal, that they violated our country's Constitution. But people often perceived "illegal" or "unconstitutional" as technical concepts, serious criticism to be sure, without understanding the actual effect. It was PROP's task to show the very real ways that bad police practices harmed and severely compromised the lives and well-being of individuals and communities of many of our fellow New Yorkers.

At the first gatherings of New Yorkers for Police Reform, people agreed that presenting in written and filmed form the stories of individuals' needlessly harsh encounters with NYPD officers would be a highly effective way to achieve this end. And so, we initiated PROP's narrative project.

As a related purpose of this effort, we aimed to present a sufficient number of these accounts to rebut the "few bad apples" argument effectively, a dubious response that department defenders frequently put forward when police wrongdoing is exposed. Our point would be that this argument belies a substantial body of evidence including not only the damning data, but also the far too many compelling stories of ordinary New Yorkers. Our point would be that the numbers and the narratives combined show that the harsh and unjust tactics employed by street cops reflect a disturbing and toxic systemwide attitude and culture.

Now on the narrative page of the PROP website, we have over 50 videos of the people describing their painful and difficult encounters with the NYPD. PROP volunteers made these videos either by arranged appointments with people who had stories to tell or by traveling to inner-city communities and approaching people on the street, many of whom proved eager to relate their unpleasant to frightening NYPD experiences.

The PROP website also contains over 30 written accounts, persuasive, credible, and unsettling, especially to people who were accustomed to seeing the police in a positive light (Police Reform Organizing Project, 2013).

Here are sample excerpts:

- Francis Destouche, a 53-year-old mechanic with a clean record, was walking home in the Bronx in October 2011 when the police stopped him for no apparent reason. They searched him, found nothing, and then accused him of "throwing something away." The police arrested and held him for 20 hours, causing him to miss his granddaughter's birth. The charges were dismissed. Destouche's lawyer stated that the stop and the arrest was a result of the NYPD's "quota policy."
- An African-American woman driving in Jamaica, Queens was pulled over because her car had a broken taillight. When she showed the officer a note explaining that she was on her way to have the light fixed, he said that then he would give her a summons for driving without a seatbelt. When she said, "But I have my seatbelt on," he responded, "Stop complaining or I'll make it worse for you."
- In 2009 Jeremy Thomas was standing across the street from his apartment building in the Bronx when the police stopped, detained, handcuffed, and searched him without any explanation. Jeremy provided the police with his identification, but was then searched inside his underwear and taken to the precinct. The police issued Jeremy a summons for disorderly conduct, which was later dismissed.
- Ramon Morales was cleaning his car outside his sister's house on Cabrini Boulevard in Manhattan in August 2009 when cops approached him, accused him of drug possession, and searched him

and the car. They found no drugs but charged him with a DWI, even though he wasn't driving. Eighteen court appearances and nearly two years later, the charges were dismissed.

- Kenrick Gray, 32, of Staten Island, was stopped, searched, and detained twice in late 2010 for no apparent reason, the second time resulting in a false arrest. His lawyer reported that racial profiling led to the stops.
- Daryl George, a 36-year-old transit worker who had never been arrested, was talking with a friend about buying an iPod in the lobby of a Brooklyn building when police came in, ordered everyone against the wall, and searched them. George didn't have any contraband, though someone else in the lobby did. The police arrested George anyway, and though the charges were dismissed and the case was sealed, he was suspended by the Transit Authority and lost five months' pay and benefits.

9.4   Conclusion

Informed and inspired by a commitment to our core principles and central mission, we at PROP have pursued these activities/strategies for the past two years. We can assess our effectiveness over that time in several ways at least. Not only because of our efforts, of course, but by any measure our main goal has been achieved. Press attention and how often and urgently candidates speak about stop and frisk and other abusive police practices demonstrate that they have become central issues in this year's NYC mayoral campaign. When I first mentioned in 2011 to some very thoughtful and politically astute people that a principal objective of the police reform movement was to inject concern about NYPD practices into the heart of the 2013 electoral debate, they gave me a disbelieving and pitiable look as if I had announced plans to don a cape, climb to the roof of a tall building, and fly. So, in the face of long odds and much skepticism, the movement that PROP helped champion has made big-size strides.

What are other signs of PROP's progress at present? The more than 1,600 "likes" on our Facebook page; over 14,000 signatures on the PROP petition; a series of well-attended public forums on a range of relevant topics; over 50 videos on our website's YouTube channel and thousands of views of the same; a steady stream of well-received reports, op-ed pieces, and letters to the editor; the thoughtful responses of all the leading mayoral candidates to PROP's voters' education guide; and, the over 45 unpaid interns and volunteers of all ages, although mostly young, and all sexual orientations and gender identities, ethnicities, races, and educational levels and class backgrounds. Our interns and volunteers carried out many PROP tasks, from collating press packets for public forums, to researching and writing reports, to making videos and designing our website, that have enabled PROP with limited funding to achieve its current impressive level of credibility and visibility in the city's policymaking arena.

Although at this point, the end of the summer of 2013, the story of the city's police reform movement is a positive tale in any telling, the final chapter has not been written. As we head for a happy ending or a disappointing denouement or, more likely, a continuing saga featuring forward movement with some pushback from hard-line law enforcement interests, here are the narrative markers yet to be recorded: the ruling of the federal judge in the *Floyd* trial, aka the stop-and-frisk case, and the final outcome of the Bloomberg administration's appeal of that ruling; the position of the leading candidates regarding the case and whether they will pledge that, if elected, they would withdraw the city's appeal and negotiate in good faith to reach a settlement that includes an outside court-appointed monitor; who will be our next mayor and how strong and direct a mandate she or he will give to the new police commissioner to implement sweeping changes in NYPD policy and practice; and the new make-up of the city council and how determined the leadership will be to continue pressing for constructive change.

Although these matters remain unresolved, one truth is certain: as with all organizing efforts of worth, PROP will maintain its commitment to action and the issue at hand; we will carry on carrying on whatever the political climate or reality; we will persevere with our advocacy strategies aimed at keeping a spotlight on police abuses and the pressure on the city's government leaders to follow through on enacting the needed NYPD reforms as a critical step toward creating a more just, livable, and inclusive city for all New Yorkers.

PROP has moved on and out. We are no longer a project operating under the auspices of the Urban Justice Center, but a stand alone, independent and incorporated nonprofit organization.

Last November, the city's voters chose by a wide margin Bill de Blasio as their mayor. De Blasio ran on a platform highly critical of stop and frisk and other abusive NYPD practices such as the Department's quota system for evaluation the performance and productivity of police officers on the street. Now, after 5 months of de Blasio's mayoralty and despite some reforms announced by Police Commissioner Bill Bratton, we at PROP have serious concerns that the daily abusive and biased practices of the NYPD have not changed and that they continue to, in effect, inflict serious harm and injustices on our city's most vulnerable groups.

References

Churchill, Winston. (1910). Retrieved September 26, 2013, from http://www.liberty-human-rights.org.uk/media/articles/pdfs/zahid-mubarek-sc-jul06.pdf

Clifford, K., Garnett, K., Najeeb, N., & Nudd, E. (2013). *Criminalizing communitites: NYPD abuse of vulnerable populations.* Retrieved September 26, 2013, from http://www.leitnercenter.org/files/WLIHRC%20and%20Prop%20Report%20-%20Spring%202013.pdf

Gangi, R. (2013). *When police are encouraged to abuse, not protect.* Retrieved September 26, 2013, from http://www.alternet.org/when-police-are-encouraged-abuse-not-protect?page=0%2C1

Police Reform Organizing Project. (2013). *In their own words, "They got bandanas on, arrest them": How productivity goals drive harsh and unjust policing.* Retrieved September 26, 2013, from http://www.policereformorganizingproject.org/wp-content/uploads/2012/04/In-Their-Own-Words-FINAL4_24_12_NB.pdf

Police Reform Organizing Project. (2013a). Retrieved September 26, 2013, from http://www.urbanjustice.org/ujc/projects/police.html

Police Reform Organizing Project. (2013b). *Voter education guide questions.* Retrieved September 26, 2013, from http://www.policereformorganizingproject.org/wp-content/uploads/2013/08/PROP-VOTER-ED-QUESTIONNAIRE-Mayor-Pub-Ad-Compt.pdf

Index